PHYSICS IN ACTION

Second Edition

BOOK 2

Hong Kong
Oxford University Press

Oxford University Press

Oxford   New York   Toronto
Petaling Jaya   Singapore   Hong Kong   Tokyo
Delhi   Bombay   Calcutta   Madras   Karachi
Nairobi   Dar es Salaam   Cape Town
Melbourne   Auckland

and associated companies in
Berlin   Ibadan

First published 1985
Second edition 1989
Third impression 1991

This book is also available in a Chinese-language edition
活用物理 第二册
©啓思出版有限公司 1989, 1990

ISBN 0 19 584293 6

Front cover: Silicon wafers produced by a local factory in the Tai Po
Industrial Estate (Courtesy of Hua Ko Electronics Co. Ltd.)

Back cover: A 256K RAM chip; a technician handling a silicon wafer;
modern electronic components (Photos by Siemens AG, Munich, Federal
Republic of Germany)

Printed in Hong Kong by Sun Fung Offset Binding Co., Ltd.
Published by Oxford University Press, Warwick House, Hong Kong

Preface

PHYSICS IN ACTION — Second Edition is a foundation physics course for Hong Kong secondary schools. It provides a complete coverage of the HKCE Physics Syllabus and incorporates all the latest changes in the curriculum.

The course adopts a modern approach which stresses experiment and enquiry and develops most of the principles of physics from experimental work. The aim is to foster learning for understanding and to reflect the nature of physics (and science) as a process or activity of enquiry. The applications of physics are given special emphasis to enhance pupils' motivation and to bring out the relevance of physics to everyday life. Extensive reference is made throughout the course to physics in action in the home, the office, transport, industry, communications and medicine, using, wherever possible, local examples.

The course is divided into two volumes. Book 1 is intended for use in Form 3−4 and Book 2 in Form 5. Each volume consists of a pupil's book, a practical workbook and a teacher's guide.

In response to the recent revision of the HKCE Physics syllabus as well as feedback from teachers, a number of changes have been made in this second edition and these are described below under each component of the course.

PUPIL'S BOOK

This contains the basic concepts and principles of physics with detailed explanation, background information and modern applications. Particular attention has been paid to the clarity of language and accuracy of illustration. Laws and theories are usually developed from practical work using genuine experimental results. Worked examples are used to illustrate particular points and to help with their understanding. Each chapter ends with a summary and problems, many of which are from local and overseas past examination papers. Numerical answers, and in many cases outlined solutions, to the problems are provided at the end of the book.

In the second edition, Chapter 24 (Electronics) has been completely rewritten to include a new section on microelectronics which covers several common electronic devices and logic gates and their applications. Other minor changes include the addition of more local applications of physics throughout the book, the addition of some recent past examination questions in the end-of-chapter problems and an expanded section on the nuclear debate in Chapter 26 (Radioactivity II).

PRACTICAL WORKBOOK

This contains experiments and demonstrations which serve to introduce and illustrate the concepts and principles covered in the pupil's book. It incorporates all the experiments in the HKCE Physics Syllabus, including those on microelectronics which have recently been added. All experiments have been fully tested in schools and sample results of many of them are quoted in the pupil's book. For each experiment, procedures are described in detail and probing questions are used to stimulate careful thought about various aspects of the experiment. As far as possible three-dimensional diagrams are used to guide pupils in setting up the apparatus correctly.

The workbook has been completely redesigned to provide spaces for answering questions, doing calculations, entering results, drawing diagrams, plotting graphs, etc. For consolidation, a summary is also included at the end of each experiment. Also, several experiments which are outside the syllabus have been deleted in order to keep the total number of experiments in the workbook to a minimum.

TEACHER'S GUIDE

This contains useful teaching hints and strategies on each section of the course as well as notes for each experiment. The notes include practical hints on the setting up of the apparatus, information on the improvising of simple equipment, ways and means of obtaining good results, the organizing of pupil experiments, teaching points, class discussion techniques, answers to some of the questions in the workbook, etc. The Teacher's Guide has been partially rewritten to comply with the changes in the workbook.

OVERHEAD PROJECTION TRANSPARENCIES

These are produced to facilitate the teaching of the course. All transparencies have been carefully developed and overlays are used as far as possible for building up diagrams or developing specific concepts and principles. Each set of transparencies is accompanied by teaching notes which give step-by-step instructions, explain concepts and principles developed, and in some cases show the working required. Questions are usually included in the teaching notes to provoke interaction between the teacher and the class.

The transparencies are available in two packs. Pack 1 consists of 33 sets covering sections on Optics, Heat, Mechanics and Waves. Pack 2 consists of 29 sets covering sections on Electricity and Magnetism, Electronics and Nuclear Physics.

Contents

Acknowledgements

The author and the publisher are grateful to Mr C.W. Tang for assistance in trying out some of the experiments in the practical workbook and in improvising some of the equipment; to Mrs V.A. Richards for improving the language of the text; Mr Stanley Chia for help with information on local examples of applications of physics; to Mr W.S. Jeffrey for permission to use material from his article, *Electricity Analogue* in the December 1978 issue of *School Science Review*; to Mr C.L. Kwan for technical information on MTR trains; to Rank Xerox Hong Kong Ltd. for information on the xerographic process; to Royden Electric Engineering Co., Ltd. for information on the full colour outdoor video display system at Happy Valley Race Course, and to Mr Vincent Chiu for comments on the problems.

We would like to thank the following for providing photographs for the book: Ricky Au and Pang Tak, 14.14, 15.11, 15.19, 15.21, 15.25, 15.26, 15.30, 15.31, 15.39, 15.40, 15.41, 15.42, 15.43, 15.44, 16.4, 16.5, 17.15, 18.7, 18.8, 18.17, 18.21, 18.24, 25.2, 25.8, 25.10, 25.22; *AA Book of the car,* © 1976 The Reader's Digest Association Ltd., 23.20; Bell Laboratories, 24.82; Lord Blackett's Estate, 25.17a, 25.18, 25.20; Bettmann Archives, 26.30, 26.31; BBC Hulton Picture Library, 23.1, 23.27; British Steel, 23.43; Cable and Wireless (Hong Kong) Ltd., p.1, 17.16, 17.31; Camera Press, 10.15, 10.16, 26.32; The Chartered Bank, 17.13; China Light and Power Co. Ltd., p.89, 23.22, 23.27, 23.42, 23.44, 23.45, 23.48; *Core Physics* by Geoff Cackett, Ron Kennedy, Alastair Stevens, © OUP 1979, 17.6, 18.1, 18.2, 18.12; Crane Maker Construction & Production System Ltd., 22.23; Crown Motors Ltd., 17.9; Robert Duffield and Eric Fox, 21.10; French Cultural Services, 17.10; Gamma Laboratory Ltd., 26.20; GEC Hong Kong Ltd., 24.29; Government Information Services, 14.3, 16.4, 17.22, 21.3, p.144 (bottom), 23.21, 24.22, 24.30; Griffin & George, 14.4, 19.11, 22.6, 25.16, 26.5; Hitachi (H.K.) Ltd., 23.10; Hong Kong Baptist Hospital, 18.36; Hong Kong Electric Co. Ltd., 19.35, 23.46; Hong Kong Telephone, 24.31; HK-TVB, 17.18; Hua Ko Electronics Co. Ltd., front cover, 24.52; IBM World Trade Corporation, 24.83; W.S. Jeffery, 20.11; Dr. S.Y. Mak, 15.27, 15.28, 15.29, 15.40; The Mansell Collection, 14.12, 17.35; Medical and Health Department, 25.7, 25.23, 25.24, 26.17a, 26.18; NASA, 17.5; Philip Harris Ltd., 20.20b, 22.36, 22.40; Philips (H.K.) Ltd., 20.38; Polaroid Corporate, 18.35; Practical Electronics (IPC Magazines Ltd.), 18.38; Rank Xerox Hong Kong Ltd., 19.36, 19.37; RS Components, 23.32a, 24.35, 24.36a, 24.47; The Science Museum, London 25.1, 25.3, 25.15, 25.17b, 25.17c, 25.19, 26.6; Sears, *Optics,* © 1949 Addison-Wesley, Reading, Ma., 16.9; The Shell Company of Hong Kong Ltd., 19.33; Siemens AG, Munich, Federal Republic of Germany, back cover; SCMP Ltd., 17.14, 18.37, 24.84, 26.34; Stanley Power Tools, 22.39; Ta Kung Bao, 26.33; Unilab, Blackburn, U.K., 20.4, 20.9, 22.13, 22.47, 24.42, 24.45, 24.59, 24.62, 24.65, 24.68; United Kingdom Atomic Energy Commission, 26.19, 26.21, 26.25, 24.66, 26.27; United States Atomic Energy Commission, p.243, 26.23, 26.24, 26.29; USIS, 16.2, 18.4; Walden Precision Apparatus Ltd., 22.41; Wing Shun Ltd., 21.1, 21.11a; Wo Kee Hong Ltd., 22.48; P.K. Wong, 14.1; Ricky Wong, 19.1, 19.3, 19.24, 19.32, 20.19, 20.20a, 21.7, 21.11b, 21.14, 22.2, 24.2, 24.4, 24.5, 24.6, 24.13, 24.24a, 24.26, 24.27; Gordon Wu and Associates Ltd., 19.30; Wellful Company, 23.24b and 23.24c.

We would like to express our gratitude to the various examination boards listed below for permission to make use of questions from their past certificate/O-level examination papers. Each question is individually acknowledged as indicated below.

Hong Kong Examinations Authority (HKCEE)

University of London University Entrance and School Examinations Council (London)

Oxford and Cambridge Schools Examination Board (O & C)

We would like to acknowledge reference made to *Nuffield Physics Pupils' Book III*, *Nuffield Physics Teachers' Guide III* and *IV*, and *Nuffield Physics Guide to Experiment IV* and *V* on pages 13, 17, 105, 115, 152, 154, 180, 190, 245 and 246; and to *Explaining Physics*, © Stephen Pople, OUP 1982, on pages 93, 104, 159, 161, 177, 178, 179, 195, 221, 222, 245, 265, 266, 270 and 278.

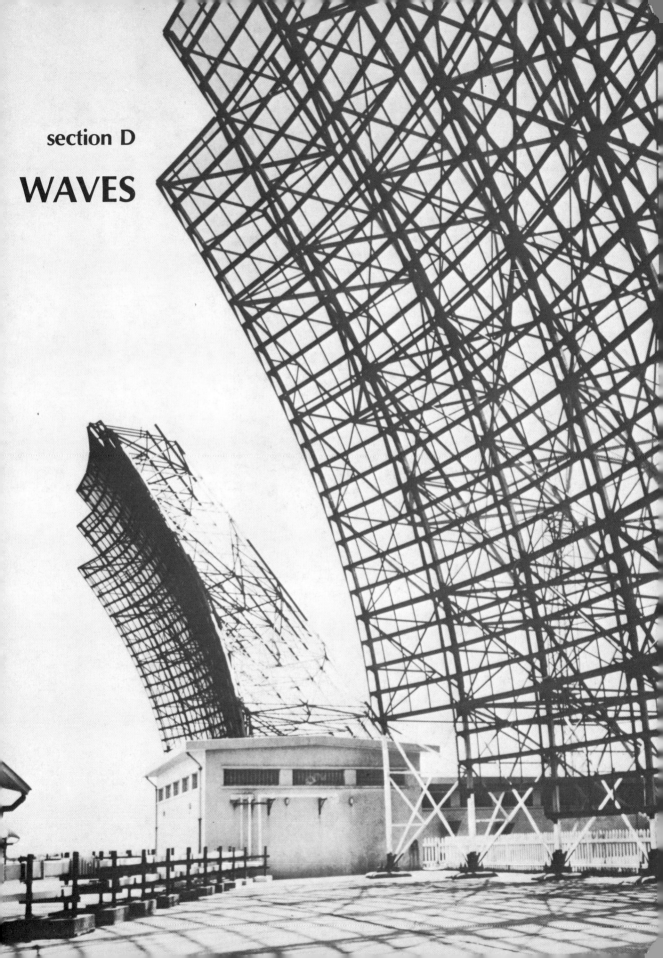

section D

WAVES

Wave Motion 14

There are many different kinds of waves, such as the water wave, the radio wave and the sound wave. What is a wave and what makes it a wave? How does a wave travel and how does it behave?

WAVE AND ENERGY

Figure 14.1 Circular ripples in a pond.

First let us look at water waves. When a stone is thrown into a pond, circular waves move outwards from the centre of disturbance (Figure 14.1). But what is it that travels outwards from the centre? If we float a cork on the water surface, it does not move outwards with the wave. The cork, and the water around it, just vibrate up and down as the wave passes (Figure 14.2), and the cork soon settles back to its resting position on the water surface after the wave has passed. Obviously it is not the water that moves outwards from the centre.

Figure 14.2 Cork vibrates up and down as wave moves outwards.

Since the wave makes the cork move up and down, the wave must be supplying energy to the cork. So the answer to the question is that *energy* is travelling out from the centre of disturbance. During a typhoon, the energy carried by water waves can often cause great damage (Figure 14.3). This wave energy is generated by the winds blowing over the surface of the sea.

Figure 14.3   Waves carry a lot of energy during a typhoon.

There is, however, another, more direct way of transmitting energy. When you kick a football resting on the ground very hard, it flies off at high speed. This is because some of the energy of your foot is transmitted to the ball. If the ball lands on a window and smashes the glass, energy is transferred to the glass. This transfer of energy, from you to the glass, occurs as a result of the motion of the ball. By contrast, in the case of water waves, energy is transmitted from the falling stone to the cork without involving travel of the water.

TRANSVERSE PULSES AND WAVES

When we considered water waves, we saw that the vibration of the water was in the *vertical* plane, while the energy was transmitted in the *horizontal* plane along the water surface. This kind of wave is a **transverse wave** (transverse means 'across').

A wave in which the vibrations are at right angles to the direction of travel of the wave is called a transverse wave.

Transverse waves can be studied using a long spring (Figure 14.4). When one end of the spring is fixed and the other end is flicked once from side to side, a disturbance called a **wave pulse** travels

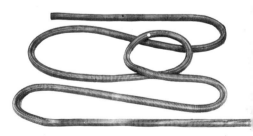

Figure 14.4   Long spring to generate waves.

transverse wave 橫波   pulse 脈衝

down the spring (Figure 14.5). The coils of the spring vibrate sideways at *right angles* to the pulse as the pulse passes them. Therefore this is a transverse pulse.

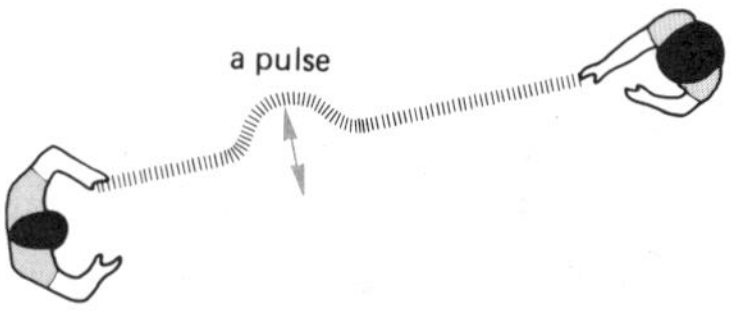

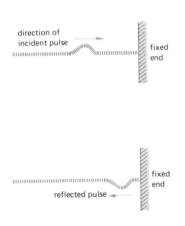

Figure 14.5 Transverse pulse along long spring.

Further investigations of pulses along the spring give some interesting results:

1. The pulse travels with a constant speed along the spring, although its size is gradually reduced.

2. The pulse speed increases the more the spring is stretched.

3. The pulse is reflected at the fixed end, and the reflected pulse is always opposite to the incident pulse (Figure 14.6).

4. If two pulses are sent from opposite ends, they will meet, cross each other and apparently continue unchanged (Figure 14.7).

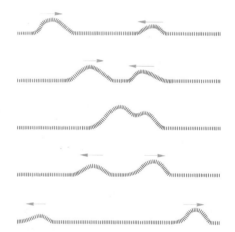

Figure 14.6   Reflection of a pulse.

Figure 14.7   Two pulses meet, pass each other and continue unchanged.

A single disturbance gives rise to a single pulse, but a series of pulses forms a **continuous wave**. If the end of the spring is flicked rapidly several times, a wave in the form of a series of humps and hollows travels along the spring (Figure 14.8). The humps are called **wave crests** and the hollows, **wave troughs**.

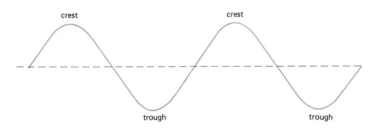

Figure 14.8   Crests are the humps; troughs the hollows.

continuous wave 連續波   wave crest 波峯   wave trough 波谷

LONGITUDINAL PULSES AND WAVES

A slinky spring can be used to transmit another kind of pulse. If one end of the slinky is fixed and the other end is given a sudden, sharp *push*, a group of compressed coils seems to travel down the spring. This region of compressed coils is called a **compression** (Figure 14.9). If instead, the end is given a sudden, sharp *pull*, a group of more separated coils seems to move along the slinky. This region of more separated coils is called a **rarefaction**.

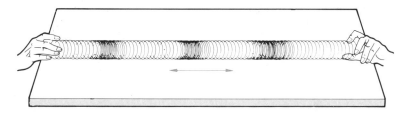

Figure 14.9 Slinky spring generating longitudinal waves.

When the end of the slinky is given several pushes and pulls, a series of compressions and rarefactions moves along the slinky in the form of a wave. This wave is clearly different from the transverse wave because the coils vibrate along the axis of the spring and in the same direction as that of the wave (Figure 14.10) and, instead of crests and troughs, there are compressions and rarefactions. This is a **longitudinal wave** (longitudinal means 'length-ways').

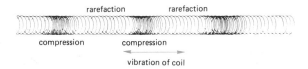

Figure 14.10 Compressions and rarefactions in longitudinal waves.

> **A longitudinal wave is a wave in which the vibrations are along the direction of travel of the wave.**

DESCRIBING WAVES

Figure 14.11 helps to explain the terms used to describe waves.

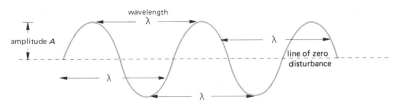

Figure 14.11 Describing waves.

Amplitude

In the case of waves along a slinky spring, the greater the movement of the hand, the greater the size of the disturbance which travels along the slinky.

compression 壓縮，密部   rarefaction 稀疏，疏部   longitudinal wave 縱波   amplitude 振幅   **5**

> **The amplitude of a wave is the size of the maximum disturbance measured from the 'zero' or resting position.**

The symbol for amplitude is A. Amplitude is measured in metres (m).

Wavelength

A wave repeats itself after a certain distance. In a transverse wave in a spring, there are series of alternating crests and troughs; whereas in a longitudinal wave, there are compressions and rarefactions.

> **The wavelength of a wave is the minimum distance in which a wave repeats itself.**

Therefore the wavelength of a transverse wave is the distance between successive crests or successive troughs; the wavelength of a longitudinal wave is the distance between successive compressions or successive rarefactions.

The symbol for wavelength is the Greek letter λ (pronounced 'lambda'). Wavelength is measured in metres (m).

Frequency

The faster the spring is flicked, the greater the number of waves produced in a given time.

> **The frequency of a wave is the number of complete waves produced in one second.**

Figure 14.12　Heinrick Hertz first produced and detected radio waves in 1888.

The symbol for frequency is f. Frequency is measured in **hertz** (Hz), which means 'per second'. This unit is named after the German physicist, Heinrick Hertz, who first produced and detected radio waves in 1888 (Figure 14.12).

If the end of the spring is flicked twice in one second, two waves are produced. The frequency of the wave is two vibrations per second or 2 Hz, the same frequency with which the end of the spring is flicked. That is, the frequencies of the wave and its source are the same.

Period

The coils of a spring vibrate as a wave passes them. In the case of water waves, the water 'particles' vibrate up and down, carrying with them a floating cork. In both cases, the vibrating

frequency 頻率　　　period 周期　　　wavelength 波長

parts do not move outwards with the wave although energy is being transmitted by them.

Vibrations are repetitive up-and-down or to-and-fro motions. We say that a particle has made a *complete vibration* if it moves up, down (or down and up) and back again to its original position. Figure 14.13 shows several examples.

Figure 14.13 One complete vibration.

The period of vibration is the time taken for a particle to make one complete vibration. It is also the time for one wave to be generated.

The symbol for period is T. Period is measured in seconds (s).

If the frequency of a wave is 2 Hz, two waves are generated in one second. It follows that the time for one wave to be generated is half a second. Obviously, frequency and period are related, and we can write

$$f = \frac{1}{T}$$

Wave speed

The wave speed is the distance travelled by a crest, or any point on the wave, in one second.

The symbol for wave speed is v. Wave speed is measured in metres per second ($m\,s^{-1}$).

TRANSVERSE WAVE MODEL

To help us understand wave motion better a wave model can be used. One simple transverse wave model consists of a spiral connected to a small motor and mounted on a transparent plastic stand. The whole assembly is put on an overhead projector (Figure 14.14). When the spiral is rotated, a travelling transverse wave is seen on the screen.

The transverse wave model can tell us a lot about the nature of wave motion (but remember that what is seen on the screen is not a real wave; it is only a simulation of a wave):

1. When a small piece of plasticine is stuck onto a coil near the left end of the spiral, it is seen as a 'particle' vibrating up and down as the wave progresses to the right. The vibrations of the particle are at right angles to the direction of travel of the wave. If the speed of rotation of the spiral is gradually increased, the particle will vibrate with a higher and higher frequency, giving rise to a correspondingly higher wave speed.

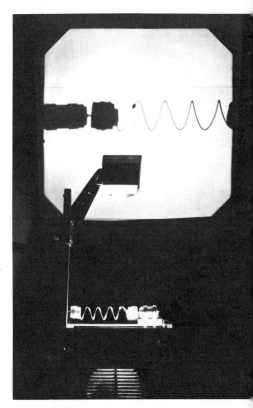

Figure 14.14 Transverse wave model demonstrating transverse wave on screen.

wave speed 波速   simulation 模擬

2. When another piece of plasticine is stuck onto the spiral next to the first, they are seen as two neighbouring particles, *a* and *b*, vibrating with the same frequency and amplitude (Figure 14.15), but not in step. *b* seems to be trying to catch up with *a*, but never succeeds. We say that the vibrations of *a* and *b* are not *in phase* and that *a leads b* or *b lags behind a*.

3. If the motor is turned off and the spiral is rotated by hand, we can make particle *a* go through one complete vibration very slowly and see how the wave progresses to the right. In Figure 14.16, which shows how the waveform shifts a short distance to the right, the solid line represents the waveform at the start, and the dotted line represents the waveform a moment later. The particles have vibrated to the new positions during that moment.

4. Figure 14.17 shows many pieces of plasticine stuck onto the spiral equal distances apart. All the particles within one wavelength vibrate in exactly the same way except that there is a phase lead from one particle to the next. But there are also particles vibrating *in phase* if we look at more than one wavelength, for example, *a* and *i*, *b* and *j*, etc. These pairs of particles are all exactly one wavelength apart. On the other hand, particles half a wavelength apart, for example, *a* and *e*, are vibrating in exactly opposite ways, that is, when one is moving down, the other is moving up, and vice versa. We say that such pairs of particles, half a wavelength apart, are exactly *out of phase*.

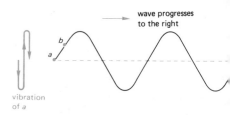

Figure 14.15 *a* and *b* vibrate with the same frequency and amplitude but not in phase. *a* is leading *b*.

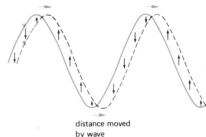

Figure 14.16 Waveform moves forward as particles vibrate to new positions.

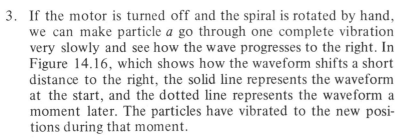

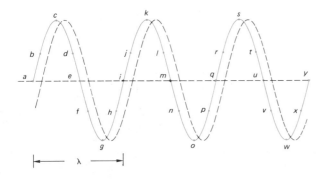

Figure 14.17 Particles at different stages in a vibration.

A more precise definition of wavelength is:

> **The wavelength is the distance between two successive particle which are vibrating in phase.**

5. Focusing on one particle, *a*, Figure 14.18 shows the new waveforms when *a*

   (a) moves to its lowest position in time $\frac{1}{4}T$ (one-quarter of a period);

in phase 同相   out of phase 異相   phase 相

(b)   returns to zero position in $\frac{1}{2}T$;

(c)   moves up to its highest position in $\frac{3}{4}T$;

(d)   returns to the starting point in T after making one complete vibration.

The wave moves forwards through a distance equal to one wavelength (λ) as a makes one complete vibration. From this we can derive an equation relating wave speed v, wavelength λ and frequency f.

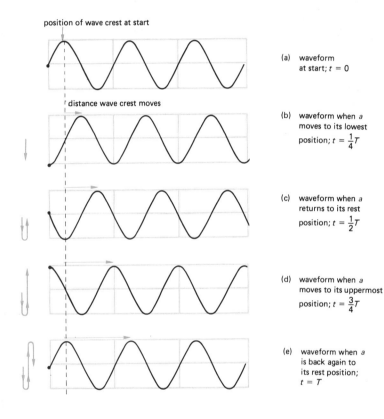

position of wave crest at start

distance wave crest moves

(a)   waveform at start; $t = 0$

(b)   waveform when a moves to its lowest position; $t = \frac{1}{4}T$

(c)   waveform when a returns to its rest position; $t = \frac{1}{2}T$

(d)   waveform when a moves to its uppermost position; $t = \frac{3}{4}T$

(e)   waveform when a is back again to its rest position; $t = T$

Figure 14.18   Particle a completes one vibration; wave moves forward by one wavelength.

A wave equation

Imagine that a is the end of a slinky spring which is flicked continuously to produce waves. If a is flicked at a frequency of 1 Hz, that is, once per second, one wave is produced which moves a distance of one wavelength (λ metres) during this second. If it is flicked at 2 Hz, two waves are produced and the wave moves a distance of 2λ metres in one second.

If it is flicked at f Hz, f waves are produced and the wave moves a distance of $f\lambda$ metres in one second. We can therefore write

$$v = f\lambda$$

9

Example 1
In 10 s, 20 waves are produced in a slinky spring.
(a) What is the frequency of the wave?
(b) If the wavelength is measured to be 0.02 m, what is the wave speed?

(a) Frequency = number of waves produced per second
$$= \frac{20}{10 \text{ s}} = 2 \text{ Hz}$$

(b) Wave speed = frequency × wavelength
$$= 2 \text{ Hz} \times 0.02 \text{ m} = 0.04 \text{ m s}^{-1}$$

Example 2
Water waves are produced by hitting the water surface with the tip of a pencil.
(a) If the wave travels 10 m in 5 s, what is the wave speed?
(b) If the pencil is hitting the water surface with a frequency of 2 Hz, find the wavelength of the wave.

(a) Wave speed = distance travelled per second = $\frac{10 \text{ m}}{5 \text{ s}}$
$$= 2 \text{ m s}^{-1}$$

(b) From $v = f\lambda$
$$\text{wavelength } \lambda = \frac{v}{f} = \frac{2 \text{ m s}^{-1}}{2 \text{ Hz}} = 1 \text{ m}$$

LONGITUDINAL WAVE MODEL

A longitudinal wave model consists of a transparent disc, called a **Crova's disc**, on which a series of circles are drawn in a special pattern. The disc is mounted on a small motor so that it can be rotated about a vertical axis and the whole assembly is placed on an overhead projector. The top of the projector is covered by a shield apart from a long narrow slit so that only a portion of the disc, along a radius, is shown on the screen (Figure 14.19a).

When the disc is rotated, a longitudinal wave is shown on the screen (Figure 14.19b). Groups of closely packed lines (compression) and groups of widely separated lines (rarefaction) progress to the right. The lines vibrate to and fro along the direction of travel of the wave.

Figure 14.19 (a) Shielded Crova's disc on overhead projector.
(b) Longitudinal wave projected on screen.

(a)

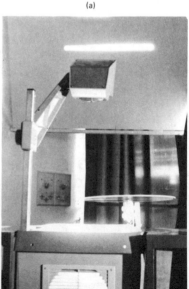

(b)

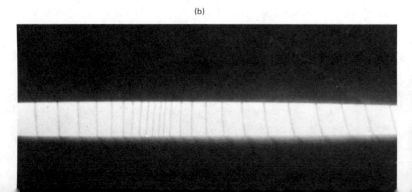

SUMMARY

Wave and energy

A travelling wave transmits energy.

Types of wave

A transverse wave is one in which the vibrations of the particles are at right angles to the direction of travel of the wave.

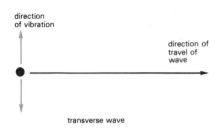

transverse wave

A longitudinal wave is one in which the direction of vibration of the particles is the same as the direction of travel of the wave.

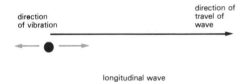

longitudinal wave

Describing waves

The amplitude (A) of a wave is the size of the maximum disturbance measured from the 'zero' or resting position. Its unit is the metre (m).

The wavelength (λ) of a wave is the distance between two successive particles vibrating in phase. Its unit is the metre (m).

Vibrations of particles at a particular instant

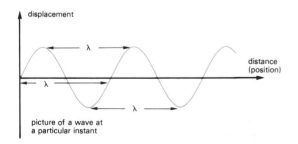

picture of a wave at a particular instant

In a water wave, the wavelength is the distance between successive crests or successive troughs. For a longitudinal wave in a spring, it is the distance between successive compressions or successive rarefactions.

Vibration of a particle in a time interval

The frequency (f) of a wave is the number of complete waves produced in one second. It is also the number of complete vibrations per second of the particles which make up the wave. Its unit is the hertz (Hz).

The period of vibration (T) is the time taken for a particle to make one complete vibration. Its unit is the second (s).

$$f = \frac{1}{T}$$

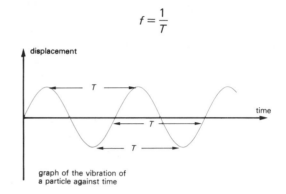

graph of the vibration of a particle against time

Wave Equation

The wave speed (v) is the distance travelled by a crest, or any point on the wave, in one second. Its unit is the metre per second (m s^{-1}).

$$v = f\lambda$$

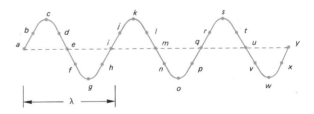

Phase difference

In a progressive transverse or longitudinal wave all the particles within a wavelength are vibrating with the same frequency and amplitude but there is a phase lead between the vibrations of a particle and the one that follows it. It is this phase difference between the particles that gives rise to the waveform.

Particles in a wave separated by exactly one wavelength are vibrating in phase; particles separated by exactly half a wavelength are exactly out of phase.

PROBLEMS

1. What is the difference between transverse wave and longitudinal wave?

2. A long spring is stretched on a smooth floor until it is 7 m long. One end of the spring is fixed and the other end is flicked to generate a wave pulse.
   (a) If the pulse takes 5 s to travel to the fixed end and back again, what will be the pulse speed?
   (b) If the free end is flicked continuously at 4 Hz, what will be the wavelength of the wave produced?

3. A water wave of frequency 10 Hz has a wavelength of 1 cm. What is its speed?

4. A train of transverse wave of wavelength 4 cm and amplitude 1 cm is moving from left to right at a speed of 1 cm s^{-1}.
   (a) What is the frequency of the wave?
   (b) Draw a diagram to represent the wave train at a certain time. Draw on the same diagram the wave train 1 second later.

5. Figure 14.20 represents a wave 0.2 s after it has started
   (a) Calculate
       (i)   the amplitude of the wave,
       (ii) the wavelength of the wave,
       (iii) the wave speed,
       (iv) the frequency of the wave.
   (b) State
       (i)   two points which are in phase,
       (ii) two points which are exactly out of phase,
       (iii) which point is on a wave crest,
       (iv) which point is in a wave trough.

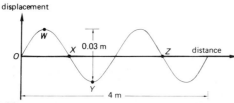

displacement

Figure 14.20

6. Figure 14.21 is the side-view of some water waves.
   (a) What is the wavelength of the waves?
   (b) The crest at X takes 2 seconds to reach the point Y. What is the frequency of the waves?

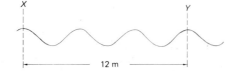

Figure 14.21

7. Figure 14.22 shows a water wave travelling from A to C in a ripple tank.
   The distance AB is 10 cm and the time taken for the vibration starting at A to reach B is 0.25 s.
   (a) Find the wavelength of the wave in the region AB.
   (b) Find the frequency of the vibration.
   (c) Find the velocity of the wave.
   (d) What are the directions of motions of particles at A and B at the moment shown?
   (e) The wave then enters into a shallow water region BC and its velocity is reduced to half its original value. What is the new wavelength and frequency of the wave in the region BC?
   (HKCEE 1978)

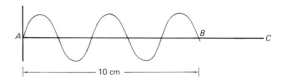

Figure 14.22

8. A transverse wave is travelling steadily from left to right through a series of particles. At a certain instant the waveform is as shown in Figure 14.23. Each of the vibrating particles is observed to perform four complete oscillations in 16 s.
   (a) Find the following quantities:
       (i)   the amplitude of the wave,
       (ii) the wavelength,
       (iii) the period,
       (iv) the frequency.
   (b) At the instant shown which of the particles P, Q, R, S, T is/are
       (i)   moving upwards,
       (ii) moving downwards,
       (iii) momentarily at rest?
   (c) What will be the position of particle Q a quarter of a period later?
   (HKCEE 1981)

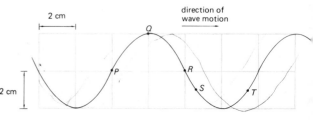

Figure 14.23

Water Waves

The properties of water waves are easily observed and their wavelength and frequency are readily measured. The criteria for wave nature can therefore be established by examining water waves.

THE RIPPLE TANK

The properties of water waves are best studied in a **ripple tank**. The apparatus consists of a large transparent plastic tray with a lamp above it. The lamp projects any water waves produced in the tray onto a piece of white drawing paper below the tray (Figure 15.1). Alternatively, the tray is placed on an overhead projector (Figure 15.2) and the images of water waves are projected onto a screen.

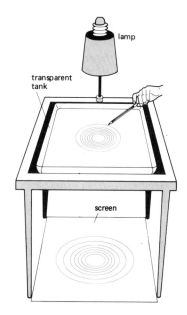

Figure 15.1 The ripple tank.

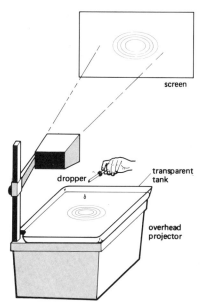

Figure 15.2 Ripple tank on overhead projector.

When the water surface in the tray is calm, the screen is uniformly illuminated. But when ripples are generated, they are seen as bright and dark lines or curves on the screen. This is because the ripples act like a series of lenses through which the light converges and diverges (Figure 15.3). The bright lines correspond to wave crests and the dark spaces in between correspond to wave troughs.

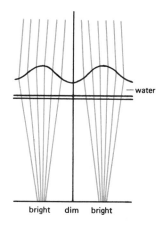

Figure 15.3 Bright lines correspond to wave crests; dark lines to wave troughs.

ripple tank 水波槽

GENERATION OF PULSES

If a drop of water from an eye dropper is allowed to fall onto the water surface, a circular pulse travels out from the point of disturbance at a constant speed. The circular shape occurs because the pulse speed is the same in all directions. The boundary of the pulse shape is called the **wavefront**.

If the straight edge of a ruler is dipped into the water, a straight pulse is generated. This pulse continues to move, with a constant speed, across the water surface as a straight wavefront.

It is readily observed that the direction of travel of the pulse is always at right angles to the wavefront. In describing a wave it is sometimes convenient to draw imaginary straight lines perpendicular to the wavefront (Figure 15.4). These lines are called **rays** and they indicate the direction of travel of the wave.

REFLECTION OF PULSES

When a barrier is placed in the path of a pulse, the pulse is reflected. The in-coming pulse is called the **incident** pulse and the one bounced back from the barrier is called the **reflected** pulse. Figure 15.5 shows a circular pulse starting from S and striking a straight barrier. The reflected pulse is also circular and seems to come from S' which is as far behind the barrier as S is in front. S' is called the **image** of S.

Figure 15.6 shows the reflection of a straight pulse from a barrier. In the figure, the **normal** is a line at right angles to the reflecting surface. The **angle of incidence** $\angle i$ is the angle between the incident ray and the normal, and the **angle of reflection** $\angle r$ is that between the reflected ray and the normal. The angle between the incident wavefront and the barrier is $\angle i$, and the angle between the reflected wavefront and the barrier is $\angle r$. It is observed that $\angle i$ is always equal to $\angle r$.

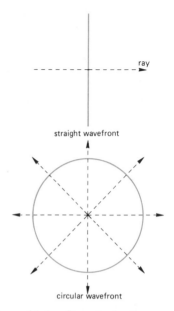

Figure 15.4   Rays, indicating direction of travel of wave, are perpendicular to wavefronts.

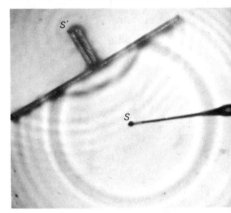

Figure 15.5   Reflection of circular wave.

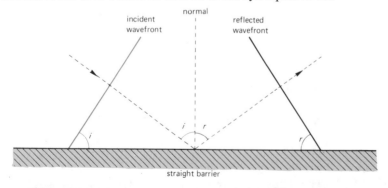

The law of reflection states that the angle of incidence is always equal to the angle of reflection.

Figure 15.6   Reflection of straight pulse at straight barrier.

14   wavefront 波陣面   reflection 反射   angle of incidence 入射角   angle of reflection 反射角

image 像   normal 法線

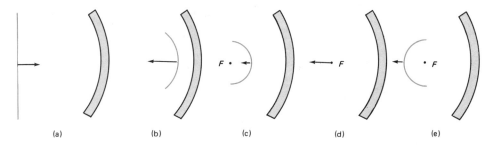

(a) (b) (c) (d) (e)

Figure 15.7 shows what happens when a straight pulse bounces back from a *concave* reflector. The series of diagrams are 'snapshots' of the wavefronts at successive points in time as the long straight pulse shrinks and converges to a point F. This point is called the **focus** of the concave reflector. Note that the pulse does not stop at F; it moves on to the left but gets fainter and fainter.

Figure 15.7 Straight pulse reflected by concave barrier.

What happens when a circular pulse is sent towards a concave barrier? The pattern of the reflected wavefront depends very much on where the incident pulse is started. Figure 15.8 shows several examples:

Figure 15.8 Circular pulse reflected by concave barrier.

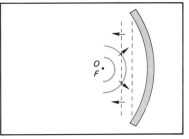

(a) *O nearer than F*

(b) *O at F*

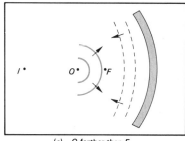

(c) *O farther than F*

(a) The pulse is started at O which is nearer the barrier than F. The reflected wavefront is also circular but is convex, and seems to come from point I behind the mirror. I is said to be the *image* of O.

(b) For a pulse started at F the reflected wavefront is straight. This is in fact the reverse of the pattern shown in Figure 15.7.

(c) For a pulse started at point O slightly further away than F, the reflected wavefront is circular, concave and converges to I.

(d) For a pulse started at a point about twice the distance of F from the barrier, the circular, reflected wavefront converges back to O.

(e) For a pulse started at a point beyond twice the distance of F from the barrier, the circular, reflected wavefront converges to I, nearer the barrier.

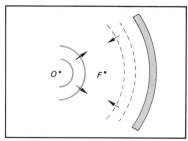

(d) *O at twice F*

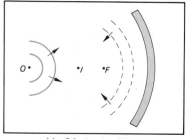

(e) *O farther than 2F*

focus 焦點 concave 凹

15

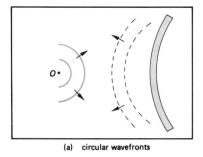

(a) circular wavefronts

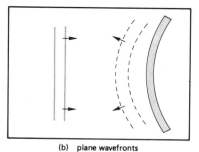

(b) plane wavefronts

Figure 15.9 Reflection of circular pulse by convex barrier.

By turning the barrier the other way around we have a convex reflector, and the reflected wavefronts of a straight and a circular pulse are shown in Figure 15.9.

GENERATION OF CONTINUOUS WAVES

Continuous waves, both circular and straight, can be produced by using a bar suspended on rubber bands. A small motor with an off-centre load on its axle is mounted on the bar. To produce continuous circular waves a dipper is attached to the bar so that it just touches the water surface (Figure 15.10a). To produce continuous straight or plane waves the dipper is removed and the bar lowered to just touching the water surface (Figure 15.10b). When the motor is started, the bar vibrates up and down and trains of waves are produced (Figure 15.11).

Figure 15.10 Generating (a) circular and (b) straight waves.

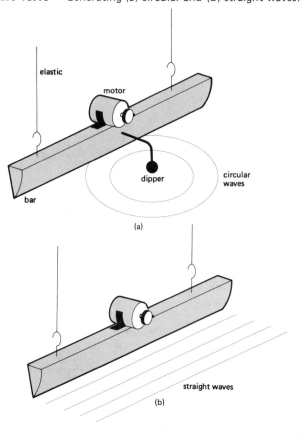

Figure 15.11 (a) Circular waves. (b) Plane waves.

(a)

(b)

convex ⌂

As we have seen, bright lines in the wave pattern represent wave crests and dark lines represent wave troughs. The wavelength of the water wave is therefore the distance between two adjacent dark or bright lines. If the speed of the motor is increased, the frequency with which the dipper strikes the water surface also increases, with the result that the spacing of the bright lines decreases — this means that wavelength is decreased. From the wave equation $v = f\lambda$, we know that frequency is inversely proportional to wavelength for a constant wave speed.

THE STROBOSCOPE

A train of waves often moves so fast that observation is difficult. One method of stopping or 'freezing' the wave pattern is to take a photograph. Another method is to use a device called a **stroboscope** (or **strobe** for short). One simple type of strobe (Figure 15.12) is a disc with usually 12 evenly spaced slits. The disc can be spun by hand using a finger hole just off the centre. The slits may be covered with tape leaving only 1, 2, 4 or 6 regularly spaced slits.

When the strobe disc is rotated, an object in front of the disc is visible every time a slit passes the eye; but is blocked the rest of the time. With a steady strobe speed, the sightings of the object are separated by fixed time intervals.

Stroboscopic viewing

To understand the principle of the stroboscope let us use it to freeze the motion of a rapidly rotating white arrow glued onto a motor-driven black disc (Figure 15.13). Consider first a simple case using a strobe with one slit (all the other slits are covered

Figure 15.12 Hand stroboscope.

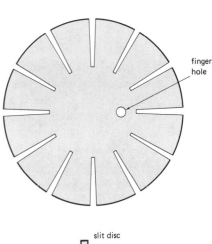

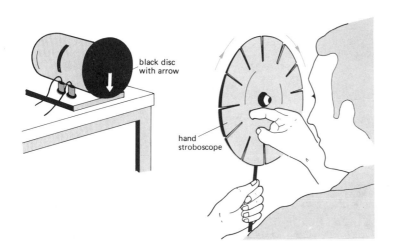

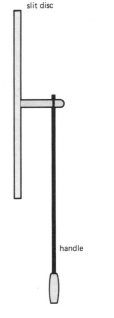

Figure 15.13 Viewing rotating arrow through stroboscope.

stroboscope 頻閃觀測器

by tape). Figure 15.14 shows how the strobe can 'freeze' the arrow when the speed of rotation of the strobe is exactly equal to that of the arrow. The arrow is at the same position every time the slit passes the eye; the arrow therefore appears to be standing still.

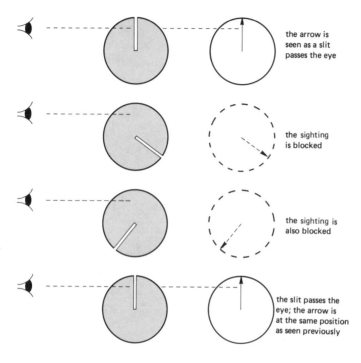

the arrow is seen as a slit passes the eye

the sighting is blocked

the sighting is also blocked

the slit passes the eye; the arrow is at the same position as seen previously

Figure 15.14   Strobe and arrow rotate at the same speed. Arrow is at the same position everytime the slit passes the eye.

If the strobe is rotated at half the speed of the arrow, the arrow still appears to be stationary although it is now making two revolutions between successive sightings (Figure 15.15). Similarly, if the strobe is rotated at one-third the speed of the arrow, the arrow makes three revolutions between successive sightings. Hence it is important that we find the *fastest* strobe speed which 'freezes' the motion of the arrow.

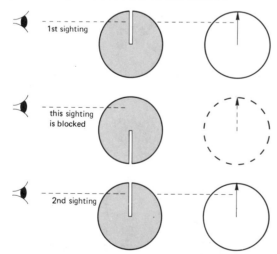

1st sighting

this sighting is blocked

2nd sighting

Figure 15.15   Strobe rotates at half the speed of arrow. Arrow again appears stationary.

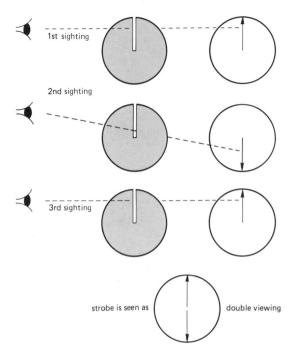

Figure 15.16 Double viewing: strobe rotates at twice the speed of arrow.

1st sighting

2nd sighting

3rd sighting

strobe is seen as   double viewing

If the strobe is rotated at twice the speed of the arrow, the arrow appears to be stationary at two positions. This is called **double viewing** (Figure 15.16).

At approximately the correct strobe speed, the arrow often wanders backwards or forwards. This is because the speed of rotation of the strobe is slightly higher or slightly lower than that of the arrow (Figure 15.17).

When the strobe speed is slightly too high, the arrow makes slightly less than one revolution and is in positions A_1 and A_2 respectively as the second and the third sighting occur. The arrow appears to rotate slowly *backwards*.

When the strobe speed is slightly too low, the arrow makes slightly more than one revolution and is in positions B_1 and B_2 respectively as the second and the third sighting occur. The arrow appears to rotate slowly *forwards*.

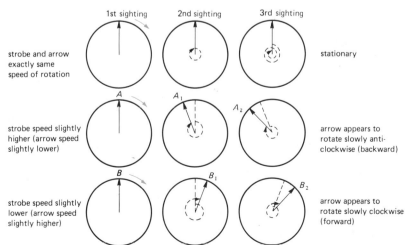

1st sighting   2nd sighting   3rd sighting

strobe and arrow
exactly same
speed of rotation   stationary

strobe speed slightly
higher (arrow speed
slightly lower)   arrow appears to
rotate slowly anti-
clockwise (backward)

strobe speed slightly
lower (arrow speed
slightly higher)   arrow appears to
rotate slowly clockwise
(forward)

Figure 15.17 Positions of arrow at successive sightings at different strobe speeds.

. . . . dotted line represents
rotation between views

19

Calculating the speed of rotation

Using a strobe with one slit, as described above, is not practical because it is just not possible to spin the strobe as fast as the motor. But a strobe with 12 slits only needs to be spun at one-twelfth the speed of the motor in order to freeze the arrow. This speed is a manageable one.

The number of sightings per second obtained with a strobe, that is, the number of slits passing the eye of the observer in one second, is called the **strobe frequency**. The strobe frequency must equal the frequency at which the arrow is seen in the same position in order to freeze the arrow. But freezing is also possible when the strobe frequency is equal to half or one-third the frequency of the motor, as explained previously. So, to find the unknown speed of rotation of the motor we must find the *maximum* strobe frequency which freezes the arrow in *one position*.

The strobe frequency is calculated by counting the number of slits in the strobe disc and measuring the time taken for the disc to rotate a fixed number of times.

Example 1

A white disc with a black arrow painted on it is rotated in a clockwise direction. It appears to be stationary when viewed through a strobe with 10 slits being rotated at the rate of 20 revolutions in 20 s. This is the maximum strobe speed without double viewing.
(a)   What is the rate of rotation of the disc?
(b)   What would be seen if the strobe rotated at the rate of 20 revolutions in 5 s?

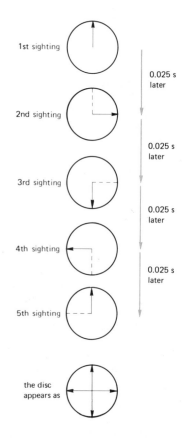

(a)   Number of slits passing the eye in 20 revolutions

$$= 10 \times 20 = 200$$

Time for 20 revolutions $= 20$ s

Strobe frequency $=$ number of slits passing the eye per second

$$= \frac{200}{20} = 10 \text{ Hz}$$

$\Rightarrow$ Rate of rotation of disc $= 10$ revs. s^{-1}

(b)   New strobe frequency $= \dfrac{20 \times 10}{5} = 40$ Hz

$\Rightarrow$ Time interval between sightings $= \dfrac{1}{40} = 0.025$ s

$\Rightarrow$ Time for arrow to make 1 revolution $= \dfrac{1}{10} = 0.1$ s

Therefore the disc appears as in Figure 15.18.

Figure 15.18   Arrow 'frozen' in four positions.

STROBOSCOPE LAMP

One difficulty in using a hand strobe is that its revolutions must be timed in order to find the strobe frequency. Also, its speed of rotation cannot easily be kept constant, and this gives rise to errors. The **stroboscope lamp** is another type of strobe which overcomes these difficulties. It consists of a lamp which flashes at regular time intervals (Figure 15.19). The flash rate can be adjusted over a wide range of frequency which is read directly on the strobe.

Figure 15.19   Stroboscope lamp.

The strobe lamp is usually used in a darkened room. Every time it flashes, the object in front of the strobe is illuminated. The maximum strobe frequency (flash rate) which freezes the motion of any vibrating or rotating object without double viewing is equal to the frequency of the object.

A strobe lamp can be used to check the rotation of, for example, a car engine. The strobe lamp is set at the correct frequency. If the engine rotation is not quite correct, a mark on the crankshaft will appear to move slowly either forwards or backwards.

The same principle is used when checking the speed of rotation of a turntable. The strobe lamp used is an ordinary lamp connected to the 50 Hz mains electricity. Although we do not notice it, the lamp flashes on and off at 100 Hz. When the turntable is viewed under the lamp, the line pattern marked on it appears to be stationary when the speed is properly adjusted (Figure 15.20).

Figure 15.20   Stroboscopic effect used to adjust turntable to the correct speed.

Figure 15.21   Ripple tank with strobe mounted in front of lens head of overhead projector.

FREEZING A WAVE PATTERN

Let us go back to the moving wave pattern in a ripple tank. The wave pattern is observed directly through a strobe. Or, with a ripple tank used on an overhead projector, the strobe may be mounted in front of the lens head of the projector (Figure 15.21). When the strobe is rotated at the correct speed either by hand or by a motor, the image on the screen is 'chopped' up at regular time intervals and the wave pattern can be frozen.

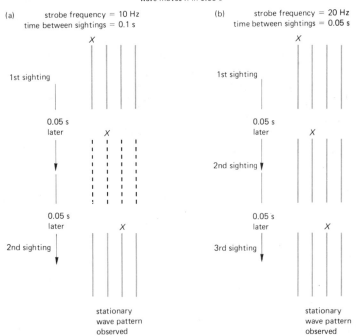

wave frequency = 20 Hz
wave moves λ in 0.05 s

(a) strobe frequency = 10 Hz
time between sightings = 0.1 s

X

1st sighting

0.05 s later

X

0.05 s later

X

2nd sighting

stationary
wave pattern
observed

(b) strobe frequency = 20 Hz
time between sightings = 0.05 s

X

1st sighting

0.05 s later

X

2nd sighting

0.05 s later

X

3rd sighting

stationary
wave pattern
observed

Figure 15.22 Wave patterns is 'frozen' if waves move on by exactly 1, 2, or more λ between successive sightings through strobe.

Figure 15.23 Wavelength is reduced to half if strobe frequency is twice that of ripples.

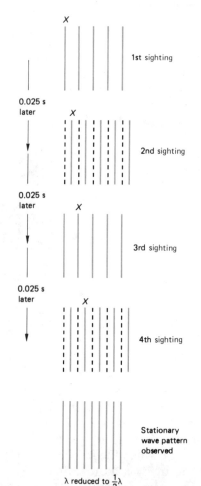

strobe frequency = 40 Hz
time between sightings = 0.025 s
wave frequency = 20 Hz
wave moves λ in 0.05 s

X

1st sighting

0.025 s later

X

2nd sighting

0.025 s later

X

3rd sighting

0.025 s later

X

4th sighting

Stationary
wave pattern
observed

λ reduced to $\frac{1}{2}$λ

The wave pattern appears stationary if the wave moves on by exactly 1, 2, or more wavelengths (λ) between successive sightings through the strobe. As in the case of the rotating arrow, the maximum strobe frequency which freezes the wave pattern is equal to the frequency of the wave.

A wave of frequency 20 Hz (Figure 15.22) has a period of 0.05 s which is the time for the wave to move a distance of one λ. In Figure 15.22a the strobe frequency is set at 10 Hz, half that of the wave, giving a time interval of 0.1 s between successive sightings. In this 0.1 s interval, the wavefronts (one of which is marked by x in the figure) move 2λ. In Figure 15.22b where the frequencies of the strobe and the wave are both 20 Hz, x moves one λ between successive sightings.

What happens if the strobe frequency is increased to 40 Hz, twice that of the wave? The wavelength appears to have reduced by half (Figure 15.23).

QUANTITATIVE WORK WITH WAVES

By using a strobe we can estimate the frequency f, wavelength λ, and speed v of waves in a ripple tank, and use these estimates to test the wave equation, $v = f\lambda$.

Estimating frequency

When the strobe is rotated at the *fastest* speed which freezes the wave pattern without any apparent reduction in wavelength, the number of slits on the strobe is counted and the time for, say, 20 revolutions is measured. The strobe frequency can then be calculated. This is the frequency of the wave.

Example 2

An observer views a wave pattern through a hand strobe with 12 slits. The strobe is rotated at the fastest rate that freezes the waves. The time for 20 revolutions of the strobe is measured to be 24 s. What is the frequency of the wave?

Number of slits passing the eye in 20 revolutions

$$= 20 \times 12 = 240$$

Time for 20 revolutions $= 24$ s

Number of slits passing in 1 s $= \dfrac{240}{24} = 10$

$\Rightarrow$ Strobe frequency $= 10$ Hz

$\Rightarrow$ Wave frequency $= 10$ Hz

Estimating wavelength

When the wave pattern is frozen, the length of 10λ can be measured with a metre rule on the screen (Figure 15.24). This distance corresponds to a magnified wavelength. The magnification can easily be measured by putting an object, for example a plastic ruler, in the ripple tank and measuring the length of the shadow cast on the screen. Then

$$\text{wavelength} = \text{apparent wavelength of screen} \times \frac{\text{object length}}{\text{shadow length}}$$

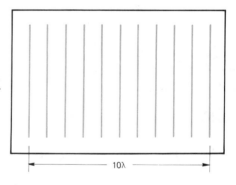

Figure 15.24   'Frozen' wave pattern.

Example 3

The image of 10 wavelengths of a wave pattern in a ripple tank measures 0.8 m on a screen. When a ruler 0.1 m long is placed in the ripple tank, its shadow on the screen is 0.5 m long. What is the wavelength of the wave pattern?

Apparent wavelength $= \dfrac{0.8 \text{ m}}{10} = 0.08$ m

Magnification of image on screen $= \dfrac{0.5 \text{ m}}{0.1 \text{ m}} = 5$ times

$\Rightarrow$ True wavelength of water wave $= \dfrac{0.08 \text{ m}}{5} = 0.016$ m

Estimating wave speed

If we have estimates of the frequency f and the wavelength λ, we can obtain an estimate of the wave speed v by substituting into the wave equation $v = f\lambda$.

A more direct method is to measure the time it takes for a straight wave pulse to travel a certain distance. Two points a measured distance apart are marked on the screen. A pencil is run along the screen between these two points. The pencil is kept is step with the pulse. The time taken to travel between the two points is measured with a stop-watch. Then

$$\text{wave speed} = \frac{\text{distance travelled}}{\text{time taken}}$$

Example 4
A pulse travels a distance of 1 m on the screen in 5 s. The image on the screen has a magnification of 5. What is the pulse speed?

$$\text{Speed of the pulse's image} = \frac{1\ \text{m}}{5\ \text{s}} = 0.2\ \text{m s}^{-1}$$

Magnification of image on screen = 5

$$\Rightarrow \text{Pulse speed} = \frac{0.2\ \text{m s}^{-1}}{5} = 0.04\ \text{m s}^{-1}$$

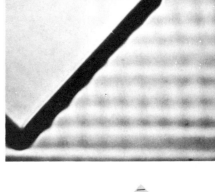

PROPERTIES OF CONTINUOUS WAVES

Using the ripple tank and the vibrating bar, we can generate continuous waves and study their behaviour. In some cases we need to use a strobe to freeze the wave pattern so that it can be observed more easily.

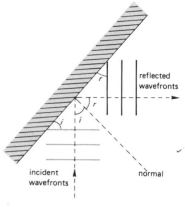

Reflection

As with a single pulse, a train of continuous waves also obeys the law of reflection, that is,

angle of incidence = angle of reflection   ($\angle i = \angle r$).

Note that only the incident and reflected *wavefronts* are observed; the rays are construction lines indicating the direction of travel of the waves (Figure 15.25).

Figure 15.25   Water waves obey the law of reflection.

Figure 15.26 shows how continuous plane waves and circular waves are reflected by a curved barrier.

Figure 15.26   (a) Plane waves converging to focus. (b) Circular waves converging to a point.

(a)

(b)

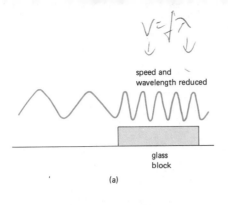

$$v = f\lambda$$

speed and wavelength reduced

glass block

(a)

(b)

Refraction

By putting a thin sheet of perspex in a ripple tank, the water in the tank is divided into two regions: a shallow and a deep region. As plane waves generated in the deep region enter the shallow region, the wavelength is reduced (Figure 15.27). The frequency remains unchanged as the same strobe frequency 'freezes' the wave in both regions. It follows from $v = f\lambda$ that the wave speed is also reduced in the shallow region.

When plane waves strike the boundary between deep and shallow waters at an angle, the direction of the waves is altered. This bending of waves at a boundary is called **refraction**. In Figure 15.28, $\angle i$ is the **angle of incidence** and is measured from the direction of travel of the incident waves to the normal; $\angle r$ is the **angle of refraction** and is measured from the direction of travel of the refracted waves to the normal. It is seen that $\angle i > \angle r$, that is, the waves bend *towards the normal* in shallow water. On the other hand, if waves move from shallow to deep water, $\angle i < \angle r$, the waves will bend *away from the normal*.

> **Refraction takes place whenever there is a change in wave speed (and a corresponding change in wavelength) when waves cross a boundary between two media.**

A lens-shaped piece of perspex converges plane waves to a focus. This is because the central part of the wavefronts has a lower speed for a longer time as it passes through the 'lens'. The waves emerging from the lens are therefore curved (Figure 15.29).

Figure 15.27 Water waves travel more slowly in shallow water.

Figure 15.28 Refraction of water waves.

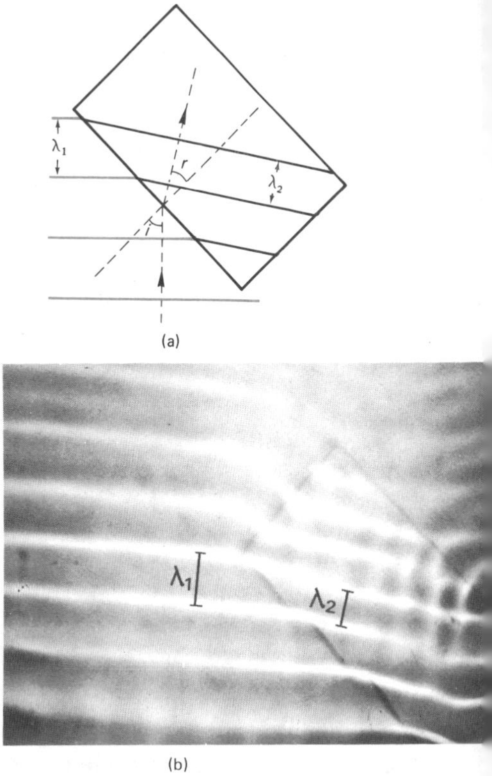

(a)

Figure 15.29 Refraction by a 'lens'.

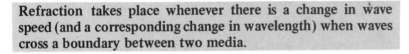

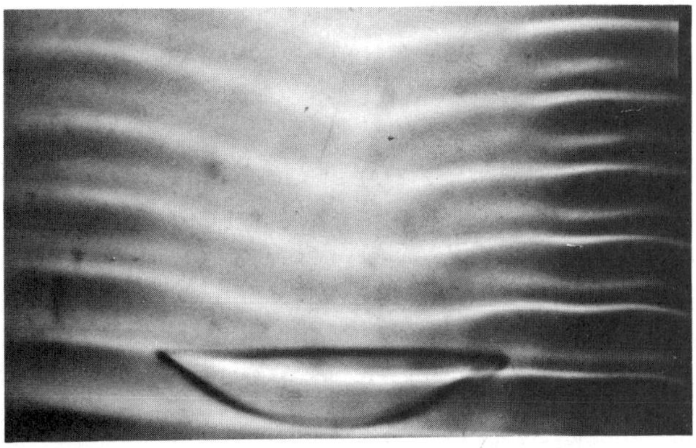

(b)

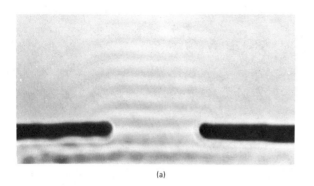
(a)

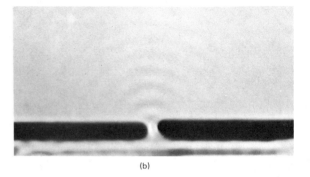
(b)

Diffraction

If plane waves are directed towards a gap between barriers in a ripple tank, they spread out into the 'shadow' of the barriers when they emerge from the gap (Figure 15.30). If the gap is reduced to about one wavelength or less, the waves that emerge are so spread out that they become semicircular.

Figure 15.30 Diffraction at (a) wide gap and (b) narrow gap.

(a)

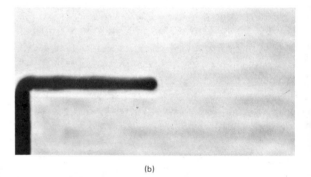
(b)

When plane waves pass the edge of an obstacle, they again bend around the edge into the 'shadow' (Figure 15.31). There is more spreading when the wavelength is increased. If the size of the obstacle is small compared with the wavelength, the waves pass round the obstacle and close up on the other side so that there is not much of a 'shadow' cast (Figure 15.32).

Figure 15.31 Diffraction of waves of (a) short wavelength and (b) long wavelength.

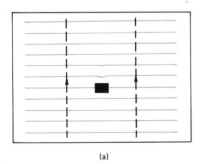
(a)

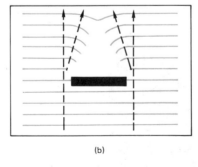
(b)

Figure 15.32 Diffraction at (a) small obstacle and (b) large obstacle.

This type of bending of waves around corners is called **diffraction**. The amount of diffraction depends on the relative size of the obstacle and the wavelength.

diffraction 衍射

Interference

When two sets of circular waves of the same frequency and wavelength cross in a ripple tank, an **interference pattern** similar to that shown in Figure 15.33 is produced. One way of producing such a pattern is to attach a pair of dippers to the vibrating bar of the ripple tank (Figure 15.34).

Let us first find out what happens when two waves meet. When we studied pulses along a spring, we found that when two pulses were sent from the opposite ends of a spring, they met, passed one another and continued unchanged, that is, when two waves pass through the same region, the resultant effect is the sum of the effects which each wave would have produced alone.

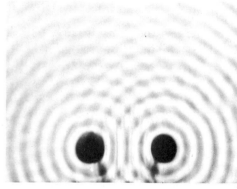

Figure 15.33   Interference pattern.

The following simple addition rules for waves therefore apply:

(a) crest + crest   = bigger crest

(b) trough + trough = bigger trough

(c) crest + trough = no wave

Cases (a) and (b) occur when the waves are in phase and case (c) occurs when the waves are exactly out of phase.

Therefore, when two waves which are in phase meet, they reinforce each other and form a wave of greater amplitude, but of the same wavelength (Figure 15.35a). This is called **constructive interference**.

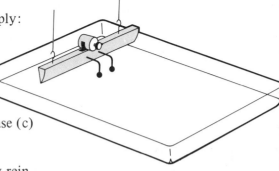

Figure 15.34   Two dippers producing two sets of interfering circular waves.

When two waves which are out of phase meet, they cancel each other and produce a wave of smaller amplitude. In the extreme case, they are exactly out of phase and cancel each other out completely (Figure 15.35b). This is called **destructive interference**.

(a)   constructive interference: 2 waves reinforce each other's effect

(b)   destructive interference: 2 waves cancel each other's effect

Figure 15.35   When two waves meet.

interference 干涉   constructive interference 相長干涉   destructive interference 相消干涉

27

Analysing the interference pattern

We can now consider how two sets of circular waves combine to form an interference pattern.

Figure 15.36 shows two overlapping sets of concentric semi-circles with centres at S_1 and S_2 respectively. They represent circular wavefronts produced in a ripple tank by two vibrating dippers *at a certain instant.* (The semicircles are wave crests.)

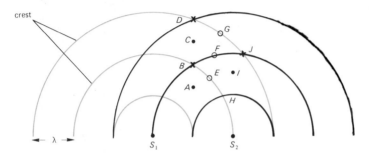

X crest meets crest
● trough meets trough
○ crest meets trough

Figure 15.36 Analyzing interference pattern.

At point A, a trough from S_1 meets a trough from S_2 and produces a larger trough. This is shown as a very dark region on the screen. At point B, a crest from S_1 meets a crest from S_2 and produces a larger crest. This is shown as a very bright region on the screen. Similarly, point C represents a large trough and point D a large crest. Hence waves from S_1 and S_2 interfere constructively at points A, B, C and D because these points are all equidistant from S_1 and S_2. Therefore, along the line joining points A, B, C and D, there is a wave of large amplitude.

Point H is at a distance of 2λ from S_1 and λ from S_2. A large crest is produced at H as a crest from S_1 meets a crest from S_2. A large crest is also produced at point J which is 3λ away from S_1 and 2λ from S_2. At point I, which is $2\frac{1}{2}\lambda$ away from S_1 and $1\frac{1}{2}\lambda$ from S_2, a large trough is produced. Hence, along the line joining H, I and J, there is also a wave of large amplitude. It can be seen that the **path difference** (symbol Δ) of any one of these points H, I or J from S_1 and S_2 is always one λ. For example,

for point H, $\Delta = \overline{HS_1} - \overline{HS_2} = 2\lambda - \lambda = \lambda$

for point I, $\Delta = \overline{IS_1} - \overline{IS_2} = 2\frac{1}{2}\lambda - 1\frac{1}{2}\lambda = \lambda$

Points E and G are points where crests from S_1 meet troughs from S_2. Point F is where a trough from S_1 meets a crest from S_2. At all these points the waves from S_1 and S_2 interfere destructively, so the line joining points E, F and G is a region of calm water. On the screen this appears as a less bright region. The path difference of any one of these points E, F or G from S_1 and S_2 is always $\frac{1}{2}\lambda$. For example,

for point E, $\Delta = \overline{ES_1} - \overline{ES_2} = 2\lambda - 1\frac{1}{2}\lambda = \frac{1}{2}\lambda$

for point F, $\Delta = \overline{FS_1} - \overline{FS_2} = 2\frac{1}{2}\lambda - 2\lambda = \frac{1}{2}\lambda$

path difference 程差

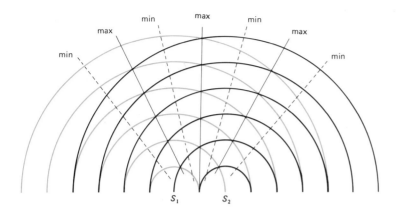

Figure 15.37 Locating lines of maxima and minima.

The complete interference pattern is obtained by locating all the lines of strong waves and of calm water (Figure 15.37). In the figure, the solid lines represent the *maxima* (large amplitude) and the dotted lines represent the *minima* (zero or near zero amplitude).

Figure 15.38 Waves from S_1 and S_2 meet at P.

Condition for interference

To see if waves from two sources S_1 and S_2 interfere constructively or destructively at a point P, we look at the path difference of point P from S_1 and S_2 (Figure 15.38).

In general, there is constructive interference when the path difference is equal to a whole number of the wavelengths, that is,

$$\Delta = \overline{PS_1} - \overline{PS_2} = 0, \lambda, 2\lambda, 3\lambda, \ldots$$

There is destructive interference when the path difference is equal to $\frac{1}{2}$, $1\frac{1}{2}$ and so on wavelengths, that is,

$$\Delta = \overline{PS_1} - \overline{PS_2} = \frac{1}{2}\lambda, 1\frac{1}{2}\lambda, 2\frac{1}{2}\lambda, \ldots$$

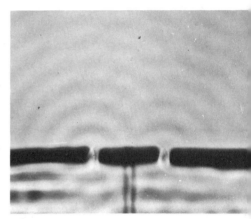

Figure 15.39 Interference pattern of diffracted waves from two gaps.

Producing interference patterns

As we have seen, an interference pattern can be produced by using two dippers attached to the vibrating bar in a ripple tank. Note that the two dippers are always vibrating in phase.

If trains of plane waves pass through two narrow gaps which are close together (Figure 15.39), interference occurs between the two sets of diffracted circular waves emerging from the gaps. This interference pattern is often very weak and difficult to observe as most of the energy transmitted by the plane waves has been blocked.

In Figure 15.40, waves travelling out directly from a dipper interfere with waves reflected from a straight barrier behind it. Interference occurs between one set of waves from the dipper and another set from its 'image' behind the barrier.

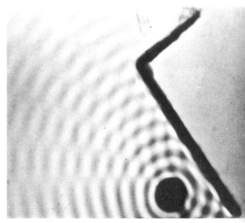

Figure 15.40 Interference pattern produced by one dipper placed in front of barrier.

29

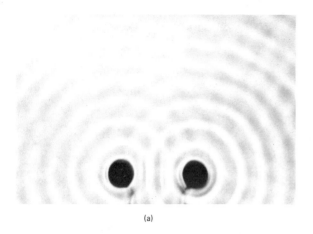
(a)

(b)

Figure 15.41 shows interference patterns produced by waves of different wavelengths. With shorter wavelength the whole pattern shrinks, so there are more closely spaced lines of maxima and minima.

Figure 15.41 Interference patterns of waves of (a) long wavelength and (b) short wavelength. With shorter wavelength, pattern shrinks, that is, there are more lines of maxima and minima.

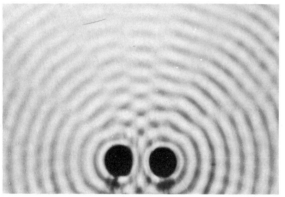

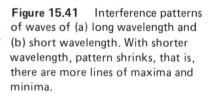

Figure 15.42 There are fewer lines of maximum and minimum interference when sources are close together.

Figure 15.42 shows that when two sources are moved closer together, the interference pattern is more spread out. There are fewer but more widely spaced lines of maxima and minima.

Simulation of interference pattern

Figure 15.43 shows a transparent plastic sheet with a large number of closely spaced concentric circles. Two such sheets are overlapped so that the centres of the circles coincide. As the two sheets are moved apart, patterns similar to interference patterns of water waves are seen, with the bright bands representing the lines of maxima and the dark bands the lines of minima. But actually what is observed is not interference; it is only a simulation.

As the two centres are moved further apart, the pattern tends to shrink: there are more lines of maxima and minima and they are more closely spaced (Figure 15.44a). When the two centres become far apart (Figure 15.44b), the 'interference' pattern

Figure 15.43 Concentric circles to simulate interference.

appears to fade away completely. This shows that, in the real situation, interference patterns can be observed only when the two sources are separated by a distance of the order of a few wavelengths. This result is very important when trying to obtain interference patterns of other forms of waves, for example light and sound.

In conclusion, water waves show reflection, refraction, diffraction and interference. The reflection and refraction of water waves are closely analogous to those of light studied in Chapters 1, 2 and 3.

Figure 15.44 (a) Sources a few wavelengths apart give distinct lines of maxima and minima. (b) Sources farther apart.

(a)

(b)

SUMMARY

Water waves show reflection, refraction, diffraction and interference.

Continuous water waves can be 'frozen' using a stroboscope. The frequency of the wave is found by measuring the maximum strobe frequency which freezes the wave pattern without any apparent reduction in wavelength.

Reflection of water waves

When water waves are reflected, they obey the law of reflection ($\angle i = \angle r$).

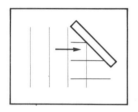
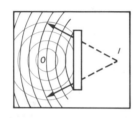
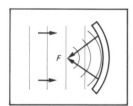
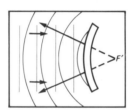

Refraction of water waves

Refraction is the change in direction of a wave as it crosses the boundary between two media. This is due to a change in wave speed of the wave between the two media.

When water waves pass from deep water to shallow water, refraction takes place:

> the wave speed decreases,
> the wavelength decreases,
> the refracted waves bend towards the normal.

When water waves pass from shallow water to deep water, the opposite occurs. In all cases of refraction the wave frequency remains unchanged.

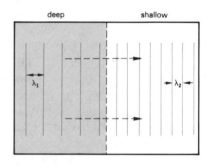
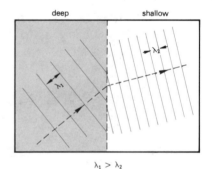

$\lambda_1 > \lambda_2$

Diffraction of water waves

Diffraction is the bending of waves around corners.

The amount of diffraction depends on the relative size of the slit or obstacle and the wavelength. The narrower the slit the more the wave spreads out.

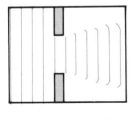
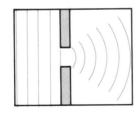

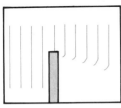
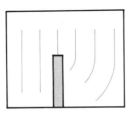

Interference of water waves

Constructive interference occurs when two waves which are in phase reinforce each other to form a wave of greater amplitude.

Destructive interference occurs when two waves which are exactly out of phase cancel each other out to give an area of calm water.

An interference pattern is produced when two circular waves which are generated in phase overlap each other.

As the distance between two sources is increased, the pattern shrinks with the lines of maxima and minima becoming closely spaced. When the distance is too great (the two sources are too many wavelengths apart), no interference pattern is observed.

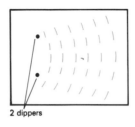

2 dippers

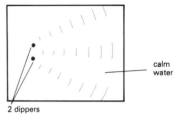

2 dippers

calm water

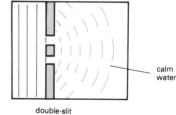

double-slit

calm water

PROBLEMS

1. When a water wave is reflected, which, if any, of the following are changed? Frequency, wavelength, wave speed.

2. Figure 15.45 shows a circular ripple hitting a straight barrier. Copy and complete the missing part of the reflected ripple.

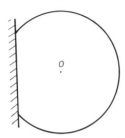

Figure 15.45

3. Figure 15.46a shows a straight ripple *ABC* travelling towards a straight barrier *XY*.
   (a) Figure 15.46b shows the position of the ripple when *B* has reached the barrier. Copy and complete the missing reflected ripple.
   (b) Draw a second diagram to show the position of the reflected ripple when *C* has reached the barrier.

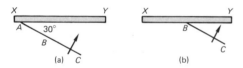

Figure 15.46

4. Copy and complete each diagram in Figure 15.47 to show what will happen to the water wave after it hits the reflector.

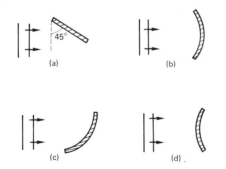

Figure 15.47

5. A water wave has a frequency of 5 Hz. Give two strobe frequencies which can freeze the wave without changing the wavelength.

6. A 10-slit stroboscope rotates 20 times in 5 seconds.
   (a) What is the strobe frequency?
   (b) What is the time interval between one sighting and the next?
   (c) How can you double the time interval between sightings without altering the rotation of the stroboscope?

7. A 12-slit stroboscope is used to view a rotating disc with an arrow painted on it. The arrow is frozen when the strobe is rotated at 2 revolutions per second. Assume this to be the highest strobe speed which does not give double viewing.
   (a) What is the rate of rotation of the disc?
   (b) What would be seen if the strobe speed is
      (i) halved,   (ii) doubled?

8. A rotating wheel has 8 spokes. A girl looks at it through a 10-slit strobe rotated at 4 times a second.
   (a) How many times can she see the wheel in 1 second?
   (b) What is the time interval between one sighting and the next?
   (c) Suppose during this time interval the wheel makes one complete rotation. Explain why the wheel appears to be at rest. Calculate the rate of rotation (in revolutions per second) of the wheel.
   (d) Next suppose during the time between one sighting and the next, the wheel makes $\frac{1}{8}$ of a rotation. Explain why the wheel also appears to be at rest. Calculate the rate of rotation of the wheel.
   (e) What are the other rates of rotation at which the wheel appears to be at rest?

9. A 6-slit stroboscope is used to freeze a wave pattern. When the stroboscope is being rotated at:
   (a) 1 revolution per second the observer sees the pattern in Figure 15.48a,
   (b) 2 revolutions per second the observer sees the pattern in Figure 15.48b,
   (c) 4 revolutions per second the observer sees the pattern in Figure 15.48c.
   What is the frequency of the wave?

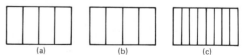

Figure 15.48

10. Water waves are generated in a ripple tank by a vibrator hitting the water surface 10 times per second. The wavelength is measured to be 2 cm.
   (a) What is the speed of the water waves?
   The frequency of the waves is now doubled by speeding up the vibrator.
   (b) What are the new wave speed and wavelength of the water waves?

11. A ruler of 10 cm length is placed in a ripple tank. It casts a shadow 40 cm long on the screen. A single ripple is produced and is found to travel 1 m on the screen in 2 s. A continuous wave is then generated with a frequency of 5 Hz.
   (a) At what speed would the waves move across the ripple tank?
   (b) What is the wavelength of the water waves?

12. A ripple tank is tilted so that the water is progressively deep from one side to the other (Figure 15.49a). Continuous straight ripples are generated in the shallow water side of the tank as shown. Copy Figure 15.49b and c and complete the pattern of the wavelengths.

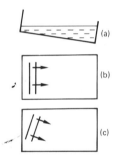

Figure 15.49

13. A pulse is started at the centre of the ripple tank in Figure 15.49a. Draw the shape of the pulse as it moves out from the centre.

14. A set of straight ripples moves into a triangular shallow region in a ripple tank. Copy and complete Figure 15.50 to show the wavefronts in the shallow region and after leaving the shallow region. Also indicate the direction of the waves.

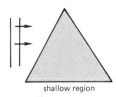

Figure 15.50

shallow region

15. (a) A vibrator sends a series of straight ripples to a barrier with a gap in it (Figure 15.51a). Redraw the diagram and complete the wave pattern on the right side.
   (b) The vibrator is now slowed down so that the water waves generated have longer wavelength. Redraw Figure 15.51b and complete the wave pattern.
   (c) Compare the two wave patterns in (a) and (b).

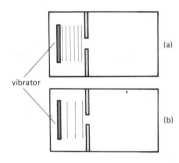

vibrator

Figure 15.51

16. (a) What are the uses of the following parts of a ripple tank in wave experiments?
       (i) a dot vibrator,
       (ii) the shallow portion of the tank.
   (b) In a ripple tank experiment, waves are generated by a straight vibrator as shown in Figure 15.52.
       (i) Copy Figure 15.52 and sketch the wave patterns at the shallow portion of the tank.
       (ii) What do you expect to be formed at the area between the reflecting barrier and the straight vibrator?

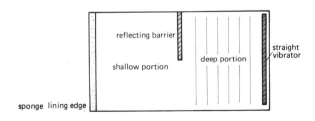

Figure 15.52

(c) A wave of wavelength 2 cm is generated by a dot vibrator placed at a distance of 2.5 cm from a plane reflecting surface as shown in Figure 15.53.

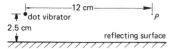

Figure 15.53

(i) What is the distance of the 'image' of the vibrator from the reflecting surface?
(ii) The distance between the 'image' and the point P in the figure is 13 cm. Would there be constructive or destructive interferences at P? Explain briefly.
(Hint: The 'image' can be considered as another wave generator.)

(HKCEE 1979)

17. (a) Water waves are viewed through a stroboscope as shown in Figure 15.54. They appear stationary when the stroboscope rotates at 3 revolutions per second and at 9 revolutions per second. However, they do not appear stationary when the stroboscope rotates at 6 revolutions per second.
    (i) Find the minimum frequency of the vibrator.
    (ii) Find the minimum velocity of the waves if the distance between two successive crests is 2 cm.

Figure 15.54

(b) A lamp is placed just above the tank. The pattern of the ripple can be projected on a white paper under the tank as shown in Figure 15.55. Explain how this happens.
(c) A straight barrier is placed in the ripple tank so that it is parallel to the wavefronts. What happens when the plane waves are reflected by the barrier?
(d) A narrow opening is made in the barrier and this opening is then made wider and wider. Draw three diagrams to show different diffraction patterns.

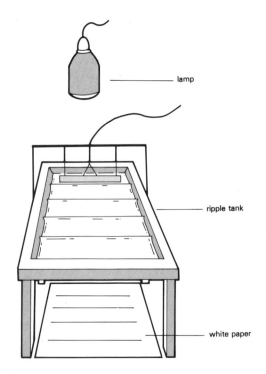

Figure 15.55

(e) If the barrier in (c) has two narrow openings, as shown in Figure 15.56, draw a diagram to show the resulting interference pattern.

(HKCEE 1982)

Figure 15.56

18. In a ripple tank experiment, a generator produces a train of straight waves travelling towards a barrier with two narrow slits. The distance between two successive wave crests is found to be 2 cm.
    (a) The ripple tank is illuminated by a stroboscope lamp. The wave motion appears to be stationary when the frequency of the stroboscope lamp is 5 Hz or 10 Hz. (No higher frequency is found to have this effect.)
       (i) What is the speed of the train of waves?
       (ii) Describe what the wave motion would appear to be if the frequency of the stroboscope lamp is slightly higher than 5 Hz.

(b) The train of waves, after passing through the narrow slits, spreads out in the pattern shown in Figure 15.57.
  (i) Explain why the wave energy is at a maximum at points A and E and is at a minimum at points B and D.
  (ii) Since very little or no wave motion is seen at points B and D, a student concludes that energy disappears there. Explain briefly where the energy goes.
  (iii) Sketch the water level along the line XC at a certain instant.
  (iv) How would the separation between A and C change if
    (1) the frequency of the generator increases, and
    (2) the separation between the two slits increases?

(HKCEE 1984)

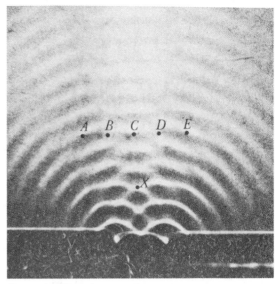

Figure 15.57

19. In a ripple tank experiment, a train of water waves are produced by a straight vibrator of frequency 10 Hz. The train of waves goes from a region A to another region B through a straight boundary PQ as shown in Figure 15.58. The two regions are of different depths. The distance between two successive crests of the waves in region A is 0.03 m while that of the waves in region B is 0.02 m.
(a) Describe briefly how to set up two regions of different depths in a ripple tank.
(b) Describe briefly how to measure the distance between the crests of two successive wavefronts.
(c) Find the speeds of the trains of water waves in
  (i) region A, and
  (ii) region B.
(d) Which of the regions, A or B, is deeper?
(e) If the wavefront in A makes an angle of 30° with PQ, what is angle θ which the wavefront in B makes with the boundary?
(f) If a straight barrier is now placed in position RS as shown in the figure, what new wave motion would you expect to find in region B? Explain briefly why this happens.

(HKCEE 1985)

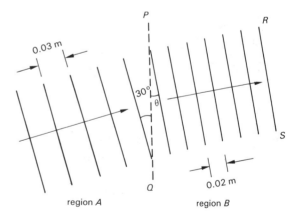

Figure 15.58

Wave Nature of Light

Light is essential for life on Earth and it is necessary to establish its nature and properties.

LIGHT AND ENERGY

Light transmits energy. The vanes of a radiometer begin to rotate as light falls on them (Figure 16.1). The reading of a thermometer rises when it is put into sunlight. A piece of paper can be burned by focusing light on it with a magnifying glass. Sunlight generates electricity in solar cells which are used, for example, in communication satellites in space (Figure 16.2), and in navigational light beacons at sea (Figure 16.3). Most importantly, sunlight is needed by green plants in order to produce food by the process of photosynthesis. Therefore, it is clear that light is a form of energy which can be changed into other forms of energy, for example kinetic, thermal, electrical and chemical energy.

Figure 16.1   Radiometer.

Figure 16.3   The Marine Department uses solar cells to operate navigational light beacons.

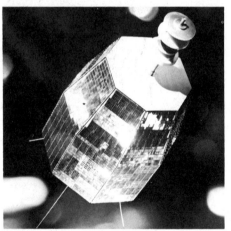
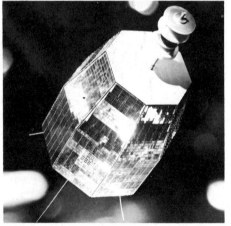

Figure 16.2   The 78-kg 8-sided communications satellite is covered with 8215 solar cells.

Light can travel through a vacuum, as with sunlight passing through the enormous vacuum in space before reaching the Earth.

Light travels with an extremely high speed of 300 million metres per second (3.00×10^8 m s^{-1}) in a vacuum and very nearly as fast in air. Light travels so fast that it can go round the equator of the Earth almost eight times in one second!

REFLECTION AND REFRACTION OF LIGHT

With water waves we looked at the wavefronts and deduced the direction of travel of the wave by drawing imaginary lines (rays) at right angles to the wavefronts. With light, we observe light beams which travel along straight lines, for example the beam from a torch. Here a *ray* is a narrow beam of light which indicates the direction of travel.

In the laboratory reflection of light is demonstrated by allowing a ray of light from a ray-box to strike a plane mirror (Figure 16.4). The light ray obeys the law of reflection: the angle of incidence is always equal to the angle of reflection.

Refraction of light is shown by allowing a ray of light to pass through a rectangular glass block (Figure 16.5). At the air-glass interface, part of the incident ray is reflected, while a second part is transmitted through the glass. The second part of the ray (transmitted ray) is refracted *towards the normal*. On emerging from the glass block the ray is refracted *away from the normal*.

Figure 16.4   Reflection at plane mirror: angle of incidence equals angle of reflection.

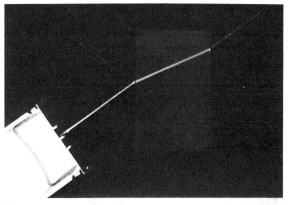

Figure 16.5   Light ray refracted twice by glass block (and partly reflected as well).

Comparing light (Chapters 1 and 2) and water waves, there is a close analogy between the reflection and refraction of light and the reflection and refraction of water waves.

WAVE OR PARTICLES?

Light rays show reflection and refraction. But these two properties are not sufficient to prove that light is a wave. Reflection and refraction can also be explained by assuming that light consists of a stream of tiny fast-moving particles shot out from the light source.

If a ball-bearing strikes a hard plane surface obliquely, it bounces off at an angle, with the angle of incidence equalling the angle of reflection (Figure 16.6).

To show refraction of particles a ball-bearing is rolled down a launching-ramp on an oblique path (Figure 16.7). It moves in a straight line at constant speed across the cardboard surface which is raised above the bench. It speeds up on reaching the sloping surface, bends *towards* the normal and continues at a *higher* speed in a straight line across the lower level surface.

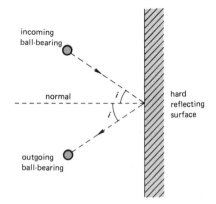

Figure 16.6 Ball-bearing striking the surface obeys the law of reflection.

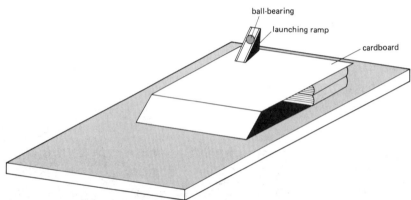

Figure 16.7 Refraction of ball-bearing.

However, there is an important difference between the refraction of a particle and the refraction of water waves. On entering a shallow region, water waves bend towards the normal and the wave speed *decreases*. When a particle enters a region in which it bends towards the normal, its speed *increases*. It has been shown that a ray of light bends towards the normal on entering from air into glass or water. So, if light is a wave, its speed in glass or water will be *lower* than in air, but if it is made up of particles, its speed will be *higher*.

The debate on whether light is a wave or is made up of particles had lasted for a long time. In 1680 the Dutch scientist Christian Huygens proposed that light was a wave. Sir Isaac Newton disagreed and suggested that light consisted of tiny fast-moving particles. The debate continued among many other scientists, and it was not until 1801 when Thomas Young demonstrated interference of light in his **double-slit experiment** that the wave nature of light was established. In 1850 Foucault succeeded in demonstrating that the speed of light in water is lower than in air. This confirmed that light is a wave.

double-slit experiment 雙窄縫實驗

DIFFRACTION OF LIGHT

When water waves emerge from a gap, they tend to spread out into the 'shadow' of the barriers. The amount of spreading depends on the relative size of the obstacle and the wavelength. Light ray also undergoes diffraction. But as the amount of bending is very small, it is extremely difficult to observe without the aid of special apparatus. Figure 16.8 shows the shadow of an opaque disc produced by placing the disc midway between a very brightly illuminated pin-hole and a photographic film. The bright spot at the centre is produced by the bending of light round the edge of the disc. Figure 16.9 shows another striking example of diffraction produced by replacing the disc with a razor blade.

In the school laboratory much simpler apparatus is used to show the diffraction of light. A number of very small holes of different sizes are made in pieces of aluminium foil which are mounted on cardboard frames. A straight-filament lamp from a ray-box is set up at a distance. The bright filament of the lamp is viewed through the fine holes by holding the foil close to one eye, with the other eye closed (Figure 16.10). As the hole gets smaller, the light source is no longer seen as a sharp bright spot. One or two rather faint, bright rings around the central bright spot begin to appear. The rings arc produced by light bending around the small hole.

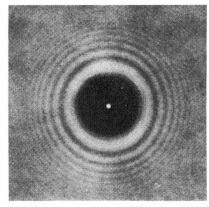

Figure 16.8   Light diffracts round the edge of an opaque disc. Note the central bright spot.

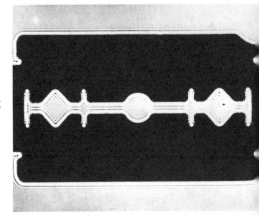

Figure 16.9   Because of diffraction, the image of the razor blade is blurred.

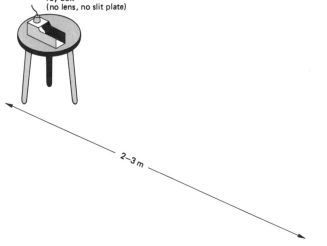

ray-box
(no lens, no slit plate)

2–3 m

aluminium
foil with holes

Figure 16.10   Observing diffraction at a slit.

The bright filament is next viewed through a narrow adjustable slit. When the width of the slit is reduced sufficiently, a diffraction pattern like that shown in Figure 16.11 is seen. The light has spread out into regions which would be in shadow if light travelled only in straight lines. (The diffraction pattern can also be seen by simply placing two pencils side by side and viewing the bright filament through the very narrow slit between them, or by holding several closely spaced pieces of hair near to the eyes.)

If the slit is covered with a red filter and then a blue filter, the red diffraction pattern is slightly more spread out than the blue one (Figure 16.12). Water waves of larger wavelength bend around a barrier more than waves of shorter wavelength. Therefore red light must have a longer wavelength than blue light.

INTERFERENCE OF LIGHT

To produce an interference pattern with water waves, the two wave sources must be:

1. of the same wave frequency,

2. in phase (more correctly, having a constant phase relationship), and

3. separated by a distance not too great compared with the wavelength.

These are also the conditions we need to produce interference of light. Two light sources of the same frequency are readily obtained, but they will never be exactly in phase. Thomas Young overcame this difficulty by using a pair of very closely spaced slits (Figure 16.13). Wavefronts pass through the single

Figure 16.11 Diffraction pattern of white light at a single slit.

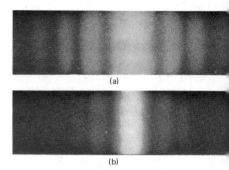

(a)

(b)

Figure 16.12 Diffraction patterns of light through (a) red filter and (b) blue filter. Red light, having a longer wavelength, is diffracted more.

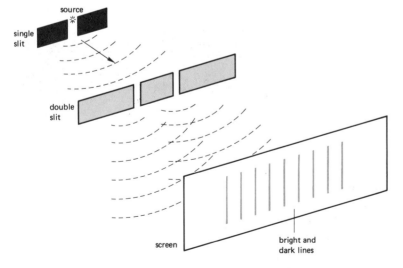

Figure 16.13 Young's double-slit experiment.

42

slit close to the light source and are diffracted when they reach the double-slit. The two sets of circular wavefronts that emerge from the double-slit interfere with each other at places where they overlap. These two sets of waves are identical in frequency and in phase because they come from the same source.

Young's double-slit experiment

Young's double-slit experiment is set up in the school laboratory as shown in Figure 16.14. A compact light source or a straight-filament lamp is used. Note that the light source should not be covered by a single slit as in Young's original apparatus because this will greatly reduce the light intensity. The straight filament itself is used as a vertical line source.

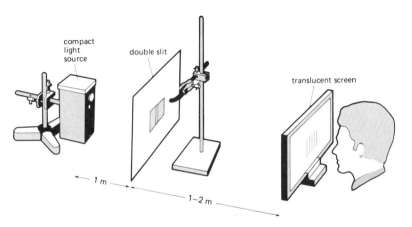

Figure 16.14 Observing interference pattern on a screen.

The double-slit is made by coating a glass slide with aquadag and making two closely spaced slits on it with a needle. Alternatively, a ready-made double-slit on a photographic negative may be used. Note that the double-slit must be mounted parallel to the *vertical* filament of the light source.

The translucent screen is placed close to the double-slit and then gradually moved away. At first only two bright lines are seen, but when the screen is more than about one metre away from the double-slit, a pattern of several faintly visible bright and dark lines or **fringes** begins to appear (Figure 16.15).

Figure 16.15 Interference pattern.

The bright and dark fringes can only be explained by assuming that light behaves as waves. Light waves have been diffracted and spread out as they pass through the slits and interference occurs in places where they cross (Figure 16.16). Where light waves reinforce each other, a bright fringe is formed; where they cancel out, a dark fringe is formed.

fringe　條紋

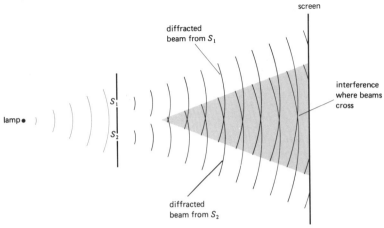

Figure 16.16 Interference occurs where the two sets of waves cross.

Thus we have

at a bright fringe: light + light = more light

at a dark fringe: light + light = no light or darkness

If light were made up of particles, it would not be possible to obtain an interference pattern, because the effects of two particles cannot add up to zero or no effect. It is now known that the wavelength of light is of the order of 10^{-7} m. Such a short wavelength explains why diffraction and interference of light are not easily observed.

Interference is a unique property of waves and it is used as the criterion of wave nature.

Effects of colour

An interference pattern can also be seen by viewing the bright, straight filament of a lamp through a double-slit held close to the eye (Figure 16.17). If the double-slit is covered in turn by a red, and a blue filter, interference patterns of different colours and different fringe spacings are observed (Figure 16.18).

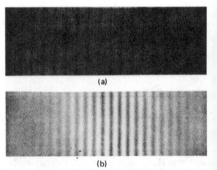

Figure 16.18 Interference fringes with different wavelengths: (a) red light, (b) blue light.

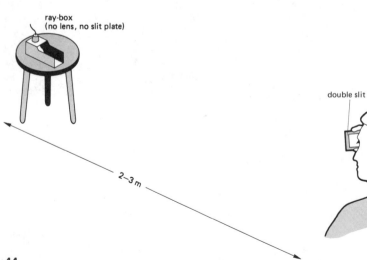

Figure 16.17 Observing interference pattern directly.

The sizes of the fringe spacings show that red light has a greater wavelength than blue light. The greater the wavelength, the wider apart become the lines of maxima and minima (Figure 16.19).

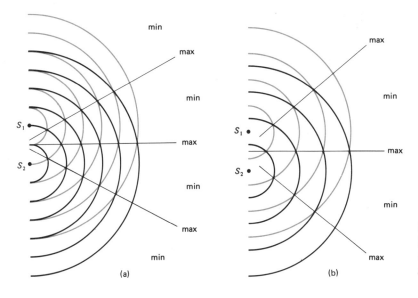

Figure 16.19 (a) Shorter wavelength, fringes close together.
(b) Longer wavelength, fringes farther apart.

More interference patterns

There are usually two types of **diffraction grating** (with a large number of very closely spaced slits) used in schools. The *coarse* grating has 1000 slits per cm, and the *fine* grating has 3000 slits per cm. With white light from a filament lamp, a coarse grating produces several coloured bands on either side of a central bright line. A fine grating produces the same pattern but with fewer and more spread out coloured bands (Figure 16.20). Each of the coloured bands, if examined closely, consists of colours ranging from red, orange, yellow, green, blue, indigo to violet. These colour bands are called **spectra** (plural of **spectrum**).

The explanation for the patterns produced by the gratings is too complicated to be dealt with here, but their appearance should be carefully noted. White light consists of seven colours which have different wavelengths so that they are diffracted to different extents by a grating and are separated out.

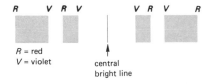

R = red
V = violet
central bright line

Figure 16.20 Spectra formed by diffraction grating.

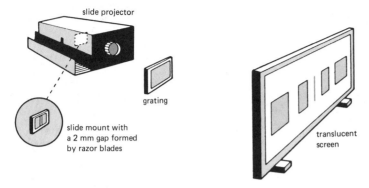

Figure 16.21 Projecting diffraction grating pattern on a screen.

The coloured bands can be shown on a screen as in Figure 16.21. A slit of about 2 mm width is made by breaking a razor blade along its axis and mounting the two halves in a slide mount. The slide is put in a slide projector which is adjusted so that a bright line is focused on the screen. When a fine grating is held in front of the projector lens, coloured bands are seen on the screen.

SUMMARY

Light transmits energy.

Light travels at a speed of 3.00×10^8 m s^{-1} in vacuum and nearly as fast in air.

Reflection of light

When light rays are reflected they obey the law of reflection ($\angle i = \angle r$).

Refraction of light

When light passes from a less dense to a more dense medium, refraction takes place and

> the wave speed decreases
> the wavelength decreases
> the refracted ray bends towards the normal

When light passes from a dense to a less dense medium, the opposite results occur. In both cases the frequency remains unchanged in the two media.

Waves or particles

The reflection and refraction of light can be explained either by assuming that light is a wave or that light is made up of particles. To determine whether light is a wave, the criterion is whether light shows interference.

Interference

To produce an observable interference pattern the two light sources used must be idential, in phase and separated by a distance that is not too great compared with the wavelength.

In 1801 Thomas Young first demonstrated interference of light using a pair of very closely spaced slits (double-slit experiment).

In an interference pattern, the greater the wavelength, the greater is the fringe spacing.

Coloured bands (consisting of the colours red, orange, yellow, green, blue, indigo and violet) are produced when white light passes through a diffraction grating.

PROBLEMS

1. Light travels at 3×10^8 m s^{-1}. How long would it take to travel 1 kilometre?

2. A ray of light strikes a rectangular glass block as shown in Figure 16.22.
   (a) Copy the diagram and show the complete path of the ray through the block.
   (b) What changes, if any, take place in the speed, wavelength and frequency of the light ray when it passes from air into glass?

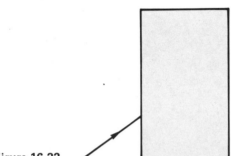

Figure 16.22

3. In a double-slit experiment, red, green and blue light are used in turn. Which colour produces the most widely-spaced and which produces the most closely-spaced fringe pattern?

4. A double-slit is held close to the eye to view a straight filament lamp at a distance.
   (a) Sketch the pattern observed.
   (b) What difference will be seen if another double-slit of smaller slit separation is used?

5. Figure 16.23 represents a double-slit experiment (not to scale).
   (a) If O is the central bright fringe, what can you say about the distances S_1O and S_2O?
   (b) If P is the first dark fringe, how do the distances S_1P and S_2P compare?
   (c) If Q is the next bright fringe, how do the distances S_1Q and S_2Q compare?

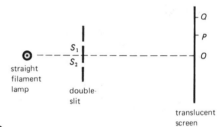

Figure 16.23

Electromagnetic Waves

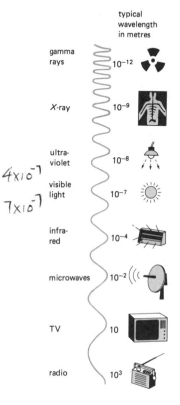

Light is only a small part of a large family of waves called electromagnetic waves. The full range of electromagnetic waves forms the electromagnetic spectrum, which includes many different types of wave useful to men.

THE ELECTROMAGNETIC SPECTRUM

The different members of the electromagnetic spectrum are shown in Figure 17.1. All have the properties of waves, that is, they show reflection, refraction, diffraction and interference. They transmit energy and all travel at the same speed, the speed of light. The wavelength λ and frequency f of each kind of wave are related to the wave speed v by the equation $v = f\lambda$, so that a short wavelength corresponds to a high frequency.

The spectrum extends from gamma rays of extremely short wavelength (of the order of 10^{-13} m) to radio waves of very long wavelength (several tens of kilometres). Each type of wave in the spectrum occupies a particular range of wavelength. But some waves overlap, for example, some waves may be called ultra-violet or X-rays depending on how they are produced.

Each kind of wave in the spectrum was discovered independently and is produced and detected in different ways. Due to the work of James Clark Maxwell all these waves were put in one family and were shown to have common properties. In his electromagnetic theory, developed in the 1860s, Maxwell showed that *theoretically* light is a form of travelling electrical and magnetic transverse waves. He calculated the speed of such **electromagnetic waves** to be nearly 3×10^8 m s^{-1} which was the same as the speed of light as measured by Fizeau in 1849. Maxwell also predicted the existence of electromagnetic waves of many different wavelengths and that they all travelled at the speed of light. Maxwell's theory was confirmed in 1887 when Hertz succeeded in producing what are now generally called **radio waves**. In the following year Hertz measured the speed of these electromagnetic waves and found it to be just the same as the speed of light, as Maxwell had predicted. In subsequent experiments Hertz also showed that radio waves had all the properties of waves. The work of Maxwell and Hertz not only

Figure 17.1 The electromagnetic spectrum.

broke new ground in physics but also set the pace for the development of new technologies such as radio, television, radar, telecommunications, etc.

THE VISIBLE SPECTRUM

Our main source of light is the Sun. There are, however, other artificial sources of light. They are either hot objects, for example the hot filament of a light bulb, or a gas discharge produced by electricity through a gas, for example a fluorescent tube.

Sunlight and light from filament lamps and fluorescent tubes appear white, but they are in fact made up of a number of different coloured lights. We have shown how white light from a filament lamp was separated into its constituent colours when it passed through a diffraction grating. As early as in 1666, Issac Newton was able to produce a similar spectrum by passing sunlight through a glass **prism**. He concluded that sunlight is a mixture of lights of different colours: red, orange, yellow, green, blue, indigo and violet. These lights are refracted to different extents by the prism and are therefore separated. The white light is said to have been **dispersed** by the prism — red light is refracted least and violet light most (Figure 17.2).

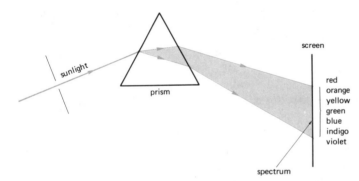

Figure 17.2 Sunlight is dispersed by prism into its constituent colours.

The wavelengths of the seven coloured light, when measured accurately, have a continuous range from 4×10^{-7} m for violet light to 7×10^{-7} m for red light, the other colours having wavelengths between these two values. The eye is sensitive to this range of wavelengths. The spectrum of white light is therefore called the **visible spectrum**. The different colours are perceived by the eye as a result of their varying wavelengths.

Figure 17.3 shows how a spectrum of white light can be produced using a prism in the school laboratory. The ray-box and the converging lens are first set up so that an image of the vertical lamp filament is formed on the screen about 1 to 2 metres away. The prism is then placed in the path of the white light and the screen is moved around as shown to capture the

dispersion 色散   visible spectrum 可見光譜

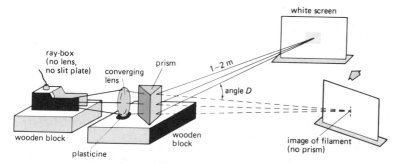

Figure 17.3 Dispersion of white light at minimum deviation.

spectrum on it. When the prism is rotated about a vertical axis, the colour spectrum shifts to and fro on the screen. The position of the prism which gives the smallest angle of deviation *D* of the spectrum from the original direction of the white light is located. The spectrum is clearest and most spread out in this position of **minimum deviation**.

INFRA-RED RADIATION — *Good absorber of IR would be good — emitted by all object with T > 0K   radiator of IR*

Detection

In 1800 William Herschel used a thermometer with a blackened bulb to investigate the spectrum of sunlight produced by a prism. He placed the bulb of the thermometer in different parts of the spectrum and observed a rise in temperature. But to his dismay, Herschel found that the temperature was highest in the region just *beyond* the red. He concluded that an invisible radiation of wavelength longer than red light was present in sunlight. He called such radiation **infra-red** (IR).

Infra-red radiation can be detected in the laboratory using a phototransistor connected to a milliammeter and a cell as shown in Figure 17.3. The amount of radiation received is indicated by the meter reading. The phototransistor is slowly moved through the spectrum from violet to red and beyond. It is found that the meter reading increases steadily, but reaches a maximum in the region just *beyond* the red. This shows that the filament lamp also emits invisible infra-red radiation.

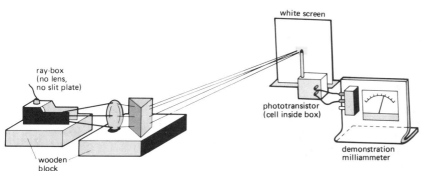

Figure 17.4 Detection of infra-red radiations with phototransistor.

colour filters 濾光鏡   infra-red radiation 紅外輻射   minimum deviation 最小偏向   **51**

Figure 17.5 Infra-red photograph of Hong Kong and Guangzhou taken from a satellite.

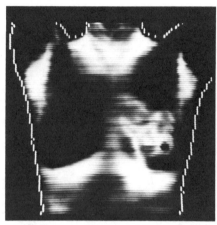

Figure 17.6 Medical infra-red photograph for diagnostic purposes.

Infra-red radiation is in fact emitted by any warm object. The amount and wavelength of the radiation depends on its temperature and colour. Below about 500°C, a body emits only infra-red and no visible light; for example, electric and soldering irons. At about 500°C a body becomes red-hot and emits infra-red as well as red light, as with the heating element of an electric fire. At about 1000°C bodies such as lamp filaments are white-hot and emit infra-red and white light. The range of wavelength of infra-red is very wide and extends from 7×10^{-7} m to about 1 mm.

Specially prepared film, sensitive to infra-red, has been used to take infra-red photographs from satellites. These photographs are useful in providing details of vegetation on the Earth's surface (Figure 17.5). Different vegetations emit different amounts and wavelengths of infra-red. Some medical conditions can be diagnosed by investigating the infra-red emissions from the skin (Figure 17.6). Jetfoils journeying between Hong Kong and Macau at night rely on an infra-red system for navigation. The system basically consists of an illuminator and a television camera. The illuminator sends out an invisible beam of infra-red radiation which is reflected whenever it encounters an obstacle, for example a sampan (Figure 17.7a). The television camera picks up the reflected signal and displays it on a television screen. The image displayed is similar to that of an ordinary television, enabling the pilot to 'see' in the dark. This system is very effective for night navigation as infra-red has a very high penetrating power. A similar device is used for sighting illegal immigrants crossing the Hong Kong border at night time (Figure 17.7b).

Figure 17.7b Use of infra-red telescope for sighting illegal immigrants crossing the Hong Kong border at night time.

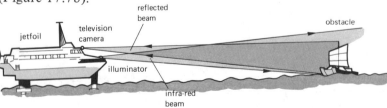

Figure 17.7a Infra-red system installed on jet-foil helps it 'see' in the dark.

Absorption and emission of infra-red

When infra-red is absorbed, the absorber shows a rise in temperature. Thus we feel warm when infra-red falls on our skin. For this reason infra-red radiation is often referred to as 'radiant heat' or 'heat radiation'.

The amount of infra-red absorbed by an object depends on the colour and nature of its surface. In the experiment shown in Figure 17.8, the blackened surface absorbs infra-red much better than the silvered surface. When the radiant heater is removed and the two flasks are filled with hot water at the same temperature, it is found that the temperature of the water in the blackened flask drops more quickly. Clearly the blackened surface emits infra-red at a faster rate than the silvered surface. These results show that a dark surface is both a good absorber and good emitter of infra-red radiation.

Reflection of infra-red

A phototransistor is placed at some distance from a radiant heater so that the meter gives only a very small reading. When a large parabolic metal reflector is placed behind the detector, the meter reading rises drastically showing that infra-red radiation must have been reflected.

Reflectors of this type are used in domestic electric heaters. They are also used to reflect infra-red from lamps to dry the paint on cars during manufacture (Figure 17.9). The giant reflector of the solar furnace at Odeillo in France (Figure 17.10) focuses sunlight (and the infra-red in sunlight) onto the furnace which is capable of producing temperatures as high as 6000°C!

Figure 17.8 A dark surface is both a good absorber and a good-emitter of infra-red radiations.

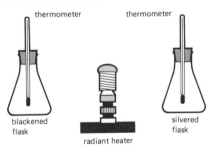

thermometer   thermometer

blackened flask   radiant heater   silvered flask

Figure 17.9 Car-paints dried by infra-red radiations.

Figure 17.10 Sunlight is focused by the huge reflector onto the solar furnace at Odeillo, France, to generate temperatures as high as 6000°C.

Refraction of infra-red

It is well known that sunlight can be focused to a point by a convex lens and set fire to a piece of paper. The large increase in temperature is due to the refraction of infra-red.

In the laboratory we can show the refraction of infra-red by passing it through a spherical flask containing a solution of iodine in carbon tetrachloride (Figure 17.11). When the flask is inserted between the radiant heater and the detector, there is a sharp rise in the meter reading.

Wave nature of infra-red radiation

It is not easy to show interference of infra-red in the school laboratory. One way, which is not totally convincing, is to project a spectrum of white light, produced by a diffraction grating, onto a screen. The phototransistor is used as a detector and is slowly moved through the spectrum from violet to red and beyond. It is found that the meter reading increases to a maximum in the small region just beyond the red. Thus it can be concluded that infra-red must have been *diffracted* by the grating in much the same way as visible light; infra-red is therefore a kind of wave.

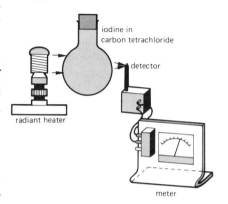

Figure 17.11 Refraction of infra-red radiations.

ULTRA-VIOLET RADIATION

About a year after Herschel discovered infra-red, the German scientist Ritter found radiation beyond the violet end of the sun's visible spectrum. This radiation, called **ultra-violet** (UV), has a shorter wavelength than visible light waves. It can be detected by certain chemicals which glow or *fluoresce* on absorbing ultra-violet. These fluorescent materials absorb 'invisible' ultra-violet and re-radiate visible light. Ultra-violet is also detected by special films which are sensitive to ultra-violet, but the camera used must have a lens made of quartz glass since ultra-violet is absorbed by ordinary glass.

The presence of ultra-violet in the spectrum produced by a filament lamp can be shown using a strip of fluorescent paper glued onto a white screen. The light is dispersed by a glass prism, and the spectrum is arranged so that the upper part falls on the fluorescent paper and the lower part on the white screen (Figure 17.12). The experiment must be carried out in a darkened room. The fluorescent paper glows *beyond* (as well as in) the violet region of the visible spectrum. If an ultra-violet filter is available, it can be used to cut off most of the visible light so that the fluorescence can be seen more easily.

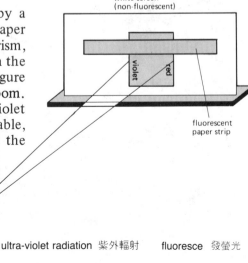

Figure 17.12 Detection of ultra-violet rays with fluorescent paper or paint.

ultra-violet radiation 紫外輻射   fluoresce 發螢光

The ultra-violet radiation in sunlight is good for health; it induces vitamin D production in the skin and is responsible for 'sun-tan' formation. However, over-exposure to ultra-violet can be harmful and can cause severe sunburn. Sun-tan lotions in fact act as filters to protect the body cells from a harmful excess of radiation. Ultra-violet is particularly harmful to the eyes. So one should *always avoid looking directly at an ultra-violet lamp*.

A mercury-vapour lamp is a convenient source of ultra-violet because it produces light with a high proportion of the radiation. The inner surface of fluorescent tubes is coated with a fluorescent material which emits a characteristic white light on absorbing ultra-violet, which is produced due to mercury vapour contained in the tubes.

Ultra-violet lamps are used by bank tellers to check signatures on savings account passbooks (Figure 17.13). The signature is marked on the passbook with fluorescent ink which glows and therefore becomes visible when viewed under ultra-violet. Ultra-violet lamps are also used for identifying fake banknotes (Figures 17.14).

Figure 17.13 Bankteller checks signature on savings account passbook with ultra-violet lamp.

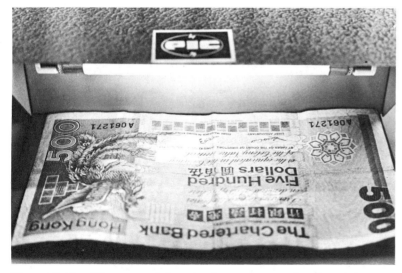

Figure 17.14 Fluorescent ink on banknote glows under ultra-violet rays.

Ultra-violet radiation is also useful for sterilization, to kill the harmful bacteria in drinking water (Figure 17.15).

The wave nature of ultra-violet radiation can be shown using a method similar to that for infra-red radiation. The spectrum produced by a diffraction grating is arranged to fall on a strip of fluorescent paper. The fluorescent paper glows beyond (as well as at) the violet end of the spectrum, showing the diffraction of ultra-violet.

Figure 17.15 The powerful ultra-violet lamp, enclosed to contain the powerful radiations, sterilizes water to be drunk directly from tap.

MICROWAVES

Hertz's discovery of radio waves has profound influence on our life; it has paved the way for many modern technologies of communications. We are able to listen to the radio, watch television programmes, communicate with people in other continents or even talk to astronauts travelling in space, all because of radio waves of one kind or another.

Radio waves vary in wavelength from less than 1 mm to several tens of kilometres. The shortest radio waves are called **microwaves**. Microwaves have wavelengths extending from 0.1 mm to about 10 m. They are distinguished from other radio waves because they are produced by a different method.

All waves produce a heating effect when absorbed, but microwaves are particularly effective on the water molecules in food. This is used in microwave ovens which cook food completely very quickly and economically.

Microwaves are used for satellite communications since only waves of this range of wavelengths can penetrate the Earth's atmosphere. There are a number of communication satellites revolving above the Earth at the rate of once every 24 hours. Since the Earth is also rotating at the same rate, these satellites appear to be stationary. Aerials to transmit and receive microwave signals can be pointed, in fixed directions, towards these satellites. Hong Kong has three huge disc-shaped aerials at Stanley (Figure 17.16). One aerial communicates with America via a satellite above the Pacific Ocean. The other two aerials work via an Indian Ocean satellite to communicate with Europe. Microwave signals are transmitted from an aerial to a satellite which amplifies and re-transmits the signal to an aerial on another continent (Figure 17.17). In this way we are able to communicate with practically any part of the world. Microwaves can be used to carry radio and television information as well as communication by telephone or telegrams, etc.

Microwaves are also used to transmit live television coverage from mobile broadcast vehicles back to the television studio (Figure 17.18). For the transmission, the transmitting and receiving aerials must be in the 'line of sight' of each other because microwaves are of such small wavelength that they cannot diffract around even the smallest obstacles.

3-cm wave transmitter and receiver

In the laboratory microwaves of wavelength about 3 cm are used to investigate wave properties. Such microwaves are often referred to as '3-cm waves'. Figure 17.19 shows the set-up of a microwave transmitter and a receiver. Both the transmitter and

Figure 17.16 The Satellite Earth Station at Stanley keeps Hong Kong in touch with the world.

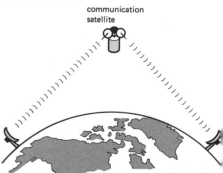

Figure 17.17 Satellite receives, amplifies and re-transmits microwave signals.

Figure 17.18 Television microwave link provides us with instant news coverage.

microwaves 微波

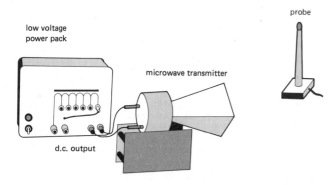

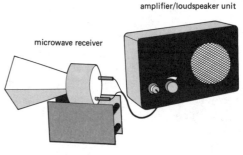

Figure 17.19 Microwaves transmitter and receiver.

receiver have 'horns' to help to direct or collect microwaves. The receiver is connected to a microammeter from which the amount of signal received can be read. Alternatively, the receiver is connected to a loudspeaker/amplifier unit which converts the received signal into sound. In this way the results of experiments can be 'heard' by the whole class. Another receiver called the **probe** has no horn and is less sensitive, but receives signals from all directions. It is used in some experiments to investigate the signal variations over a small area.

Reflection of microwaves

Microwaves, like all other waves, obey the law of reflection. In Figure 17.20 the receiver detects a maximum signal when the angle of incidence equals the angle of reflection. Microwaves are also reflected by a parabolic metal reflector to converge to a point, the focus (Figure 17.21).

Microwaves are of small wavelength and are reflected by objects of small size. This property of reflection is used in **radars** (standing for *RA*dio *D*etection *A*nd *R*anging) which are commonly installed in airfields, aircraft and ships for direction finding and navigation purposes.

A radar system consists of a transmitter, an aerial and a receiver (Figure 17.21). The transmitter sends out a narrow beam of

Figure 17.20 Microwaves obey the law of reflection.

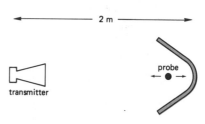

Figure 17.21 Microwaves reflected by parabolic reflector converge to a point.

Figure 17.22 Radar station.

radar 雷達

microwaves, in short pulses, through the aerial, which whirls round continuously to scan the surrounding area. Distant objects in the path of the beam reflect some of the radiation back to the receiver. The direction in which the beam is transmitted and received gives the direction of the object, for example an aircraft. The time lag between the transmitted pulse and the reflected pulse gives an indication of the distance of the object from the radar.

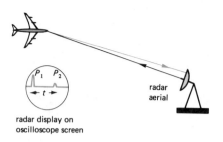

Figure 17.23 Estimating how far away the aeroplane is.

The information is usually displayed on the screen of an oscilloscope. Figure 17.23 shows a transmitted pulse P_1 and a weaker echo pulse P_2. The time taken for the pulse to travel to the aircraft and back is found from the separation between P_1 and P_2 on the screen.

Using the formula

$$\text{speed} = \frac{\text{distance travelled}}{\text{time taken}}$$

we can find the distance of the reflected object. The speed is 3×10^8 m s^{-1} since all electromagnetic waves travel at this speed.

Example 1
A radar pulse is reflected by an aircraft and is received 4×10^{-5} s after it is transmitted. What is the distance of the aircraft from the radar station?

The time for the pulse to travel to the aircraft and back is 4×10^{-5} s. Hence the time for the one way journey is 2×10^{-5} s.
Speed of radar pulse is 3×10^8 m s^{-1}

Hence distance travelled = speed × time taken

$$= 3 \times 10^8 \text{ m s}^{-1} \times 2 \times 10^{-5} \text{ s}$$

$$= 6 \times 10^3 \text{ m}$$

$$= 6 \text{ km}$$

The aircraft is 6 km away.

Refraction of microwaves

Microwaves change their speed and wavelength when they pass through different materials and this can result in a change in the direction of travel.

When microwaves enter a hollow perspex prism filled with paraffin oil, they are bent or refracted (Figure 17.24). When microwaves pass through a hollow perspex 'lens' filled with

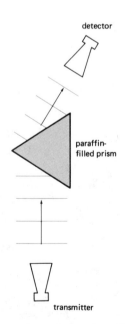

Figure 17.24 Refraction of microwaves by a prism.

paraffin oil, the radiation is focused more or less to a point (Figure 17.25). If the 'lens' is removed, the receiver response immediately weakens.

Figure 17.25 Refraction of microwaves by a 'lens'.

Diffraction of microwaves

In Figure 17.26, a large metal plate blocks about half the signal from the transmitter. As the receiver is moved from X to Y, it detects microwaves even when it is in the 'shadow' of the obstacle. This indicates that the radiation must have been diffracted.

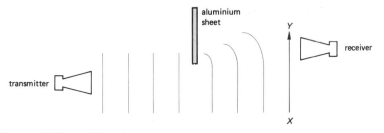

Figure 17.26 Diffraction of microwaves at a straight edge.

Figure 17.27 shows how microwaves diffract through a gap. The receiver detects microwaves on either side of the gap as it is moved from X to Y. The narrower the gap, the more the microwaves are spread out.

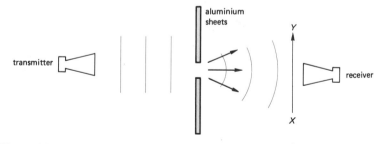

Figure 17.27 Diffraction of microwaves at a gap.

Interference of microwaves

To show that radiation from the transmitter is a wave, we must demonstrate that it shows interference (Figure 17.28).

The two slits through which the microwaves pass are formed by three metal plates. The separation of the slits should be of the order of several wavelengths of the microwaves.

As the receiver is moved from X to Y, a series of maximum and minimum responses is obtained. The two slits through which the waves pass act as two sources of microwaves which are *in phase*. When their waves combine, the two sources produce constructive and destructive interference. If one of the slits is 'closed up', no such interference pattern can be obtained.

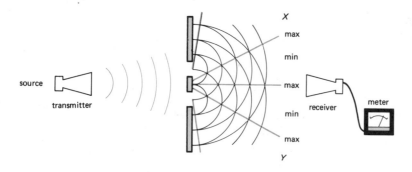

Figure 17.28   Interference of microwaves.

Another method of producing interference is shown in Figure 17.29. As the probe is moved away from the metal plate along XY, a series of alternating maximum and minimum responses is detected. In this arrangement, interference is due to the combination of reflected waves from the metal plate and direct waves from the transmitter. Interference can also be detected when the metal plate is quickly moved across XZ, with the position of the probe and the transmitter being fixed.

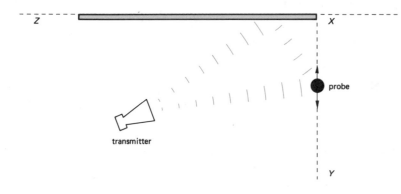

Figure 17.29   Interference occurs when reflected waves from mirror meet direct waves from transmitter.

Example 2
What is the frequency of the waves, wavelength 3 cm, emitted by a microwave transmitter?

Wave speed of microwaves (and all other electromagnetic waves) in air is very nearly 3×10^8 m s^{-1}.

Using the formula $v = f\lambda$

$$f = \frac{v}{\lambda} = \frac{3 \times 10^8 \text{ m s}^{-1}}{3 \text{ cm}}$$
$$= \frac{3 \times 10^8 \text{ m s}^{-1}}{0.03 \text{ m}}$$
$$= 10^{10} \text{ Hz} = 10 \text{ GHz}$$
$$(1 \text{ gigahertz} = 10^9 \text{ hertz})$$

The frequency of the 3-cm waves is 10^{10} Hz or 10 GHz.

RADIO WAVES

Radio waves other than microwaves cover a very large range of wavelength. The entire range is divided into a number of smaller *bands* according to wavelength. The various bands have different applications and are usually allocated by law to different types of radio service. The commonly known wavebands include long wave, medium wave and short wave for radio communication and broadcasting, and VHF (very high frequency) and UHF (ultra high frequency) for FM radio and television broadcasting. Their approximate ranges of wavelength and frequency together with their applications are given in Table 17.1. Note that the wavebands of VHF and UHF overlap with the wavelengths of microwaves.

Table 17.1

Radio waves	Wavelength (approximate)	Frequency (approximate)	Application
Long waves	600 m – 20 km	15 kHz – 500 kHz	radio communication
Medium waves	100 – 600 m	500 kHz – 3 MHz	AM radio broadcasting
Short waves	10 – 100 m	3 MHz – 30 MHz	AM radio broadcasting, radio communication
VHF (very high frequency)	1 – 10 m	30 MHz – 300 MHz	FM radio broadcasting
UHF (ultra high frequency)	0.1 – 1 m	300 MHz – 3000 MHz	TV broadcasting

Reflection of radio waves

Long waves are suitable for communication over large distances, but the curvature of the Earth limits the range of the signals transmitted (Figure 17.30a). This range seldom exceeds 80 km. To extend the range, **repeaters** are used (Figure 17.30b) to receive and then re-transmit the signals to the final receiving station. For greater distances short waves which can be reflected off a layer in the upper atmosphere called the ionoshpere are used.

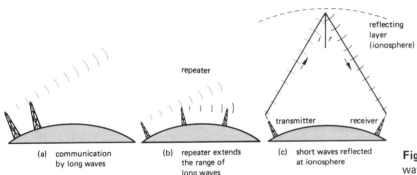

reflecting layer (ionosphere)

repeater

transmitter   receiver

(a) communication by long waves

(b) repeater extends the range of long waves

(c) short waves reflected at ionosphere

Figure 17.30 Reflection of radio waves.

On encountering this reflecting layer, the radio waves obey the law of reflection (Figure 17.30c). The Tropospheric Scatter Station on Cape D'Aguilar Peak (Figure 17.31) provides communications between Hong Kong and Taiwan based on this reflection of short radio waves.

Medium and short waves have a smaller range and are therefore suitable for local radio broadcasting. In such broadcasting the *amplitude* of the radio waves changes according to the sound broadcast. This is called **amplitude modulation** (AM). Local stations also use VHF waves when the *frequency* of the radio waves changes according to the sound broadcast. This second method which is called **frequency modulation** (FM) is being increasingly used as it provides a better quality of sound reproduction. The broadcasting frequencies of the local radio stations are shown in Table 17.2.

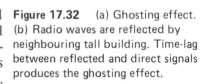

Figure 17.31 Tropospheric Scatter Station of Cable and Wireless at Cape D'Aguilar Peak.

Table 17.2

	AM	FM
RTHK 1 (Chinese)	783 kHz	—
RTHK 2 (Chinese)	—	94, 103 MHz
RTHK 3 (English)	567 kHz	—
RTHK 4 (English)	—	91, 100 MHz
RTHK 5 (BBC relay/Chinese)	—	96, 105 MHz
Commercial 1 (Chinese)	864 kHz	102.4 MHz
Commercial 2 (Chinese)	675 kHz	104.6 MHz
Commercial (English)	1044 kHz	—

Television broadcasting relies on UHF radio waves, often referred to as TV waves, of wavelength about 1 m. Because of the small wavelength, TV waves are reflected by obstacles such as buildings, hills and even aeroplanes. This reflection produces what is called a 'ghosting' effect on a television screen (Figure 17.32).

Figure 17.32 (a) Ghosting effect. (b) Radio waves are reflected by neighbouring tall building. Time-lag between reflected and direct signals produces the ghosting effect.

(a)

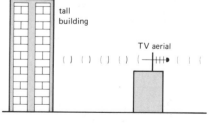

(b)

amplitude modulation 調幅　　frequency modulation 調頻

Most of the signal is received directly by the aerial but some of it is reflected back from an obstacle and reaches the aerial slightly later. The two signals are received at two slightly different times and produce two pictures side by side on the screen. The ghost picture is of couse fainter since it comes from the weaker reflected signal. This is common in Hong Kong where buildings are usually very close together. In some cases, an aerial may be surrounded by highrise buildings and it has to rely solely on reflected signals from a neighbouring building rather than direct signals from the transmitting station.

Diffraction of radio waves

The extent to which waves are diffracted depends on the relative size of the obstacle and the wavelength (Figure 17.33). Long wavelengths (low frequency) are diffracted more than short wavelengths (high frequency).

Figure 17.33 Radio waves of longer wavelengths are diffracted more at an obstacle.

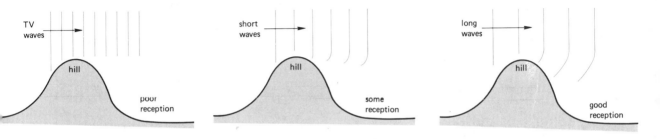

Interference of radio waves

The picture on a television screen often pulsates when an aeroplane flies low overhead. This is a result of interference of TV waves, with the low-flying aeroplane acting as a reflector. The signal travelling directly to the aerial interferes with the signal reflected from the aeroplane (Figure 17.34). The interference is seldom completely destructive as the reflected signal is usually much weaker.

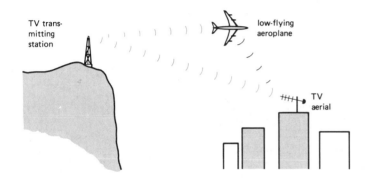

Figure 17.34 Interference of TV waves.

Example 3
RTHK Radio 3 broadcasts at a frequency of 567 kHz. What is the wavelength of the radio waves it emits?

All radio waves travel in air at a speed of 3×10^8 m s^{-1}.

Using the formula $v = f\lambda$

$$\lambda = \frac{v}{f} = \frac{3 \times 10^8 \text{ m s}^{-1}}{567 \text{ kHz}}$$

$$= \frac{3 \times 10^8 \text{ m s}^{-1}}{567 \times 10^3 \text{ Hz}} = 529 \text{ m}$$

The wavelength of the waves is 529 m.

Example 4
RTHK Radio 5 (FM) broadcasts at a frequency of 105 MHz. What is the wavelength of the radio waves it emits?

Using the formula $\lambda = \frac{v}{f} = \frac{3 \times 10^8 \text{ m s}^{-1}}{105 \text{ MHz}}$

$$= \frac{3 \times 10^8 \text{ m s}^{-1}}{105 \times 10^6 \text{ Hz}} = 2.86 \text{ m}$$

The wavelength of the waves is 2.86 m.

Example 5
TVB Jade Station broadcasts on Channel 21 which has a frequency range extending from 470 to 478 MHz. This channel bandwidth of 8 MHz carries both sound and vision signals. What is the range of wavelength of the TV waves used?

For $f = 470$ MHz, $\lambda = \frac{v}{f} = \frac{3 \times 10^8 \text{ m s}^{-1}}{470 \text{ MHz}}$

$$= \frac{3 \times 10^8 \text{ m s}^{-1}}{470 \times 10^6 \text{ Hz}} = 0.638 \text{ m}$$

For $f = 478$ MHz, $\lambda = \frac{v}{f} = \frac{3 \times 10^8 \text{ m s}^{-1}}{478 \text{ MHz}}$

$$= \frac{3 \times 10^8 \text{ m s}^{-1}}{478 \times 10^6 \text{ Hz}} = 0.628 \text{ m}$$

The wavelength range of the TV waves of Channel 21 extends from 0.628 m to 0.638 m.

X-RAYS

Radiations of higher frequency and smaller wavelength than ultra-violet rays are known as X-rays. X-rays were discovered in 1895 by Röntgen who found that they were invisible but could penetrate solid materials. Röntgen also found that X-rays

X-ray X 射綫

affected photographic film in the same way as light does. One of his early X-rays photograph is shown in Figure 17.35. X-rays pass through flesh more easily than through bone.

The penetrating properties of X-rays make them very useful for 'looking inside' things without opening them. We are all familiar with the chest X-ray picture which helps the doctor to diagnose lung diseases. However, prolonged exposure to X-rays is dangerous and causes severe damage to body tissues.

GAMMA RADIATION

The gamma radiation (p.250) emitted by some radioactive substances is even more dangerous than X-rays. These are rays of extremely short wavelength, of the order of 10^{-13} m.

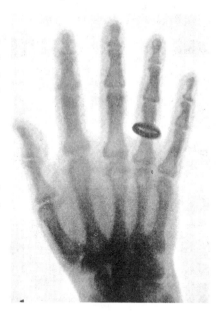

Figure 17.35 X-ray photograph of Mrs Röntgen's hand.

SUMMARY

All electromagnetic waves show the wave properties of reflection, refraction, diffraction and interference. They all travel at 3×10^8 m s^{-1} and obey the wave equation $v = f\lambda$.

The electromagnetic wave spectrum consists of the following waves in order of decreasing wavelength.

Waves	Typical wavelength	Sources	Detectors	Uses mentioned in text
Radio waves	10^{-2} m to 10^3 m	Radio & TV transmitter	Aerial & TV set Radio set Radio receiver	Radio & TV broadcast Radio communications
Microwaves	10^{-2} m	Microwave transmitter	Microwave receiver	Microwaves oven Satellite telecommunication TV microwave link Radar
Infra-red	10^{-4} m	Warm or hot objects Sun	Skin Blackened thermometer Phototransistor IR photographic film	Satellite IR photography Medical IR photography for diagnostic purposes IR navigation system Solar furnace
Visible light	4×10^{-7} m to 7×10^{-7} m	Hot objects Sun Fluorescent substances	Eyes Photographic film Photocell	
Ultra-violet (UV)	10^{-8} m	Very hot objects Mercury lamp (Dangerous)	UV photographic film Fluorescent paper or materials	Causes sun-tan Fluorescent light Checking fake banknotes and and bankbook signature Sterilization of drinking water
X-rays	10^{-10} m	X-ray tube (Dangerous highly penetrating)	Photographic film	Medical diagnosis
Gamma rays	10^{-13} m	Radioactive substances, e.g. radium (Dangerous, highly penetrating)	Photographic film Geiger-Muller counter (See Chapter 25)	Radiotherapy Tracers Thickness gauge Carbon dating Nuclear power station (See Chapter 26)

PROBLEMS

1. A ray X of red light is directed towards a glass prism (Figure 17.36).
   (a) Copy Figure 17.36 and show how the light leaves prism at P.
   (b) What changes, if any, take place in
      (i) the wavelength,
      (ii) the speed of the red light as it is reflected at O (ray Y)?
   (c) What changes, if any, take place in
      (i) the wavelength,
      (ii) the speed of the red light as it enters the prism at O (ray Z)?
   (d) The ray X of red light is now replaced by a ray of white light. Describe what is now seen on the screen. Explain how this happens.

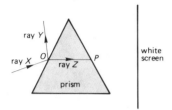

Figure 17.36

2. The Earth continually receives electromagnetic radiation from the Sun, producing a warming effect. Why doesn't the Earth eventually get as hot as the Sun?

3. Name one type of electromagnetic wave which
   (a) produces sun-tan,
   (b) has the shortest wavelength,
   (c) is reflected off the Earth's atmosphere,
   (d) passes through flesh.

4. A microwave oven uses microwaves of wavelength 12 cm. What is the frequency of the wave generated in the oven?

5. Commercial Radio broadcasts at 1044 kHz. What is the wavelength used?

6. (a) Figure 17.37 shows an experimental set-up to study the interference of 3 cm microwaves. Microwaves emitted from a transmitter at T pass through two narrow slits A and B where $TA = TB$. The microwaves are picked up by a receiver at X where $XA = XB$. The receiver is connected to a loudspeaker through an amplifier. The loudness of sound from the loudspeaker indicates the intensity of the microwaves received.
      (i) Given that the velocity of light is 3×10^8 m s^{-1}, what is the frequency of the 3 cm microwaves?
      (ii) What is the path difference of the microwaves from A and B at X?
      (iii) Are the waves at constructive or destructive interference at X?
      (iv) Would the sound from the loudspeaker be loud or soft?
      (v) Describe briefly the variation of the loudness of the sound from the loudspeaker when the receiver is being moved along XY.

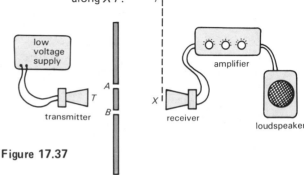

Figure 17.37

   (b) Figure 17.38 shows another experimental set-up using the same microwave transmitter and receiver. 3 cm microwaves are emitted from the transmitter. A metal plate M is moved from P to Q. Describe the variation of the loudness of the sound from the loudspeaker. Explain briefly with the aid of a diagram.
   (c) Give two examples of applications of microwaves.

(HKCEE 1986)

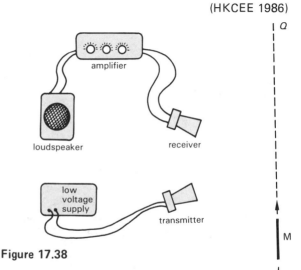

Figure 17.38

Sound Waves 18

Sound also travels in the form of waves, but sound waves are very different in nature from electromagnetic waves.

PRODUCTION OF SOUND

If you put your fingers gently on your throat when you are speaking, you will feel your throat vibrating. These vibrations produce the sound. Other sound sources all vibrate when they emit sound. A tuning fork looks slightly blurred when it is struck because the prongs are vibrating rapidly backwards and forwards. If the fork is allowed to touch the surface of some water, the water is splashed by the vibrations of the prongs (Figure 18.1). A few, light, plastic beads placed in the cone of a loudspeaker bounce up and down when the loudspeaker is emitting sound (Figure 18.2).

Energy has to be supplied to a sound source to produce vibrations. The vibrations of the sound source cause the surrounding air to vibrate. Vibrations of the air then cause our ear-drums to vibrate. This causes the sensation of sound. Our ear-drums require energy to vibrate, and obviously this energy comes from the sound source. Sound is therefore a form of energy which can be transmitted through the air from a vibrating source to our ears.

Figure 18.1 Vibrating tuning fork.

Figure 18.2 Sound is produced by vibrations of speaker.

TRANSMISSION OF SOUND

Sound can travel through air to our ears. But can it travel through a vacuum as do light or other electromagnetic waves? In 1654 Otto von Guericke carried out an experiment to find out. We can repeat his experiment in the laboratory using the apparatus shown in Figure 18.3. When the electric bell is switched on, it can be clearly heard. As air is gradually pumped out of the bell jar, the sound dies away and finally becomes very faint although the striker can still be seen hitting the gong. The sound never disappears completely because some of it can still be transmitted through the elastic supports to the surrounding air.

tuning fork 音叉

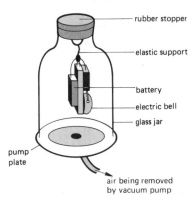

Figure 18.3   Sound does not travel through vacuum.

rubber stopper
elastic support
battery
electric bell
glass jar
pump plate
air being removed by vacuum pump

Figure 18.4   Astronauts can only talk to each other via a radio.

Astronauts in space or on the Moon (Figure 5.4) cannot talk to each other even though they may be very close together. They have to rely on a radio transmitter/receiver system to communicate with each other because radio waves, unlike sound, can travel through a vacuum.

Figure 18.5   Toy telephone: sound is transmitted along string.

Air is not the only medium through which sound will travel. A toy telephone built from two boxes and a length of string functions (Figure 18.5) and this shows that sound travels along string. If you press your ear to one end of a metal railing and the other end is tapped, the sound travels much faster through the metal railing than it does through the air. Sound also travels through water. Divers can hear the sound of an approaching motor-boat. Fish are attracted by sound and fishermen nowadays use electronic sound to attract fish into their nets.

Sound does not travel through a vacuum but it can travel through a material medium which may be a solid, a liquid or a gas.

WAVES PROPERTIES OF SOUND

Interference

Sound is energy sent through a material medium from a vibrating source. But is sound energy transmitted by means of a wave? Sound will show the property of interference if it is a wave.

medium 介質

To produce interference two sound sources of the same frequency are required. This can be arranged by connecting two identical loudspeakers in parallel to a signal generator (Figure 18.6). The signal generator produces signals of variable frequency which can be read off a scale. In this way the two loudspeakers emit sounds of the same frequency which are also in phase. In order to produce an observable interference pattern, the two wave sources must be separated by a distance of the order of a few wavelengths. Therefore an estimate of the wavelength of the sound produced is required.

Figure 18.6   Experiment to demonstrate interference of sound.

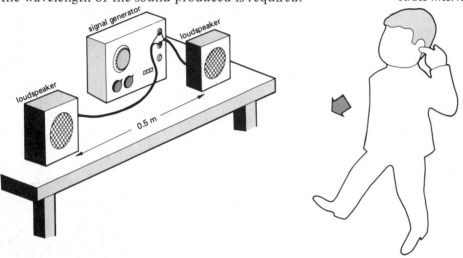

Example 1

A signal of frequency 2 kHz is fed into two loudspeakers. What should be the distance between the two loudspeakers if they must be placed three wavelengths apart?

Speed of sound waves in air $= 340$ m s^{-1}

Frequency of the sound $\quad = 2$ kHz $= 2000$ Hz

From the wave equation $\quad v = f\lambda$

$$\Rightarrow \quad \lambda = \frac{v}{f} = \frac{340 \text{ m s}^{-1}}{2000 \text{ Hz}} = 0.17 \text{ m}$$

$$\Rightarrow \quad 3\lambda = 3 \times 0.17 \text{ m} = 0.51 \text{ m}$$

The two loudspeakers should be separated by about 0.5 m.

A possible arrangement is to place the two loudspeakers about half a metre apart and set the signal generator at 2 kHz. Walking slowly across in front of the loudspeakers, the loudness of the sound rises and falls. This series of loud and soft sounds is the series of maxima and minima of the interference pattern.

Pupils were asked to stand where the sound was loudest and they found themselves forming lines going out from the loudspeakers (Figure 18.7a). These lines indicate an interference pattern similar to that produced with water waves in a ripple

(a)

(b)

tank. With the signal generator set at a lower frequency, the interference pattern becomes more widely spaced (Figure 18.7b) because with a lower frequency, the wavelength of the sound becomes greater and the two sound sources are now fewer wavelengths apart. This experiment is conducted in an open space to avoid undesirable reflections of sound.

In the above experiment the ear was used to detect and locate the position of loud and soft sounds. A more sensitive detector is a microphone connected to a **cathode ray oscilloscope** (CRO). Figure 18.8 shows the pattern (trace) produced on the CRO screen when someone whistles into the microphone. The microphone receives the sound signal and converts it into electrical signal which is displayed on the screen. The trace looks like a transverse wave, but this does not necessarily mean that sound is a transverse wave. In fact, we shall shortly see that it is *not*. Nevertheless, the trace gives us a lot of information about the sound wave. The interference pattern can be investigated by moving the microphone across in front of the two loudspeakers (Figure 18.9). The positions of maxima are where the amplitude of the trace is largest and the positions of minima are where the amplitude is smallest.

Figure 18.7 (a) Pupils standing along lines of maximum loudness. (b) The lines become spaced out when sound of a lower frequency is emitted.

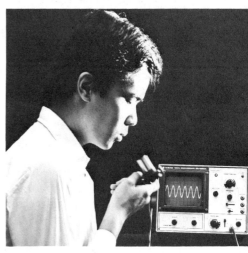

Figure 18.8 Waveform of sound produced by whistling.

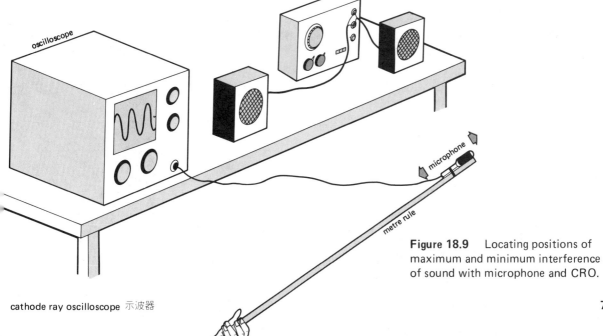

Figure 18.9 Locating positions of maximum and minimum interference of sound with microphone and CRO.

cathode ray oscilloscope 示波器

Diffraction

Someone can be heard talking behind a doorway although he cannot be seen. A doorway is of comparable width to the wavelength of much speech and music. It is therefore not surprising that sound is diffracted at doorways and that we can hear round corners. As with water waves, sound waves of low frequency (long wavelength) are more readily diffracted.

Reflection

When a loudspeaker connected to a signal generator is pointed at a plane surface such as a wooden board or a metal plate, the reflected sound signal can be detected using a microphone connected to a CRO (Figure 18.10). As the microphone is moved, the maximum sound signal is received when the directions are such that the angle of incidence is equal to the angle of reflection, that is, sound waves obey the law of reflection.

Sound waves are reflected readily from hard, flat surfaces such as walls or cliffs. The reflected sound forms an **echo**.

Refraction

A balloon filled with carbon dioxide is placed between a loudspeaker and a microphone (Figure 18.11) and the strength of sound reaching the microphone increases. The sound waves are focused onto the microphone showing that sound travels more slowly in carbon dioxide than in air.

Figure 18.10 Sound obeys the law of reflection.

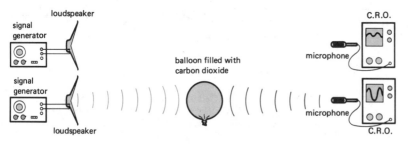

Figure 18.11 Refraction of sound.

THE NATURE OF SOUND

Sound energy is transmitted as waves through a material medium. But how is this taking place? Figure 18.12 shows a candle flame placed in front of a loudspeaker which is emitting a low note. The flame moves backwards and forwards, indicating that the air around it is also moving in a similar direction. These vibrations of the air are along the direction of travel of the sound, indicating that sound is a *longitudinal* wave.

Figure 18.12 Sound is a longitudinal wave.

echo 回聲

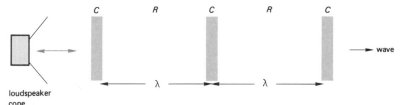

C = compression
R = rarefaction

Figure 18.13 Compressions and rarefactions travel outwards from loudspeakers.

A sound wave produced by a loudspeaker, or any other source, consists of a series of compressions and rarefactions in the air (Figure 18.13). The loudspeaker has a cone which is made to vibrate backwards and forwards by an electric current. When the cone moves forwards the air in front is compressed and when it moves backwards the air is rarefied. The cone vibrates continuously, producing successive regions of compressed and rarefied air. These compressions and rarefactions progress through the air but the air as a whole does *not* move outwards.

For a longitudinal wave, the wavelength λ is the distance between successive compressions (or successive rarefactions). The frequency f is the number of complete wavelengths produced per second. It is also the number of compressions (or rarefactions) produced per second by the vibrating source. The wave speed v of sound depends on the medium through which it travels. The wave equation $v = f\lambda$ applies for a longitudinal wave.

SPEED OF SOUND

'Clap-echo' method

The speed of sound was first measured in 1640 by Mersenne. He measured the time interval between making a sound and hearing its echo reflected from a known distance away. He estimated the speed of sound to be approximately 315 m s^{-1}. If we can find a large wall facing an open space at least 100 m away (which is not easy in Hong Kong), we can use Mersenne's idea to estimate the speed of sound. By clapping two pieces of wood together we can obtain an echo from the wall (Figure 18.14). During the time interval between clapping and hearing the echo, sound has travelled to the wall and back. The time of one echo is too short to be measured accurately, so it is necessary to clap regularly and adjust the clapping rate to a steady rhythm (so that the echos are heard mid-way between the claps). By measuring the time for a number of claps and knowing the distance from the wall, the speed of sound can be calculated.

Example 2
A pupil stands 150 m from a large wall facing an open space. He claps two pieces of wood at a steady rate to obtain a clap-echo-clap-echo rhythm. His partner who is counting the claps, starts a stop-watch on the count of zero and stops it on the count of

Figure 18.14 Measurement of speed of sound by 'clap-echo' method.

73

10. The reading on the stop-watch is 17.6 s. From these results calculate the speed of sound.

Time for 10 clap-clap intervals $= 17.6$ s

Time for 10 clap-echo intervals $= \frac{1}{2} \times 17.6$ s $= 8.8$ s

$\Rightarrow$ Time for 1 clap-echo interval $= 0.88$ s

During this time, 0.88 s, sound travels from the pupil to the wall and back.

$\Rightarrow$ Speed of sound $= \dfrac{\text{distance}}{\text{time}} = \dfrac{2 \times 150 \text{ m}}{0.88 \text{ s}}$

$= 341 \text{ m s}^{-1}$

The race between light and sound

In the early eighteenth century, more accurate measurements of the speed of sound were carried out by timing the interval between seeing the flash of a distant cannon and hearing its 'boom'. It was assumed that the flash was seen at the very instant the cannon was fired. Is it justified to ignore the time taken for the light from the flash to reach the observer?

Example 3
A cannon is fired at a distance of 20 km from an observer. Calculate and compare the time taken by (a) the light from the flash, and (b) the sound from the 'boom' to reach the observer. The speed of light is 3×10^8 m s^{-1} and that of sound is 340 m s^{-1}.

Time for light to reach the observer $= \dfrac{\text{distance}}{\text{speed of light}}$

$= \dfrac{20 \times 10^3 \text{ m}}{3 \times 10^8 \text{ m s}^{-1}}$

$= 6.7 \times 10^{-5} \text{ s}$

Time for sound to reach the observer $= \dfrac{\text{distance}}{\text{speed of sound}}$

$= \dfrac{20 \times 10^3 \text{ m}}{340 \text{ m s}^{-1}}$

$= 58.8 \text{ s}$

Comparing the two times:
$$\dfrac{58.8 \text{ s}}{6.7 \times 10^{-5} \text{ s}} = 8.8 \times 10^5 \approx 10^6$$

The time taken by the sound is almost one million times greater than the time taken by the light. It is therefore very reasonable to assume that the time taken for light to travel from the cannon to the observer is negligible.

The speed of sound depends very much on the nature and temperature of the medium through which it travels. Table 18.1 gives some examples of the speeds of sound in different media.

Medium	Speed of sound /m s^{-1}
Air at 0°C	331
Air at 20°C	343
Water at 20°C	1460
Metals	2000 to 7000
Rock	1500 to 3500

Table 18.1

MUSICAL NOTES

A **note** is a sound produced by the regular vibration of, for example, a tuning fork or a musical instrument. A **noise**, which is not pleasant to hear, is caused by irregular vibrations.

Pitch and loudness

In the case of visible light, different frequencies and intensities of the light waves produce different colour and brightness sensations in the eye. How do the frequency and intensity of sound waves affect our hearing?

Using a loudspeaker driven by a signal generator, notes of different frequencies and loudness are produced and heard (Figure 18.15). As the frequency is increased, by varying the frequency control, the **pitch** of the note becomes higher and higher. The pitch of a note depends on the frequency of the sound.

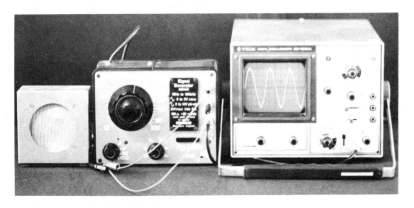

Figure 18.15 Waveform of note from signal generator is displayed on CRO.

When a cathode ray oscilloscope is also connected to the signal generator, the note can be 'seen' on the CRO screen. Remember that although the trace on the screen looks like a transverse wave it represents a longitudinal sound wave.

When the volume of the signal generator is turned up, a louder note is heard but the pitch remains the same. More energy is now supplied to the vibrating cone of the loudspeaker, enabling it to vibrate with a larger amplitude. As a result, more sound energy reaches our ears and we hear a louder note. When a tuning fork is struck very hard or a violin string is bowed strongly, a loud note is also heard.

note 音，樂音，律音   noise 噪音   pitch 音調，音高   loudness 響度

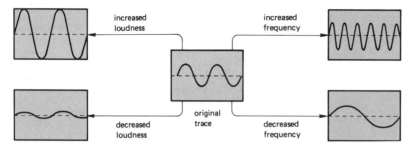

Figure 18.16 Changing the loudness and pitch of a note.

Note		Frequency /Hz
C	doh	256
D	ray	288
E	me	320
F	fah	340
G	soh	384
A	lah	427
B	te	480
C′	doh′	512

Table 18.2

Figure 18.16 shows how changes in the frequency and loudness of the note affect the trace on the CRO screen. As the frequency of the note increases, it pitch increases and the number of waves on the CRO trace increases. When the loudness of the note increases, the amplitude of the CRO trace increases, indicating an increase in the amplitude of the longitudinal sound wave.

A loudspeaker connected to a signal generator is a convenient sound source of standard frequency. Another source is a tuning fork which produces a note of a known single frequency. Sets of eight tuning forks are usually available in the laboratory and they cover the eight notes in the **musical scale**: doh, ray, me, fah, soh, lah, te, and doh′. Their frequencies are in Table 18.2.

Doh with frequency of 256 Hz is **middle C** and doh′ with twice the frequency (512 Hz) is a note one **octave** above middle C.

Quality

When the note produced by a tuning fork (or by a loudspeaker driven by a signal generator) is displayed on a CRO screen, the trace looks like a **sine wave** (Figure 18.17a). This is the simplest form of sound wave and is often referred to as a *pure* note.

When notes from musical instruments are displayed on a CRO, the waveforms are more complex. Figure 18.17b, c and d show the waveforms produced by a Chinese er-hu, a Chinese flute and a French horn respectively, all sounding the middle C. Each instrument has its own characteristic waveform and is said to have a typical sound **quality**. It is this difference in quality which enables us to distinguish notes from different instruments, for example 'doh' from a violin or from an er-hu.

Using more advanced mathematics it can be shown that such a complex wave is the sum or **resultant** of a sine wave of a particular frequency (the **fundamental note**) added to a number of multiples of this frequency (the **harmonics**) with different

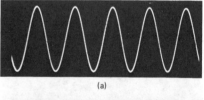

(a)

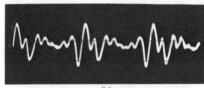

(b)

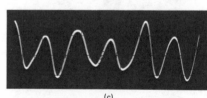

(c)

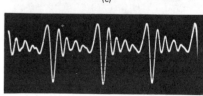

(d)

Figure 18.17 Waveforms of (a) tuning fork, (b) er-hu, (c) Chinese flute and (d) French horn. All sounding the middle C.

octave 八度   musical scale 音階   quality 音色

amplitudes. Figure 18.18 shows the resultant waveform when a fundamental frequency f_0 is added to its second harmonic $2f_0$ of smaller amplitude. If more harmonics are added, the resultant waveform will look more and more like the waveforms of musical notes in Figure 18.18. Therefore the quality of a musical note depends on the *number* and *amplitude* of the harmonics which accompany the fundamental frequency.

Figure 18.18   Addition of waves.

fundamental

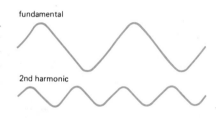

2nd harmonic

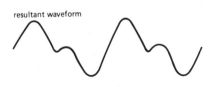

resultant waveform

STATIONARY WAVES

When a musical instrument is sounded, longitudinal sound waves are produced and transmitted through the air. What kind of vibration is being set up in such an instrument? We are particularly interested in stringed instruments such as guitars and violins, and in wind instruments such as flutes and organ pipes.

When a long spring is stretched on a smooth floor, with one end fixed and the other end repeatedly flicked sideways, a train of waves is produced. If the spring is flicked slowly at first and then with increased frequency, special wave patterns are formed. At certain frequencies one or more vibrating loops of large amplitude are formed on the spring and the whole pattern does not seem to move backwards or forwards. This is called a **stationary** or **standing wave**.

A typical stationary wave is shown in Figure 18.19. There are positions on the spring which have no displacement at any time; these are called **nodes** (labelled N). Midway between the nodes are positions which vibrate with the largest amplitude; these are called **antinodes** (labelled A). The distance between two successive nodes (or antinodes) is half a wavelength.

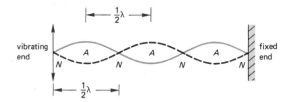

Figure 18.19   Typical stationary waves.

How is a stationary wave formed? A continuous wave sent along a spring is reflected from the fixed end, the reflected wave being out of phase with the incident wave. A stationary wave is formed when the incident wave meets the reflected wave coming back in the opposite direction.

Stationary wave in a stretched spring

It is not easy to maintain a steady stationary wave pattern on the long spring. A better method is to produce stationary waves on an elastic string by means of a **vibration generator** which is

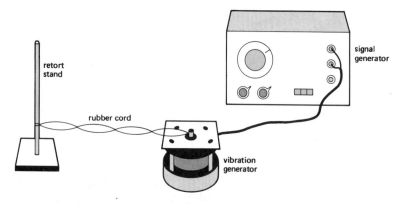

Figure 18.20   Stationary waves in a stretched string.

driven by a signal generator (Figure 18.20). As the frequency of the vibration is varied, stationary waves are only found to be set up at certain frequencies (Figure 18.21). The string produces a single loop when it is vibrated at the lowest possible frequency, the fundamental frequency. Doubling and trebling this frequency produce two and three loops respectively. The string is said to vibrate at its second and third harmonics.

The string is vibrating too fast to see its movement. But a stroboscope lamp, flashing at a rate *near* that of the vibrator frequency, can be used to 'slow down' the movement of the string.

Wave model

To find out more about 'particle' motion in a stationary wave we can again use the transverse wave model (p.7). In place of a spring, a *sine-wave curve* is now mounted on the stand. When the wave model is operated, a stationary wave is projected onto the screen. When small pieces of plasticine are stuck on the curve, the vibrations of the 'particles' can be observed. Within one loop, all the particles vibrate *in phase* but with *varying amplitudes*, and the vibrations in one loop are *antiphase* with those in an adjacent loop. For example, referring to Figure 18.22, particles A, E, I are the nodes and C, G, K are the antinodes; the vibrations of B, C, D are antiphase with those of F, G, H.

Travelling waves transmit energy but stationary waves *store energy*. In a vibrating string there is a continuous energy conversion between elastic potential energy and vibrational kinetic energy. This stored energy in a stationary wave can, however, be used to produce travelling sound waves. This occurs when a guitar string is plucked or when a violin string is bowed.

Figure 18.21   The mode of vibrations changes with frequency. (a) Frequency f. (b) Frequency $2f$. (c) Frequency $3f$.

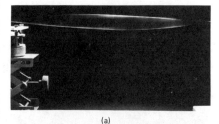

(a)

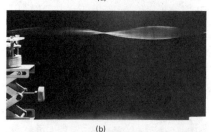

(b)

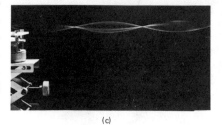

(c)

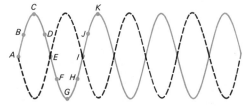

Figure 18.22   Vibrations of particles in a stationary wave.

Longitudinal stationary waves

Longitudinal stationary waves can also be produced. The elastic string in Figure 18.20 is replaced by a chain of rubber bands with matchsticks inserted through the knots (Figure 18.23). The vibration generator is turned to stand on its side so that it now vibrates along the length of the string. When the vibrator is operated, stationary wave patterns are set up at certain frequencies (Figure 18.24). The positions of nodes and antinodes can easily be identified.

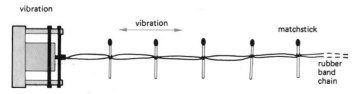

Figure 18.23   Rubber band chain.

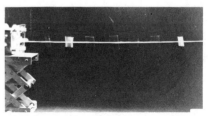

Figure 18.24   Longitudinal waves in rubber band chain.

Replacing the Crova's disc on the longitudinal wave model (p.10) with a **Cheshire's disc**, the 'particle' motion in a stationary longitudinal wave can be studied on the screen (Figure 18.25).

Figure 18.25   Simulations of longitudinal waves.

In wind instruments, such as flutes, musical notes are produced by stationary longitudinal waves set up in an air column in the instrument.

RESONANCE

Figure 18.26 shows a number of pendulums suspended from a stretched horizontal wire. If one pendulum is set swinging, all the others are somewhat affected, but the one of the *same length* soon vibrates with a large amplitude. This second pendulum has the same **natural frequency** as the first and is said to resonate with it. All objects have a natural frequency of vibration. The vibration can be started and increased by another object vibrating at the same frequency. This phenomenon is called **resonance**.

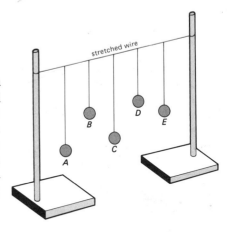

Figure 18.26   Pendulums of the same length have the same natural frequency of vibration.

When the stretched wire on a **sonometer** (Figure 18.27) or a guitar is plucked, a note of a certain frequency is produced.

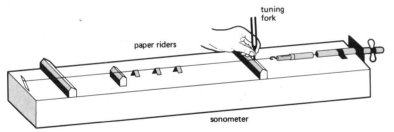

Figure 18.27   Wire is set in resonant vibration by tuning fork.

resonance 共振   sonometer 弦音計   natural frequency 自然頻率

This frequency varies with the vibrating length and tension of the wire. If the wire is adjusted to produce the same note as a tuning fork of known frequency, resonance can occur. This is done by striking the tuning fork and holding its stem on one of the bridges on the sonometer. Small paper riders on the wire jump off if the wire is set in resonant vibration. This is a standard method for determining the unknown frequency of vibration of a stretched string.

A vibrating string itself produces a rather faint note. But if it is mounted on a sounding or **resonance box**, as with a sonometer, a guitar or any other string instrument, a much louder note can be heard. This is because the wooden box, and the air it encloses, are forced to vibrate at the same frequency as the string.

Figure 18.28 Vibration generator.

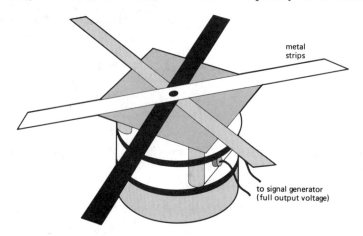

metal strips

to signal generator (full output voltage)

An even more impressive demonstration of resonance can be carried out with the vibration generator. Three metal strips, spaced about 60° apart, are mounted on the apparatus (Figure 18.28). As the frequency of the vibrator is gradually increased, it will be found that each of the six lengths in turn vibrates with maximum amplitude when its natural frequency corresponds to the vibrator frequency.

Resonance occurs in everyday life. A low flying aeroplane may make a window pane vibrate and this may even break it. A washing machine may sometimes vibrate very vigorously when in use. This can, however, be remedied by re-distributing the clothing inside, thereby changing the natural frequency.

Large structures such as suspension bridges can also be made to vibrate at their natural frequency. The collapse of the Tacoma Narrows Bridge, U.S.A., in 1940 was due to gusts of wind of the right speed to cause resonant vibration. (Figure 18.29). To prevent this kind of disaster, natural frequencies of new bridges are now checked by testing scaled-down models in wind tunnels. Resonance may also occur in a bridge when soldiers march in step over it, so the soldiers will be told to break step.

Figure 18.29 The Tacoma Narrows Bridge, completed in July, 1940, collapsed four months later, after near resonant vibrations caused by a strong wind.

resonance box 共振箱

A microwave oven (Figure 18.30) is a special cooking device which uses neither a gas fire nor an electric heating coil; it utilizes the effect of resonance. Microwaves of frequency equal to the vibrational frequency of water molecules (about 2.5×10^9 Hz) are generated in the oven. These cause resonant vibrations of the water molecules in the food. The water becomes very hot and this cooks the food, but the dish on which the food is placed does not become hot. Microwave ovens cook very fast and the food is heated 'right-through' and not from the outer surface inwards.

Figure 18.30   Microwave oven.

VIBRATION OF STRINGS

When a stretched string is plucked, a stationary wave is set up and a note is emitted. The string can vibrate in various ways and some of these are shown in Figure 18.31. In all cases, the two fixed ends of the string must be nodes. The distance between two successive nodes (or antinodes) is half the wavelength. When the stationary wave has one loop, the fundamental note is emitted. When there is more than one loop, **overtones** are produced. As shown in Figure 18.31, the first overtone (that is, the first possible mode of vibration after the fundamental) has twice the fundamental frequency and is therefore a second harmonic. Similarly, the second overtone is a third harmonic. In a musical instrument, a string vibrates in several ways at the same time depending on where it is plucked or bowed and this determines the quality of the note.

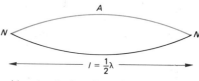

(a)   string vibrating at fundamental frequency f_0

(b)   string vibrating at $2f_0$ (first overtone)

The fundamental frequency f_0 at which a string of a given material vibrates depends on its length l, tension T and thickness t. Using a sonometer or guitar, it is found that

  f_0 decreases as l increases;

  f_0 increases as T increases;

  f_0 decreases as t increases.

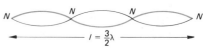

(c)   string vibrating at $3f_0$ (second overtone)

Figure 18.31   Modes of vibration in a string.

More precise relationships can be investigated using the sonometer and a set of tuning forks of known frequencies. The wire is set to vibrate in resonance with the tuning forks by varying its vibrating length and tension. This determines the frequency of the vibrating wire. The 'paper-rider' method described previously is used to locate the exact positions of resonance. The following graphs can then be plotted:

  f_0 against l at constant tension;

  f_0 against T at constant length.

It is found that: $f_0 \propto \dfrac{1}{l}$ and $f_0 \propto \sqrt{T}$

overtones 泛音

And if wires of different mass per unit length m are used,

$$f_0 \propto \frac{1}{\sqrt{m}}.$$

The formula relating all these quantities can be shown to be:

$$f_0 = \frac{1}{2l} \sqrt{\frac{T}{m}}$$

VIBRATION OF AIR COLUMNS

In wind instruments musical notes are produced by longitudinal stationary waves set up in an air column in a tube open at one or both ends. A tube open at one end and closed at the other is called a **closed tube**; one with both ends open is an **open tube**. When a disturbance is made at one end of the tube, sound waves travel to the other end where they are reflected. Interference occurs between the incident and reflected waves and a stationary wave is formed.

An air column can vibrate in various ways. Some of the possible modes of vibration for a closed tube are shown in Figure 18.32. The closed end of the tube must always be a node as the air there cannot vibrate longitudinally. On the other hand, at the open end the air vibrates most freely and there is always an antinode. As a longitudinal stationary wave is difficult to draw, it is customarily represented diagrammatically by a transverse wave as shown. The fundamental note is emitted when the mode of vibration is simplest. Overtones occur when there are more nodes and antinodes in the column. As shown in Figure 18.32, the first and second overtones are respectively the third and fifth harmonics. Hence, unlike the vibrating string which has *all* the harmonics, the closed tube has only the *odd* harmonics, $3f_0$, $5f_0$, .., accompanying the fundamental frequency f_0. A similar excercise for an open tube shows that it has *all* the harmonics.

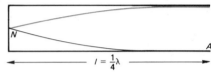

(a) air column vibrating at fundamental frequency f_0

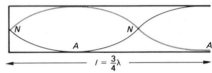

(b) air column vibrating at $3f_0$ (first overtone)

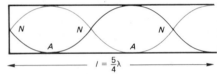

(c) air column vibrating at $5f_0$ (second overtone)

Figure 18.32 Modes of vibration in an air column.

Example 4

A boy blows hard across the mouth of a closed tube of length 0.33 m. What is the frequency of the fundamental note emitted? What would the frequency be if the tube were open at both ends? Speed of sound is 340 m s^{-1}.

For closed tube: wavelength λ = 4 × length of air column

$$= 4 \times 0.33 \text{ m} = 1.32 \text{ m}$$

$$\text{frequency } f = \frac{v}{\lambda} = \frac{340 \text{ m s}^{-1}}{1.32 \text{ m}}$$

$$= 258 \text{ Hz}$$

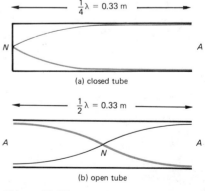

Figure 18.33

For open tube: wavelength λ = 2 × length of air column
= 2 × 0.33 m = 0.66 m

frequency $f = \dfrac{340 \text{ m s}^{-1}}{0.66 \text{ m}} = 515$ Hz

ULTRASONICS

Human beings can only hear sounds within a certain range of frequency. For a young person the **audio range** is from about 20 Hz to 20 kHz, but the range varies from person to person and also decreases with age. Sound waves with frequency above 20 kHz are called **ultrasonic** waves.

Bats use ultrasonic waves to help them move in the dark. They emit 'beeps' at frequencies ranging from 20 kHz to 120 kHz which are reflected from solid objects. From the time taken for the signal to return, the bats can tell how far away an obstructing object lies. Bats can successfully avoid wires as small as 0.5 mm in diameter.

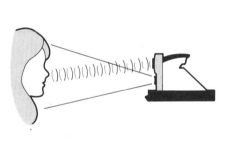

An echo-location system, using ultrasonic waves, called **sonar** was first developed during World War II for detecting submarines (Figure 18.34). It works on the same principle as the navigation system of bats. Today sonars are used by fishing boats to detect schools of fish and to measure the depth of the sea. Sonars are also used in cameras for autofocusing. The camera sends out ultrasonic signals which bounce back from the object being photographed (Figure 18.35). The time lapse is measured by the camera, and an electronic control circuit in the sonar system uses the time lapse to adjust the lens to proper focus.

Ultrasonics have been used for some time for diagnosis in medicine. Ultrasonic beams are focused on different parts of the body and the reflections from some of the organs are used to form an electronic picture. This technique is particularly useful for studying those parts of the body where X-ray photography is hazardous. Figure 18.36 shows the image of an foetus in a pregnant woman, taken by an ultrasonic scanner.

Figure 18.34 Sonar to detect submarines.

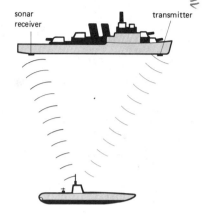

Figure 18.35 Sonar autofocus camera.

Figure 18.36 Foetus depicted by ultrasonic scanner.

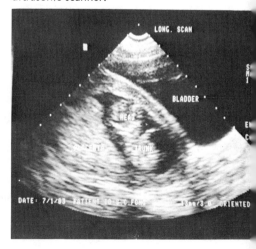

ultrasonic wave 超聲波   sonar 聲納

(a)

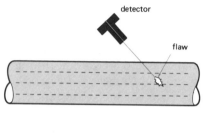

Figure 18.37 (a) Ultrasconic flaw detector checking a rail. (b) The flaw reflects ultrasonic waves.

detector

flaw

(b)

Ultrasonics have many uses in industry. They are used to detect flaws and cracks in, for example, a railway track (Figure 18.37a). The ultrasonic waves are reflected from a flaw and this appears as an echo. Ultrasonics are also used for cleaning small and delicate objects such as jewellery, watch movements, etc. The object is put in a bath of liquid and exposed to ultrasonic waves (Figure 18.38). The vibrations help the liquid to remove dirt from the surface.

Small ultrasonic control units are now increasingly used to operate televisions, slide projectors, and hi-fi sets by remote control.

Figure 18.38 Ultrasonic cleaner.

SUMMARY

What is sound

Sound is produced by vibrating object.

Sound does not travel through a vacuum; it travels through a material medium: a solid, a liquid, or a gas.

The speed of sound depends on the nature and temperature of the medium through which it travels.

Sound waves

Sound shows reflection, refraction, diffraction and interference and is therefore a wave.

Sound is a longitudinal wave, that is, one in which the vibrations are along the same line as the direction of travel of the wave.

Musical notes and resonance

A note is sound produced by the regular vibration of a source. A noise is a sound caused by irregular vibrations.

Frequency of vibration↑ ⇔ Pitch of note↑
Amplitude of vibration↑ ⇔ Loudness of note↑

Different musical instruments may produce notes of the same pitch. The notes do not sound alike to the ear. The note from each instrument is accompanied by its own harmonics. The number and amplitude of the harmonics are characteristic of the instrument; they determine the quality of the note.

Stationary waves

A stationary wave is produced when an incident wave combines with its reflected wave.

In a stationary wave, nodes are where the particles are at rest at all times, and antinodes are where they vibrate with maximum amplitude.

The separation between two adjacent nodes (or antinodes is half a wavelength.

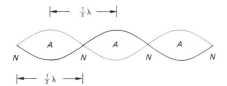

A travelling wave transmits energy but a stationary wave stores energy.

Resonance and Musical instruments

Musical notes are produced when stationary waves are set up in the strings of a string instrument or in an air column of a wind instrument.

Resonance is said to occur in a system, e.g. a stretched string or an air column, when it is set vibrating with a source which is vibrating at the natural frequency of vibration of the system.

The frequency f_o of the fundamental note emitted by a vibrating string depends on the length l, tension T and mass per unit length m of the string:

$$f_o \propto \frac{1}{l}; \quad f_o \propto T; \quad f_o \propto \frac{1}{m}$$

The frequencey f_o of the fundamental note emitted by an air column of length l depends on the length of the column: $f_o \propto \frac{1}{l}$ for both closed and open tubes.

A vibrating string has all the harmonics, $2f_o$, $3f_o$, $4f_o$, . . . accompanying the fundamental note f_o.

A closed tube has only the odd harmonics, $3f_o$, $5f_o$, $7f_o$. . .; but an open tube has all the harmonics.

Audio range of the human ear

The human ear can hear sounds of frequencies ranging from 20 Hz to 20 kHz.

Ultrasonics are sound waves of frequency above 20 kHz. They have wide applications in communications, medicine and industry.

PROBLEMS

1. A girl sees a flash of lightning in the sky. Five seconds later she hears the bang. How far is she away from the thunderstorm? Take the speed of sound in air as 340 m s^{-1}.

2. In a clap-echo experiment, a boy stood 200 m away from a wall and clapped two pieces of wood with a steady rhythm so that he heard the echos in between the claps. His partner timed 20 time intervals between claps and found it to be 50 s. What value do these results give for the speed of sound in air?

3. When a boy whistled into a microphone connected to an oscilloscope, he observed a wave trace on the screen. What type of wave was viewed on the screen, and how did it differ from the sound wave controlling it?

4. Figure 18.39 shows the traces of three notes on an oscilloscope. Assuming that the oscilloscope controls are not changed, which trace represents
   (a) the loudest note,
   (b) the highest pitch?

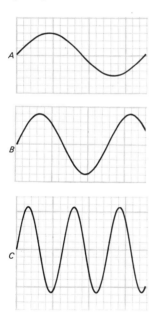

Figure 18.39

5. A stretched string is tuned to a frequency of 256 Hz. Briefly explain how you would produce a note of 512 Hz
   (a) by altering only the length of the string,
   (b) by altering only the tension in the string.

6. A stretched string 40 cm long is tuned to resonate with a tuning fork of frequency 256 Hz. Assume that the string vibrates at its fundamental mode. Take the speed of sound in air as 340 m s^{-1}.
   What is the wavelength of
   (a) the vibration in the string,
   (b) the sound note emitted?

7. A vertical glass tube contains water, the level of which can be varied. A 512 Hz tuning fork is sounded over the open end of the tube and the note heard is loudest when the water level is 16.2 cm below the open end. What value do you obtain for the speed of sound in air from the experiment?

8. A tube of length 67 cm open at both ends is found to resonate with a tuning fork of frequency 256 Hz. Calculate
   (a) the wavelength of the vibration in the tube,
   (b) the speed of sound in air.

9. In an experiment on sound interference, two loudspeakers S_1 and S_2 (Figure 18.40) are connected in parallel to a signal generator. The signal generator is set at 1.4 kHz. A boy walks in front from X to Y. As the walks along, he hears a loud sound at O, then a soft sound at P and another loud sound at Q. The distance between S_1 and S_2 is 1 m, the perpendicular distance between S_1S_2 and XY is 8 m, and the distance between O and Q is 2 m. Calculate
   (a) the distance S_1Q and S_2Q,
   (b) the path difference $S_2Q - S_1Q$,
   (c) the wavelength of the sound emitted.
   (d) the speed of sound in air.

Figure 18.40

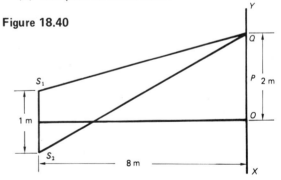

10. (a) A source of sound, S (Figure 18.41), is placed in front of a large plane reflector, R.
    (i) A microphone, M, which is connected to a cathode ray oscilloscope, is moved along the line AB perpendicular to the reflector. The oscilloscope shows maxima and minima of sound intensity.

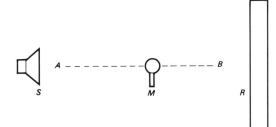

Figure 18.41

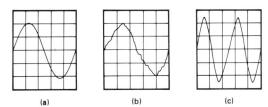

(a)　　　　　(b)　　　　　(c)

Figure 18.42

 Explain this and name the maxima and minima.

(ii) The distance between 11 successive minima is 2.5 m. Assuming the speed of sound to be 340 m s^{-1} find the frequency of the source.
 Why is it better to use eleven successive minima instead of two to determine the frequency of the source?

(iii) State, giving your reason, what you would expect to happen to the distance between the minima as the frequency of the source is increased.

(b) Figure 18.42a, b and c represent the traces on an oscilloscope of sound waves produced by three different instruments. Compare the pitch, quality and intensity of the three sounds. (Give your reasons.)

(London June 1979)

11. Figure 18.43 shows an elastic string with beads fixed on it at equal intervals. One end of the elastic string is connected to a vibrator and the other to a wall. The vibrator then vibrates to and fro along the direction of the elastic string. Figure 18.44 shows the positions of some of the beads at different times.

(a) What kind of wave motion is produced in this case?

(b) Find the frequency of the wave motion set up in the string.

(c) Which bead(s) has/have the
 (i) largest amplitude, and
 (ii) smallest amplitude?

(d) If the separation between any two beads in Figure 18.43 is 2 cm, find the velocity of the wave formed.

(e) Sketch the displacement-time graph of bead 7 from 0 s to 0.04 s, taking the displacement to the right as positive.

(HKCEE 1983)

Figure 18.43

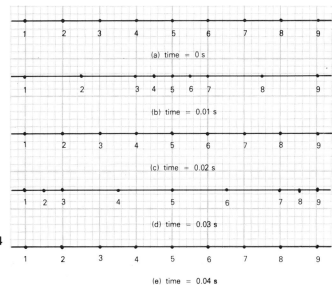

Figure 18.44

section E

ELECTRICITY, MAGNETISM and ELECTRONICS

Electrostatics

Over two thousand years ago, the Greeks discovered that amber, when rubbed with fur, exerted a force on nearby objects. The phenomenon is now called static electricity — given its name by the Greek word for amber, 'elektron'.

ELECTRIC CHARGES

Plastic materials can be charged with **static electricity** by friction (Figure 19.1). A plastic rod rubbed with a dry, woollen cloth attracts small pieces of aluminium foil or paper. The plastic rod is said to be exerting an **electric force**; it is carrying an **electric charge**.

When two thin, flexible acetate strips are rubbed with a *dry* duster and then held side by side, they *repel* each other (Figure 19.2a). A rubbed polythene strip also repels another rubbed polythene strip (Figure 19.2b) but a rubbed acetate strip and a rubbed polythene strip *attract* each other (Figure 19.2c). This suggests that the electric charges on the acetate and polythene strips are of different kinds. Experiments with other materials provide further evidence that a general rule applies to forces between the two different kinds of charges:

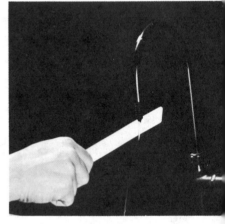

Figure 19.1 Rubbed plastic rod attracts stream of running water.

> **like charges repel; unlike charges attract**

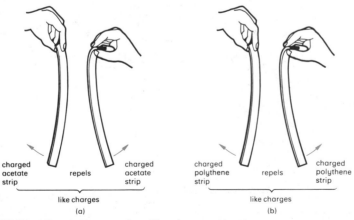

| charged acetate strip | repels | charged acetate strip | charged polythene strip | repels | charged polythene strip | charged acetate strip | attracts | charged polythene strip |

like charges (a)   like charges (b)   unlike charges (c)

Figure 19.2 Like charges repel; unlike charges attract.

electrostatics 靜電學   electric charge 電荷

Figure 19.3 shows the repulsion between hairs carrying the same kind of charge.

The two kinds of charges are called positive (+) and negative (−). When rubbed with a dry duster or a dry woollen cloth, acetate and perspex become positively charged while polythene and PVC become negatively charged.

Where charges come from

Matter is made up of tiny particles called atoms. An atom is thought to consist of yet smaller particles, some of which carry electric charges. Figure 19.4 shows a model of the atom. At the centre of the atom is the **nucleus** which is made up of particles of similar mass called **protons** and **neutrons**. Surrounding the nucleus are particles of very much smaller mass called **electrons**. A proton has a positive (+) charge, an electron has an *equal* negative (−) charge while a neutron is uncharged.

Figure 19.3   Repulsion between hairs carrying the same kind of charge.

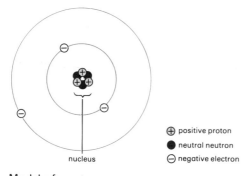

nucleus

⊕ positive proton
● neutral neutron
⊖ negative electron

Figure 19.4   Model of an atom.

Generally, an atom has an equal number of protons and electrons and so is electrically **neutral**. When two materials are rubbed together, electrons from the atoms of one material may be transferred to the other material. This upsets the balance of positive and negative charges within each material and results in one material having more electrons than usual and the other material having less.

When an acetate strip is rubbed with a dry duster, the duster pulls electrons away from the atoms on the surface of the acetate strip. This leaves the acetate strip with *less* electrons and the duster with more (Figure 19.5). The acetate strip therefore becomes positively charged and the duster negatively charged. When a polythene strip is rubbed with a dry duster, the opposite happens. In this case, it is the polythene strip that pulls electrons away from the duster. With *more* electrons than usual, the polythene strip is left with a negative charge while the duster gains an equal quantity of positive charge (Figure 19.6).

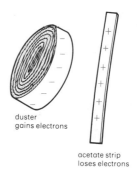

duster
gains electrons

acetate strip
loses electrons

Figure 19.5   Rubbing transfers electrons from acetate strip to duster.

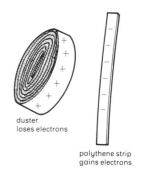

duster
loses electrons

polythene strip
gains electrons

Figure 19.6   Rubbing transfers electrons from duster to polythene strip.

nucleus 原子核   proton 質子   neutron 中子   neutral 中性   **91**

Note that rubbing materials together does not create electric charges; it merely separates the positive and negative charges which already exist within the materials.

Quantity of charge

An uncharged object becomes positively charged if it loses electrons and negatively charged if it gains them. The more electrons an object loses or gains, the greater is the positive or negative charge on it.

Charge, symbol Q, is a quantity of electricity and is measured in **coulombs** (C). One coulomb is the charge on about 6 million million million (6×10^{18}) electrons.

The charge on a rubbed polythene rod is typically around one thousand millionth of a coulomb (10^{-9} C). This is a very small charge, and yet the rod still carries about 1000 million extra electrons.

Conductors and insulators

Plastic materials can readily be charged by rubbing. This is because the transferred electrons remain on the plastic material and do not escape easily. Materials, like plastics, which do not allow electrons to readily flow through them are called **insulators**.

On the other hand, a metallic object cannot be charged unless it is held on an insulating handle. The charge that results is lost almost as soon as it is gained. This happens because electrons flow through the object or surrounding materials until the balance between positive and negative charges is restored. Materials which allow electrons to readily flow through them are called **conductors**. Metals are the best conductor of all because the outermost electrons of the atoms

Table 19.1

Good conductor	Poor conductor	Insulator
metals, especially gold, silver, copper, aluminium	water	rubber
	human body	plastics, e.g. acetate, perspex, polythene, PVC
	earth	
	moist air	glass
carbon	semiconductors, e.g. silicon, germanium	dry air

conductor 導體   insulator 絕緣體   coulomb 庫倫

are loosely held and so can move freely between atoms. Most non-metals are poor conductors of electricity because they have few, or no, *free electrons*. Table 19.1 shows some of the common conductors and insulators.

ATTRACTION OF UNCHARGED OBJECTS

A charged object will attract any nearby uncharged object. If an uncharged plastic strip is held near a rubbed acetate strip and a rubbed polythene strip in turn, the uncharged strip is attracted in each case. A plastic ruler rubbed with a piece of dry woollen cloth will pick up small pieces of aluminium foil or paper.

Such attraction can be explained by considering the effect of a charged acetate rod on a small piece of aluminium foil placed beneath it (Figure 19.7). Free electrons in the aluminium are pulled towards the positively charged rod so that the top end of the foil becomes negatively charged while the bottom end is positively charged. The charged rod attracts the top end of the foil and repels the bottom end. Since the top end is closer to the rod, the force of attraction is greater than the force of repulsion and so the foil is pulled towards the rod.

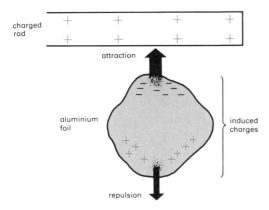

Figure 19.7 Charged object attracts uncharged objects by causing induced charges.

The charged rod will also attract small pieces of paper. Being an insulator, the paper has no free electrons, but the charge on the rod distorts the atoms in the paper, pulling the electrons a little closer towards the rod and pushing the nuclei a little further away. The paper behaves as if it has a negative charge at the top end and a positive charge at the bottom end and is therefore attracted by the rod.

In the above two examples, the aluminium foil and the paper appear to be charged because of the presence of a nearby charged object. They are said to be carrying **induced charges**.

induced charges 感應電荷

EHT SUPPLY

An extra high tension (EHT) power supply which supplies a voltage of up to 5000 volts provides an alternative, and probably more effective method of charging an object. Figure 19.8 shows two thin, flexible metal-coated plastic strips, each hung from an insulating rod on a retort stand. One strip is connected to the + terminal of the EHT supply and the other to the − terminal, but *neither terminal is earthed*. When the supply is switched on, electrons are drawn from one strip and driven to the other strip. As a result, one strip becomes positively charged and the other negatively charged and therefore they *attract* each other.

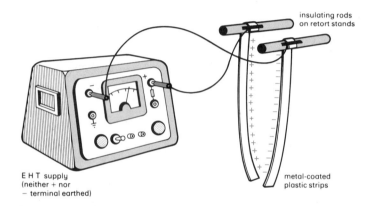

E H T supply
(neither + nor
− terminal earthed)

insulating rods
on retort stands

metal-coated
plastic strips

Figure 19.8 Attraction between strips charged by EHT supply.

However if, both strips are connected to the +terminal of the EHT supply (Figure 19.9), *the negative terminal being earthed,* the strips both become positively charged and therefore *repel* each other. This suggests that the general rule for forces between charges is also applicable to objects charged by an EHT supply. A further experiment using a strip charged by friction and another strip charged by an EHT supply (Figure 19.10), again shows that like charges repel and unlike charges attract. Electric charges are therefore the same, whether produced by friction or a power supply, because electrons are identical, that is, only the method of producing the charge varies, not the charge itself.

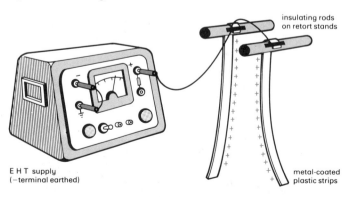

E H T supply
(−terminal earthed)

insulating rods
on retort stands

metal-coated
plastic strips

Figure 19.9 Repulsion between strips charged by EHT supply.

extra high tension 超高電壓

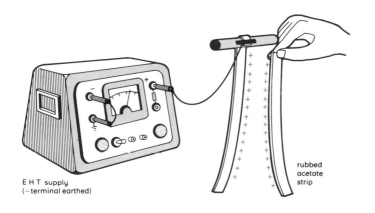

Figure 19.10 Repulsion between strip charged by rubbing and strip charged by EHT.

EHT supply
(–terminal earthed)

rubbed
acetate
strip

VAN DE GRAAFF GENERATOR

A **van de Graaff generator** produces a large and continuous supply of electric charge. Figure 19.11 shows a school model in which a rubber belt is driven by a plastic roller. The belt rubs against the roller and becomes charged. The charge produced is carried by the moving belt up to the metal dome where it is collected. A large quantity of charge therefore builds up on the dome.

The generator may be used to demonstrate a number of interesting experiments. In Figure 19.3 (p.91), the boy, standing on an insulating plastic stool, touches the metal dome and becomes negatively charged. Because they carry the same type of charge, his hairs repel each other and so stand on end.

When a metal sphere, connected to the earth with a lead (Figure 19.12), is brought near the metal dome, electric sparks are produced. This happens as electric charges pass from the dome through the air to the sphere and then to the earth.

Figure 19.11 Charge is built up on dome of van de Graaff generator.

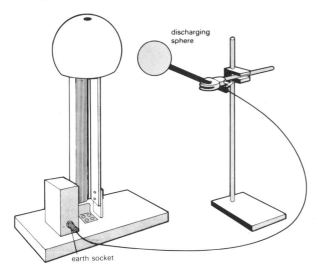

discharging
sphere

earth socket

Figure 19.12 Electric sparks indicate transfer of charge from doom to sphere through the air.

van de Graaff generator 范德格拉夫起電機

When the charges on the dome are passed to the earth via a sensitive microammeter (Figure 19.13a), the meter pointer deflects. If a dry cell is connected to the meter through a very high resistance (Figure 19.13b), the meter pointer is also deflected as an electric current flows through the circuit. This shows that the flow of charges is identical to the flow of an electric current.

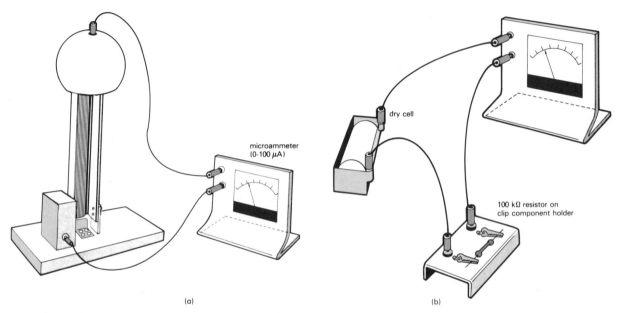

(a)

(b)

Figure 19.13　Electric current is flow of electric charge.

GOLD-LEAF ELECTROSCOPE

The **gold-leaf electroscope**, shown in Figure 19.14, is used for detecting small charges. When a rubbed acetate rod is brought near the metal cap, the leaf rises. The positively

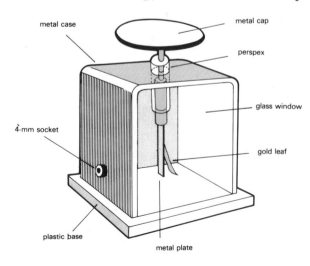

Figure 19.14　Gold-leaf electroscope.

electroscope 驗電器

charged rod attracts free electrons in the plate and leaf up towards the cap so that the cap becomes negatively charged and the plate and leaf positively charged. Charges on the plate and leaf repel each other (Figure 19.15). As a result, the leaf rises. On removing the charged rod, the extra free electrons in the cap are no longer attracted to the rod and return to the plate and leaf, and so the leaf falls.

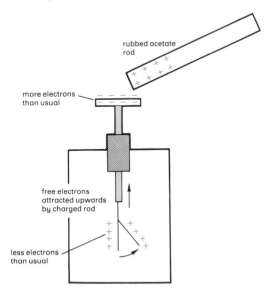

Figure 19.15 Free electrons in gold-leaf and metal plate attracted upwards by positively charged rod.

The leaf also rises when a negatively charged polythene rod is brought near the cap (Figure 19.16). The rise of the leaf occurs because, free electrons in the cap are pushed downwards, that is, repelled by the negatively charged rod.

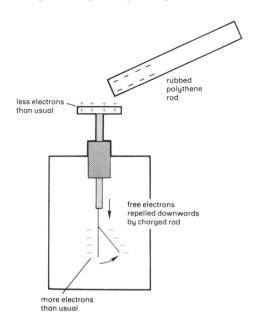

Figure 19.16 Free electrons repelled downwards by negatively charged rod.

Testing for polarity of charges

When a charged rod is rubbed firmly across the edge of the metal cap, some of the charge is transferred to the electroscope and the leaf rises. Once charged, an electroscope can be used to find out whether the charge on an object is positive or negative. Figure 19.17a shows an electroscope which has been given a negative charge; the cap, plate and leaf all contain more electrons than usual.

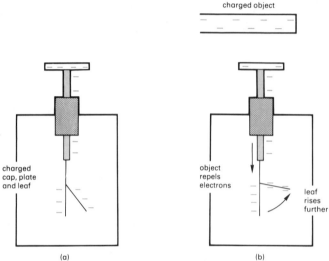

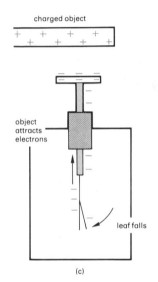

If a negatively charged rod is held near the cap (Figure 19.17b), some of the free electrons in the cap are repelled and flow downwards into the plate and leaf. This increases the repulsion between leaf and plate, and so the leaf rises further. However, on removing the rod, the extra free electrons flow back to the cap and the leaf falls to its previous position.

If a positively charged rod is brought near the cap (Figure 19.17c) the reverse occurs, that is, free electrons in the plate and leaf are attracted towards the cap. The leaf therefore falls slightly.

However, the leaf also falls if an uncharged rod is held near the cap. This occurs because the negatively charged electroscope induces a positive charge on the near end of the rod and a negative charge on the far end (Figure 19.17d). The induced positive charge on the rod then causes the leaf to fall.

In general, if an object held near a charged electroscope causes the leaf to rise further, it has the same kind of charge as the electroscope; if it causes the leaf to fall, it has a different kind of charge or is uncharged. Hence, only a rise of the leaf can conclusively demonstrate the polarity of the charge on the object.

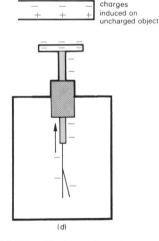

Figure 19.17   Rod carrying charge different from that on electroscope causes leaf to rise further.

polarity 極性

CHARGING BY INDUCTION

A positively charged rod is held near two small metal cans, A and B, which are placed touching each other, on insulating tiles as shown in Figure 19.18. The rod pulls free electrons in can B towards can A. As a result, a negative charge is *induced* in can A on the side near the rod, and a positive charge on can B on the far side. If the two cans are then separated *while the charged rod is held in position,* the can near the rod (can A) ends up with a negative charge while the can away from the rod (can B) ends up with an equal but positive charge. This is a charging process by **induction**. It is a process which does not involve any loss of charge from the charged rod.

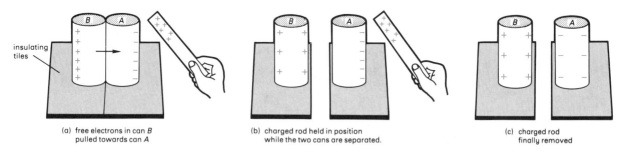

(a) free electrons in can B pulled towards can A

(b) charged rod held in position while the two cans are separated.

(c) charged rod finally removed

Figure 19.18 Charging two cans by induction.

Figure 19.19 shows how a single can is charged by induction. As before, a positively charged rod is held near the can and this causes induced charges to appear on the can as shown. With the rod held in position, the can is touched momentarily with a finger. This allows electrons to flow in from the earth to replace the missing electrons. First the finger and then

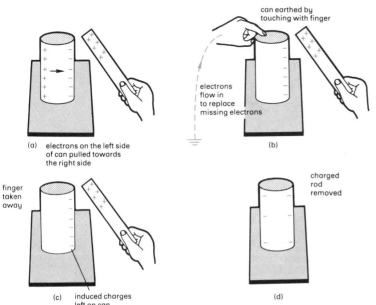

(a) electrons on the left side of can pulled towards the right side

can earthed by touching with finger

electrons flow in to replace missing electrons

(b)

finger taken away

(c) induced charges left on can

charged rod removed

(d)

Figure 19.19 Charging one can by induction.

induction 感應

the charged rod are removed and the can is left with a net negative charge. Using a negatively charged rod, the can can be given a positive charge in a similar way. Note that the charge induced on the can is always different from that on the rod.

A gold-leaf electroscope can also be charged by induction. This method is more effective than charging by contact with a charged object. The process is shown step-by-step in Figure 19.20.

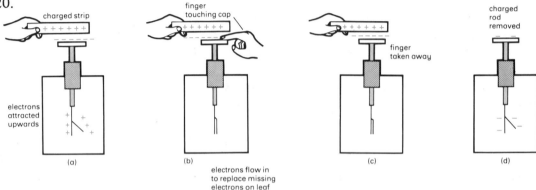

Figure 19.20   Charging electroscope by induction.

CHARGE SHARING AND EARTHING

Charge an electroscope and touch the cap with a small, uncharged conducting sphere (Figure 19.21). The leaf will fall slightly. This happens because some charge is taken away from the electroscope – in fact, charge is shared between the electroscope and the conducting sphere. If a larger sphere is used, the leaf falls even further because a larger sphere takes a larger share of charge. If the cap is now touched with a finger, the leaf falls completely. Being a (poor) conductor, the human body puts the electroscope in contact with the largest available object of all, the earth, and so practically all the charge leaves the electroscope. This process of sharing charge with the earth is called **earthing**.

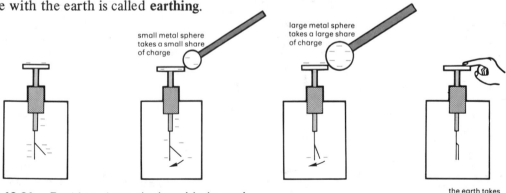

Figure 19.21   Earthing: charge sharing with the earth.

earthing 接地

ELECTRIC FIELD

Around an electric charge or a charged object, other electric charges or charged objects are subjected to forces of either repulsion or attraction. We say there is an **electric field**. It is represented by a series of arrowed lines called **electric field lines**.

Where a positive charge experiences repulsion, a negative charge would experience attraction. Therefore, by convention, an electric field line shows the path along which a positive charge would move, if free to do so. The arrow gives the direction of the acting electric force. Figure 19.22 shows the electric field lines between a positively and a negatively charged sphere.

Electric field patterns due to charged conductors of different shapes can be shown using the apparatus in Figure 19.23.

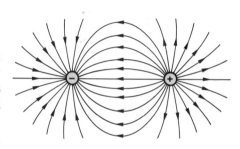

Figure 19.22 Electric field lines due to one positive charge and one negative charge.

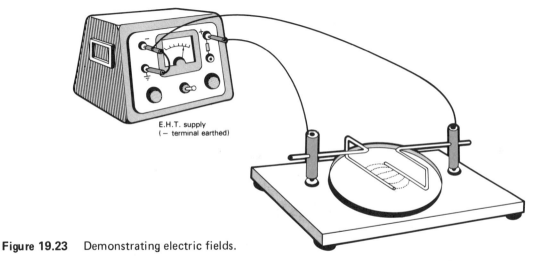

E.H.T. supply
(− terminal earthed)

Figure 19.23 Demonstrating electric fields.

Two electrodes connected to the terminals of an EHT are dipped into a dish of castor oil. When the EHT is switched on, an electric field exists across the electrodes. When a little semolina powder is sprinkled on the surface of the oil, the tiny particles become charged and line up in the direction of the electric field (Figure 19.24).

Figure 19.24 Electric field patterns: (a), (b) and (c) electrodes connected to different terminals; (d) electrodes connected to the same terminal.

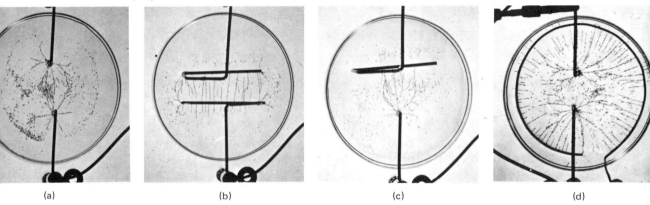

(a)   (b)   (c)   (d)

electric field 電場   electric field lines 電力線   castor oil 蓖蔴油   semolina powder 粗粒小麥粉   **101**

ELECTRIC POTENTIAL

A charge experiences a force in an electric field. If it is moved against the force from one point to another (Figure 19.25a), work has to be done and energy, symbol E, has to be supplied. As a result, the charge gains **electrical potential energy**. This situation is analogous to that of a mass raised in the earth's gravitational field; the mass gains gravitational potential energy equal to the work done in raising it against gravity (Figure 19.25b).

Two points in an electric field are said to be at different **electric potentials** if work has to be done in moving a charge from one point to the other. The **potential difference** (symbol V), or **p.d.** for short, between two points in an electric field is defined as (Figure 19.26):

> The potential difference between two points in an electric field is the work in joules which has to be done to move 1 coulomb of positive charge from one point to the other.

As the charge gains electrical potential energy as a result of the work done, potential difference between two points can also be defined as:

> The potential difference between two points in an electric field is the electrical potential energy gained per coulomb of positive charge in moving from one point to the other.
>
> $$\text{Potential difference} = \frac{\text{electrical potential energy}}{\text{charge}}$$
>
> $$V = \frac{E}{Q} \qquad \text{or} \qquad E = VQ$$

Potential difference is measured in joules per coulomb or **volts**, abbreviated to V.

If the positive charge in Figure 19.25a is allowed to return from B to A, work is done by the electric force and the electrical potential energy previously gained is lost, or rather, changed into other forms of energy.

ACTION OF A POINT

The charge on a conductor stays on its outside surface and tends to accumulate where the surface is most sharply curved. When a pin is stuck on the dome of a van de Graaff generator most of the charge on the dome is concentrated at the pin.

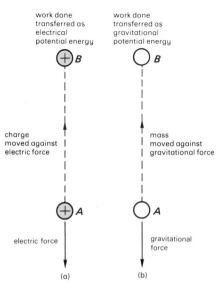

Figure 19.25 Electrical and gravitational potential energy.

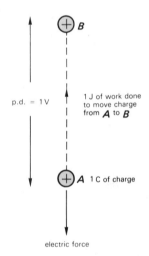

Figure 19.26 One volt is one joule per coulomb.

There is so much charge that it 'leaks' away, carrying with it a stream of air which is often called an **electric wind**.

The electric wind can be felt by a hand placed a few centimetres away from the pin or demonstrated by holding a candle flame held close to the pin (Figure 19.27). If a 'windmill' is fixed on top of the dome (Figure 19.28), the electric wind from the spikes of the windmill propels the windmill to turn around.

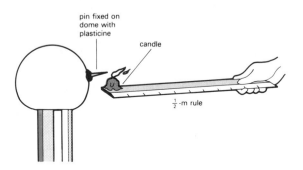

Figure 19.27   Candle flame flickering in electric wind.

Figure 19.28   'Windmill' propelled by electric wind.

The action of a point is explained by considering the effect of the high concentration of negative charge in the pin on the nearby air molecules. The electric field of the charged pin is so strong that it removes electrons from the air molecules around it. Some of these electrons become attached to other molecules. As a result, the pin is surrounded by a large number of molecules which have either lost or gained electrons. When this happens, the air is said to be **ionized** and the charged molecules so formed are called **ions** (Figure 19.29). The positive ions are attracted towards the negatively charged pin, collect electrons from it to become neutral molecules, and so the charge on the pin falls rapidly. At the same time, negative ions are repelled by the pin producing a stream of air. It appears as if a stream of electrons flows out from the pin, but in fact it is the negative ions in the air which are pushed away.

A sharp point with a positive charge on it loses charge by a similar process. But in this case it is positive ions which are repelled by the point.

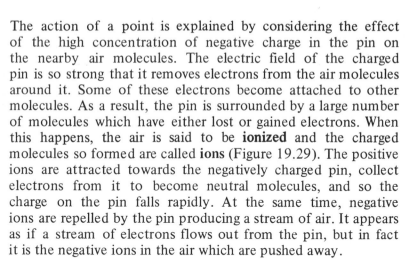

Figure 19.29   Point action explained.

ionized 電離   ion 離子

Lightning conductor

A lightning conductor is usually installed on a tall building (Figure 19.30) to prevent it from being struck by lightning during a thunderstorm. It consists of a copper strip with one end fixed to a metal plate buried in the ground (Figure 19.31) and the other end attached to sharp spikes above the rooftop.

Clouds are charged when they are blown around by wind. A thundercloud is one in which a large quantity of positive or negative charge accumulates. If, for example, a negatively charged thundercloud gathers over a building, a positive charge is induced on the roof. The force of attraction between the positive and negative charges may be so strong that electrons suddenly jump from the cloud to the roof producing a flash of lightning.

The lightning conductor helps to reduce the risk to the building in two ways:

1. Streams of positive ions flow out from the spikes reducing the induced charge on the roof and cancelling out some of the charge on the cloud. This lowers the chance of lightning striking the building.

2. If lightning does occur, the lightning conductor provides a route for electrons to pass into the ground without causing damage to the building.

ELECTROSTATIC HAZARDS

In industry, charges produced by friction can be very troublesome. Sheets of paper become charged and stick to each other, thus becoming difficult to separate. Wool, cotton and artificial fibres attract dust when charged and become dirty. In some cases, sparks produced by electric charge may cause fires or even explosions. An oil truck carries a metal chain at the back touching the road as it moves (Figure 19.32). This helps to pass into the ground any charge which may develop in the tyres. For similar reasons, when an aircraft is being refuelled (Figure 19.33), a cable connects its wheel to the oil tank,

Figure 19.30 Lightning conductor on top of Hopewell Centre.

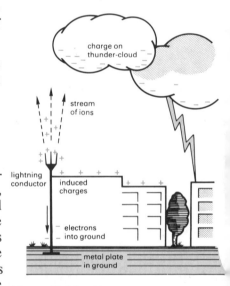

Figure 19.31 How lightning conductors work.

lightning conductor 避雷針

Figure 19.32 Metal chain safeguards truck against electric sparks which may cause fire and explosion.

Figure 19.33 Cable at wheel of aircraft is another safety measure against electrostatic hazards.

which is also connected to ground. Tyres for aircrafts, sometimes for oil trucks too, are made of conductive rubber so that any charge developed on the aeroplane body during flights is conducted to the ground on landing.

APPLICATIONS OF ELECTROSTATICS

Electrostatics has many applications in industry which are relevant to everyday life.

Electrostatic precipitation

Fly-ash from factory chimneys poses serious air pollution problems. This is especially true of coal-fired power stations which can produce many tens of tonnes of fly-ash everyday. An electrostatic method is used to remove or 'precipitate' the fly-ash. Its working principle can be demonstrated using a van de Graaff generator. A plastic cylinder with metal ends is fixed on the dome (Figure 19.34) and a drawing pin is placed in it, pointing upwards. The cylinder is filled with smoke and when the generator is started and the metal lid earthed, the smoke quickly clears. A very strong electric field is set up in the cylinder and the smoke particles become charged and attracted to the pin.

In a chimney, fly-ash is precipitated by applying a high voltage between wires strung inside the chimney and metal plates on the inside of the chimney walls. The wires are negatively charged and give a similar charge to the ash particles which are then attracted to the positive plates. The chimneys of the coal-fired Castle Peak Power Station are fitted with electrostatic precipitators (Figure 19.35). A cement factory has been built near the power station to make use of the fly-ash which is produced in large quantities.

Photocopying

Photocopiers (Figure 19.36) are now widely used in schools and offices. They print by an electrostatic process. Inside the photocopying machine a rotating, light-sensitive drum is given a positive charge by a charged grid which moves over

electrostatic precipitation 靜電沉積法

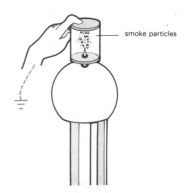

Figure 19.34   Demonstrating electrostatic precipitation.

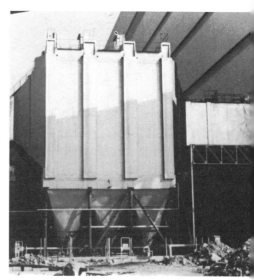

Figure 19.35   An electrostatic precipitator.

Figure 19.36   Inside a photocopier.

105

it (Figure 19.37). A system, usually of optical fibre lenses, then projects the image of the document to be copied onto the drum. Positive charges on the drum disappear from the exposed areas, but remain in areas which correspond to the black or printed part of the original document. A negatively charged powder (toner) is poured over the drum and adheres to the positively charged image. A sheet of paper then passes over the drum and a positive charge underneath it attracts the powder from the drum to the paper. The powder image is softened and fused into the paper by heating it for a few seconds. Hence a dry, clean and permanent copy of the original document is produced. The process of electrostatic printing is illustrated step by step in Figure 19.37.

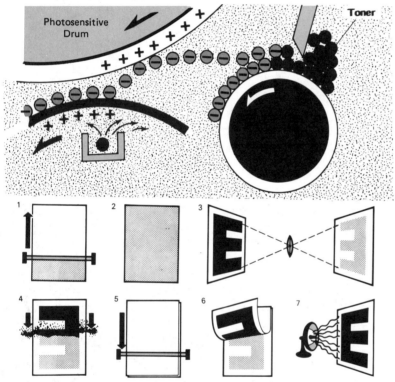

Figure 19.37   The photocopying process explained.

1. The surface of the photo-sensitive drum is sensitized by an electrically charged grid which moves across it.

2. The coating of the drum is now fully charged positively.

3. The original document (E) is projected onto the drum. Positive charges disappear in areas exposed to light.

4. A negatively charged powder (toner) is dusted over the drum and adheres to the positively charged image.

5. A sheet of paper is now passed over the drum and receives a positive charge.

6. The positively charged paper attracts powder from the drum, forming a direct positive image.

7. The print is fixed by heating it for a few seconds to form the permanent image.

SUMMARY

What is matter

Matter is made up of atoms.

Inside an atom, there are electrons and a nucleus. The nucleus is made up of protons and neutrons.

Electron has negative charge; proton has positive charge; neutron has no charge.

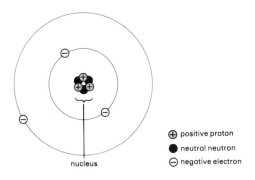

positive proton
neutral neutron
negative electron

nucleus

Charge and matter

By nature, atoms are neutral, that is, the number of protons in an atom is equal to the number of electrons.

An object becomes positively charged if it loses electrons. Conversely, if an object gains electrons, it becomes negatively charged.

What is charge

Charge is a quantity of electricity and is measured in coulombs (C).

Like charges repel; unlike charges attract.

The charge on an electron is -1.6×10^{-19} C.

Materials which allow electrons to flow through them are called conductors. Materials which do not allow electrons to flow are called insulators. Conductors have many *free electrons* which move between atoms.

Insulators, on the other hand, have very few or no free electrons.

Methods of charging

An object can be charged by rubbing against another object. As a result, one object becomes positively charged while the other object becomes negatively charged.

An object can also be charged by using an EHT power supply.

A van de Graaff generator gives a very large continuous supply of charge. The charge on the dome, if allowed to flow through a microammeter, deflects the meter pointer, indicating an electric current.

Both insulators and conductors can be charged by friction. Conductors, on the other hand, can also be charged by induction or charge sharing.

The process of charge sharing with the earth is called earthing.

The process of charging two conductors by induction is shown below.

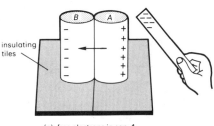

insulating tiles

(a) free electrons in can *A* repelled towards can *B*

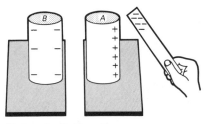

(b) charged rod held in position while the two cans are separated.

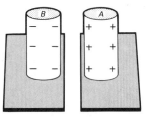

(c) charged rod finally removed

The process of charging one conductor by induction is shown below.

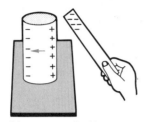

(a)   electrons on the right side of can repelled towards the left side

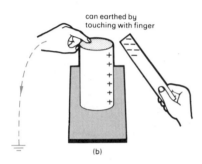

can earthed by touching with finger

(b)

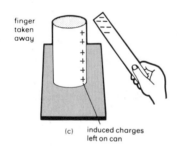

finger taken away

(c)   induced charges left on can

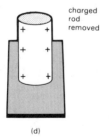

charged rod removed

(d)

Electric field

A charged object attracts or repels other charges near it. We say that there is an electric field.

An electric field is represented graphically by electric field lines which indicate the paths along which a positive charge would move.

If we have to supply energy E to move a positive charge Q from one point A to another point B, then the potential difference V_{AB} between A and B is defined as

$$V_{AB} = \frac{E}{Q}$$

Potential difference is measured in volts (V).

Point action

Gas molecules can be ionized by a sharp point on a charged object. The ions produced can carry charge to or from the sharp point.

Electrostatic precipitation and photocopying are two of the important applications of electrostatics.

PROBLEMS

1. Name the material which, when rubbed with a dry woollen cloth becomes (a) positively charged, (b) negatively charged. Explain in terms of electron transfer what has happened in each case.

2. Why does a conductor have to be held by an insulating handle if it is to be charged? What happens if the conductor is held in the hand?

3. Two identical metal-coated plastic strips, hung from insulating rods, are connected to an EHT supply set at 5000 V.
   (a) One strip is connected to the + terminal and the other to the − terminal of the EHT supply. Describe what happens
      (i) when the strips are brought close to each other,
      (ii) when the strips are allowed to touch each other (after they have been disconnected from the supply).
   (b) Both strips are connected to the − terminal of the EHT, the + terminal being earthed. Describe what happens
      (i) when the strips are brought close to each other,
      (ii) when the strips are allowed to touch each other (after they have been disconnected from the supply).

4. A metal sphere on an insulating stand is connected to the + terminal of an EHT supply, the − terminal being earthed. Describe and explain what happens when a conducting polystyrene ball, hung on a nylon thread, is brought near to the metal sphere.

5. Explain why a rubbed acetate strip attracts a stream of running water.

6. A negatively charged rod is held near a metal sphere on an insulating stand (Figure 19.38).
   (a) Copy the diagram and add any induced charges that would appear on the sphere.
   (b) What can be done to the sphere in order to leave it with a positive charge?

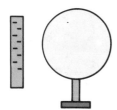

Figure 19.38

7. A negatively charged polythene rod is brought near the cap of an electroscope. Figure 19.39 shows successive steps in charging the electroscope by induction.

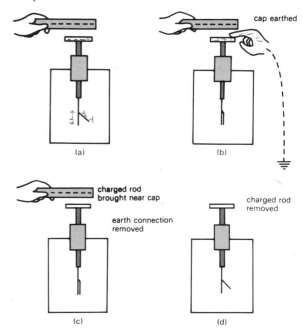

Figure 19.39

   (a) Copy the diagram and add the sign of the charge, if any, at
      (i) the cap,
      (ii) the leaf of the electroscope.
      (iii) What would be the effect if the rod is removed before the finger?
      (iv) If the polythene rod touches the cap, will the same results be obtained?
   (b) Describe what happens to the leaf when
      (i) a positively charged acetate rod,
      (ii) a negatively charged polythene rod,
      (iii) an uncharged rod
      is in turn brought near the cap of the electroscope.

8. (a) In a factory, rubber sheets were put under the machines to lower down the noise level. Soon the workers protested because they sometimes received an electric shock when they touched the machines. No leakage from the mains cable was found. Explain and suggest how you would eliminate the electric shock.
   (b) In the manufacture of nylon thread, some bits of nylon fluff may stick to the thread. However this could be overcome by maintaining a high humidity in the room. Suggest reasons for this.

9. Two straight, parallel electrodes are dipped into a dish contain castor oil. The electrodes are connected to an EHT supply, one to the $+$ terminal and the other to the $-$ terminal. When semolina particles are sprinkled over the castor oil, they settle down into positions showing an electric field pattern.
   (a) Sketch the pattern observed.
   (b) Explain why the semolina particles settle down into positions showing a special pattern.
   (c) Explain why castor oil is used, and not, for example, water or other liquids.
   (d) What would be the effect on the pattern, if the two parallel electrodes are placed closer together?

10. If the p.d. between the dome of a van de Graaff generator and the earth is 40 000 V, how much work has to be done in carrying a charge of 5×10^{-6} C from the base to the dome?

11. If 60 J of work has to be done to carry 5 C of charge across two parallel metal plates, what is the p.d. across the metal plates?

12. A small metal sphere A is suspended by an insulating thread, as shown in Figure 19.40a, and carries a charge of -10^{-8} C.

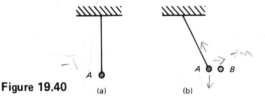

Figure 19.40 (a) (b)

   (a) Another insulated metal sphere B carrying a charge of $+3 \times 10^{-8}$ C is held near A. Sphere A is attracted and rests in the position shown in Figure 19.40b. Draw a diagram showing all the forces acting on sphere A in the equilibrium position.
   (b) The spheres A and B are then allowed to touch each other. Describe and explain briefly what happens. *share electrons, no attraction, suspense*
   (c) If the charges were shared equally between A and B after contact, what would be the charge on each? *0.*

(HKCEE 1980)

13. (a) A and B (Figure 19.41a) are two conducting spheres on insulating stands. A is charged to a high positive potential and B, which is earthed, is brought near to it. Draw a diagram showing the resulting charge distribution on B.

(b) B is replaced by the earthed metal needle C (Figure 19.41b), which is the same distance from A as was B. Draw a diagram to show the charge distribution on C, and explain why in this case A loses its charge much more quickly than it did in (a).

(c) Lightning conductors with pointed tops are put on high buildings to prevent the buildings being damaged by lightning but it is foolish to walk across an open space carrying an open umbrella in thundery conditions. Give the physical reasons for the above statement.

(London Jan 1979)

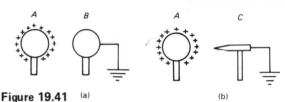

Figure 19.41 (a) (b)

14. A pin is placed on the cap of an electroscope (Figure 19.42). When a charged polythene rod is brought near it, the leaf rises.
   (a) State the sign of the charge on the polythene rod.
   (b) Sketch the distribution of the charge on the electroscope and the tip of the needle when this charged polythene rod is held near.
   (c) When the rod is removed, the leaf of the electroscope remains in the rising position. Why has the electroscope become charged?
   (d) Has the rod lost some of its charge?

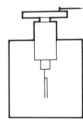

Figure 19.42

15. (a) A girl, after combing her hair on a dry day, holds the comb near small pieces of paper. What will be observed if the comb is made of
    (i) plastic, and
    (ii) aluminium?
    Explain briefly in each case.
   (b) Two similarly charged metal-coated balls, A and B, are suspended from two insulating threads as shown in Figure 19.43.
    (i) Copy the diagram into your answer book and draw on the diagram all the forces acting on the two balls.
    (ii) If the ball A is earthed by touching, what would happen to the two balls? Explain briefly.
   (c) Describe briefly how you would test whether a body is positively or negatively charged in a laboratory.

(HKCEE 1985)

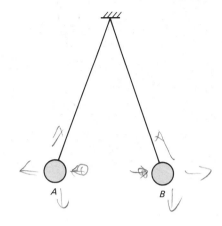

Figure 19.43

Electric Circuits 20

A potential difference applied across the two ends of a conductor causes the free electrons in the conductor to flow through it. Different conductors offer different resistances to the electron or current flow. Increase the potential difference and a greater current flows.

ELECTRIC CURRENT

Figure 20.1 represents two lamps connected by copper wires to a battery made up of two cells. The symbols used in the diagram have been selected from the chart on the inside back cover. The complete conducting path through the lamps, wires and battery is called a **circuit**. When the circuit is connected up, a **current**, symbol *I*, flows through the circuit and, as a result, the lamps light. Current indicates the rate at which charge is flowing.

Figure 20.1 A simple electric circuit.

The SI unit of current is the **ampere**, abbreviated to 'A'. A current of one ampere is equivalent to a flow of about 6 million million million (6×10^{18}) electrons per second, but this is *not* the proper definition of the unit. The ampere is defined in terms of the force exerted between two wires each carrying a current. This can be demonstrated using the apparatus in Figure 20.2. Two aluminium strips are mounted parallel and close to each other. When a current flows up one strip and down the other, the two strips repel each other. The larger the current, the greater is the force of repulsion. This force is explained by *the magnetic effect of a current*, which will be treated in detail in Chapter 22.

The definition of the ampere is given on p.293.

In practice, currents are measured using an **ammeter** (Figure 20.3) which is connected into a circuit so that a current flows through it. The working principle of an ammeter will be explained in Chapter 22, p.161.

On an ammeter the terminal coloured red, or marked +, should be connected to the side of the circuit which leads to the positive terminal of the battery. If it is connected the wrong way round, the ammeter will be damaged.

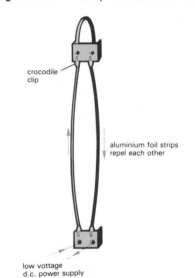

Figure 20.2 Aluminium foil strips, each carrying current flowing in opposite directions, repel each other.

Figure 20.3 An ammeter.

Conventional current

When the first battery was invented at the beginning of the nineteenth century, it was not known how charge moved in a circuit or in what direction. Scientists then agreed to take an electric current as a flow of positive charge from the positive terminal of a battery through a circuit to the negative terminal. About 100 years later, it was found that a current in a conductor was in fact a flow of negatively charged electrons moving in the *opposite* direction (Figure 20.4). However, the **conventional current** is still being used today. This is perhaps because it is difficult to change a convention two hundred years old, or because it is not really necessary to change. Apart from direction, a conventional current is equivalent to a flow of electrons in the opposite direction.

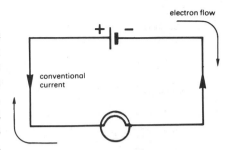

Figure 20.4 Electrons flows in the direction opposite to the direction of the conventional current.

Current through a simple circuit

Three ammeters are connected as in Figure 20.5 to measure the current at different points in the previous circuit. All three ammeters read the same, showing that *the current is the same at every point throughout a circuit.*

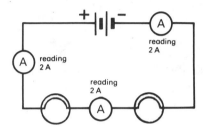

Figure 20.5 Current is the same at every point throughout the circuit.

When the battery is connected up, an electric field is created in the connecting wires and lamps of the circuit, causing the free electrons there to accelerate. The motion of the electrons is hindered by their collisions with the atoms. As a result, the electrons move through the circuit in a chain *at a constant rate* (Figure 20.6). The rate of flow of electrons at any point in the circuit must be the same, otherwise some electrons would be accumulating or leaking away somewhere.

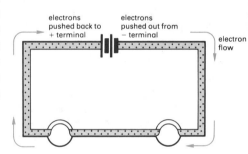

Figure 20.6 Free electrons move through the circuit in a chain at a constant rate.

Charge and current

Current is the rate at which charge is flowing in a circuit. Hence current and charge are related by the equation:

$$\text{current} = \frac{\text{charge}}{\text{time}}$$

or   charge = current × time

$$I = \frac{Q}{t} \quad \text{or} \quad Q = It$$

Charge is measured in coulombs, abbreviated to 'C'. One coulomb was earlier referred to as the charge on about 6 million million million electrons (p.93). But its formal definition is based on the ampere which is a SI base unit:

1 coulomb is the charge passing any point in a circuit when a steady current of 1 ampere flows for 1 second.

1 coulomb = 1 ampere second;   1 C = 1 A s

Example 1

How much charge passes a point in a circuit when a steady current of 2 A flows for 10 s?

A current of 2 A means that 2 C of charge flows in 1 s.

⇒ Charge flowing in 10 s = 2 A × 10 s = 20 A s = 20 C.

When a current of 2 A flows for 10 s, 20 C of charge passes any point in the circuit.

ELECTRICAL POTENTIAL ENERGY

When the circuit in Figure 20.1 (p.112) is connected up, the lamps light. Energy stored in the battery is being changed into the light and internal energy of the lamps. This energy is transferred by electrons moving through the circuit.

The free electrons in the conducting path are driven through the circuit from the battery terminal of lower potential to that of higher potential, that is, from the negative to the positive terminal. At the battery some electrons gain electrical potential energy. As they move through the circuit, they pass the lamps, and all their potential energy is changed into the light and internal energy of the lamps. Some electrons in the circuit then flow back towards the positive battery terminal. In this way, a chain of electrons 'drifts' continuously through the circuit, transferring electrical potential energy from the battery to the lamps.

Note that a battery does not give a supply of electrons; it transfers electrical potential energy to the free electrons which already exist in the conducting path, driving them through the circuit.

The energy transfers taking place in the circuit can be represented by a 'hill diagram' as in Figure 20.7. The diagram refers to the positive charges of a conventional current moving through the circuit. The charges move 'uphill' through the battery and gain electrical potential energy. They then move 'downhill' and transfer to the lamps light energy and internal energy.

Typical energy changes are indicated in the 'hill diagram'. Each coulomb of charge receives 4 joules of potential energy from the battery. 3 joules of potential energy are changed into light and internal energy as the charge passes through the first lamp, and the remaining 1 joule as it passes through the other lamp. There is negligible energy change in the connecting wires.

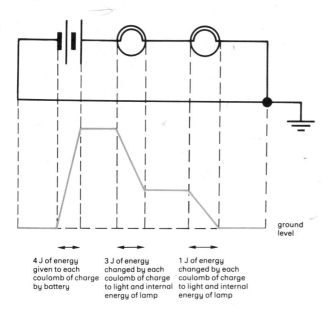

4 J of energy given to each coulomb of charge by battery

3 J of energy changed by each coulomb of charge to light and internal energy of lamp

1 J of energy changed by each coulomb of charge to light and internal energy of lamp

ground level

Figure 20.7 'Hill diagram': moving *'uphill'* through battery, charges gain potential energy moving *'downhill'*, they transfer energy to the lamps.

e.m.f. and p.d.

The **electromotive force (e.m.f.)** of a battery indicates the potential energy given to each coulomb of charge *within* the battery.

> **The e.m.f. of a battery is 1 volt if each coulomb of charge is given 1 joule of electrical potential energy.**

The battery in Figure 20.7 has an e.m.f. of 4 volts since it gives each coulomb of charge 4 joules of potential energy.

The **potential difference (p.d.)** or **voltage**, symbol V, across each lamp in the circuit indicates the electrical potential energy which changes to other forms of energy when 1 coulomb of charge passes through the lamp.

> **The p.d. between two points in a circuit is 1 volt if 1 joule of electrical potential energy is changed into other forms of energy when 1 coulomb of charge passes between the points.**

The p.d.s across the lamps are 3 volts and 1 volt respectively since the potential energy changes are 3 joules and 1 joule when 1 coulomb of charge passes through the lamps. The p.d. across any of the connecting wires is zero as there is no potential energy change at the wires.

electromotive force (e.m.f.) 電動勢   potential difference (p.d.) 電勢差，電位差

It follows that p.d. is potential energy per unit charge, that is:

$$p.d. = \frac{\text{potential energy}}{\text{charge}}$$

$$V = \frac{E}{Q} \qquad \text{or} \qquad E = QV$$

E.m.f. and p.d. are both measured in volts, abbreviated to 'V'.

$$1 \text{ volt} = 1 \text{ joule coulomb}^{-1} \qquad (1 \text{ V} = 1 \text{ J C}^{-1})$$

The e.m.f. of a battery is measured using a **voltmeter** (Figure 20.8) connected across its terminals (Figure 20.9). The p.d. across each of the two lamps is measured by connecting a voltmeter across each lamp (Figure 20.10).

Figure 20.8   A voltmeter.

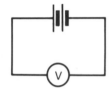

Figure 20.9   Use of voltmeter to measure the e.m.f. of a battery.

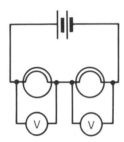

Figure 20.10   Use of voltmeter to measure the p.d. across the lamps.

Figure 20.11   Electricity analogue.

ELECTRICITY ANALOGUE

Figure 21.11 shows a **electricity analogue** for illustrating potential difference. It consists of an array of polystyrene spheres mounted on the ends of small springs which in turn are mounted on a wooden board. The spheres represent atoms in a conductor. The board is inclined and a ball bearing, representing a free electron, is rolled down it from the upper end. The ball moves down the board in a random way, colliding with the spheres on its way and setting them in vibration. The motion of the ball bearing can be compared to that of the charges in a current.

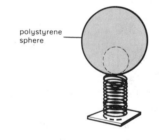

polystyrene sphere

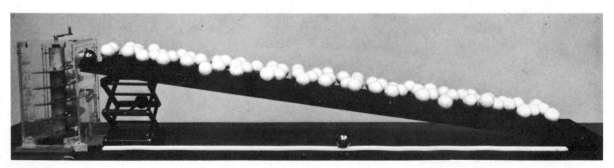

On moving down the inclined board the gravitational potential energy of the ball is changed to kinetic energy of the polystyrene spheres. In a similar way, the electrical potential energy carried by an electron is changed to internal energy as the electron moves through a conductor.

A screw type device represents a 'cell'. Applying energy to the screw by turning it, raises the ball to the top end of the inclined board, thereby giving the ball potential energy and creating a potential difference. Electrons will only flow through a conductor if there is a p.d. across its ends.

On reaching the bottom end of the inclined board, the ball returns to the cell by means of a friction-compensated slope which represents a 'good conductor'.

The motion of the ball is resisted as it collides with the spheres on its way down the board. An electron drifting through a conductor also experiences resistance to its motion.

Increasing the height of the upper end of the board shortens the time of travel of the ball. Increasing the p.d. across a conductor increases the rate of flow of electrons.

Example 2
A p.d. of 12 V is applied across a ray-box lamp. How much electrical potential energy is changed into light energy and internal energy when a current of 2 A flows through the lamp for 10 s?

>Charge flowing past the lamp in 10 s
>$= 2\,A \times 10\,s = 20\,A\,s = 20\,C$ ($Q = It$)

>A p.d. of 12 V means that there is a potential energy change of 12 J when 1 coulomb of charge passes through the lamp.
$\Rightarrow$ Total energy change due to 20 C of charge
>$= 20\,C \times 12\,V = 240\,C\,V = 240\,J$ ($E = QV$)

>240 J of electrical potential energy is changed into light energy and internal energy when a current of 2 A flows for 10 s through the lamp.

OHM'S LAW

In 1826 a German scientist, Georg Ohm, carried out experiments with different metal wires to investigate how the current through each was related to the p.d. across its ends. The experiment can be repeated using apparatus set up as in Figure 20.12. The wire used is an alloy called eureka which does not get heated up easily when a current flows through it. The rheostat, to be explained later, is used to vary the current.

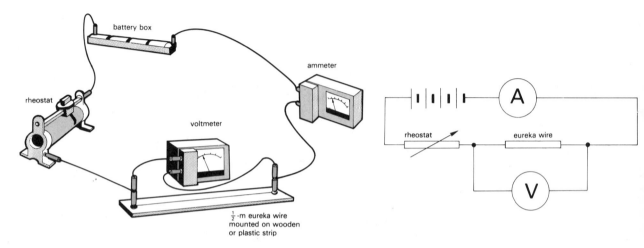

Figure 20.12   Investigating relation between p.d. across conductor and current through it.

A set of typical results is shown in Table 20.1.

Table 20.1

p.d. across wire V/V	0.8	1.6	2.4	3.3	4.2
Current through wire I/A	0.2	0.4	0.6	0.8	1.0

When p.d. is plotted against current on a graph, a straight line through the origin is obtained (Figure 20.13). This means that the p.d. across the wire is directly proportional to the current flowing through it:

$$\text{p.d.} \propto \text{current} \qquad \text{or} \qquad V \propto I$$

Experiments with other wires produce similar results. These can be summed up by **Ohm's law**:

> The p.d. across the ends of a conductor is directly proportional to the current flowing through it, provided that the temperature and other physical conditions are constant.

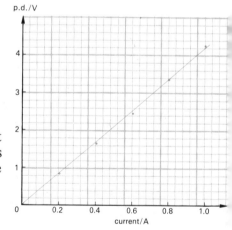

Figure 20.13   Ohm's law.

RESISTANCE

The Ohm's law experiment is repeated using a thicker eureka wire of the same length. Table 20.2 shows a set of typical results which are plotted on the same graph as before for comparison purpose (Figure 20.14).

Table 20.2

p.d./V	0.18	0.39	0.60	0.80	1.0
Current/A	0.2	0.4	0.6	0.8	1.0

Once again, the p.d. and current are directly proportional to each other, but for any given p.d. the current through the second (thicker) wire is greater than that through the first. The second wire is a better conductor than the first, and is said to offer a smaller **resistance**, symbol R, to the current flow.

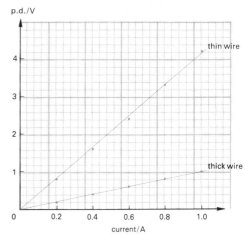

Figure 20.14 Thicker wire offers smaller resistance to current flow.

The resistance of a conductor is defined as:

$$\text{resistance} = \frac{\text{p.d. across conductor}}{\text{current through conductor}} \quad \text{or} \quad R = \frac{V}{I}$$

Note, however, that Ohm's law is *not* applicable to all conductors. In cases where Ohm's law is not obeyed, the resistance

of the conductor is still given by the ratio $\frac{V}{I}$, but it now

changes according to the current flowing.

Resistance is measured in **ohms**, abbreviated to 'Ω' (Greek letter omega).

A conductor has a resistance of 1 ohm if a current of 1 ampere flows through it when a p.d. of 1 volt is applied across its ends.

$$1 \text{ ohm} = 1 \text{ volt ampere}^{-1} \quad (1\ \Omega = 1\ V\,A^{-1})$$

Measuring resistance

The resistance of, for example, a ray-box lamp or a radio-type resistor, can be found by measuring the current I through it when a known p.d. V is applied across it (Figure 20.15). The

resistance R is then calculated using Ohm's law: $R = \frac{V}{I}$.

This is called the **voltmeter-ammeter method**.

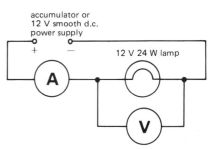

Figure 20.15 Measuring resistance of tungsten filament of ray-box lamp.

For a more accurate result, the rheostat is adjusted so that a number of pairs of V and I readings can be obtained. The resistance is the average of all the $\dfrac{V}{I}$ values.

Effect of temperature on resistance

Figure 20.16 shows a circuit diagram for investigating how the resistance of a lamp filament changes with temperature.

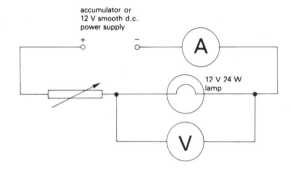

Figure 20.16 Investigating effect of temperature on resistance.

As the current is increased from a low value, the brightness of the lamp increases, and so does the filament temperature. At its operating voltage, 12 V, the filament is white hot and its temperature is above 3000°C.

Table 20.3 shows a set of typical results. The V-I graph plotted is a curve (Figure 20.17) indicating that the p.d. is *not* proportional to the current, that is, Ohm's law is not obeyed. The calculation of the ratios $\dfrac{V}{I}$ shows that the resistance of the filament increases as the temperature rises. The resistance of most metals increases with temperature, though some increase more than others.

Table 20.3

p.d./V	2	4	6	8	10	12
Current/A	0.5	0.8	1.2	1.4	1.7	1.9
Resistance/Ω	4.0	5.0	5.0	5.7	5.9	6.3

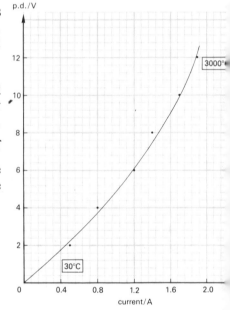

Figure 20.17 Increase in temperature increases resistance of tungsten filament.

RESISTANCE OF A METAL WIRE

The resistance of a wire depends on its length and thickness and also on the conducting property of the material from which it is made. By experimenting with wires of different lengths and thicknesses it can be shown that:

1. For the same wire the resistance R is directly proportional to its length l, that is $R \propto l$. This means that doubling the length doubles the resistance.

2. For wires of the same length and material, the resistance R is inversely proportional to its cross-sectional area A, that is $R \propto \dfrac{1}{A}$.

   This means doubling the cross-sectional area halves the resistance.

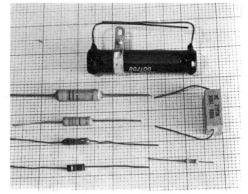

Figure 20.18 Some types of resistors.

RESISTORS

Resistors (Figure 10.18) are devices especially made to provide resistance. One type has a long length of alloy wire, coiled to take up less space. Another type provides resistance with a thin layer of carbon.

Variable resistors are used in electronic devices such as 'volume' and 'dimmer'. These are called **potentiometers** (Figure 20.19). Large current version used in the school laboratory are called **rheostats** (Figure 20.20). It consists of a coil of resistance wire wound on a tube with a sliding contact on a metal bar above the tube.

Figure 20.19 Variable resistor (or potentiometer).

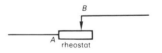

(b) circuit symbol

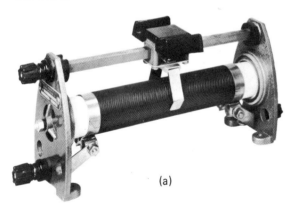

(a)

Figure 20.20 A laboratory rheostat.

Connected as in Figure 20.21, a variable resistor is used to vary the current flowing through a circuit. Moving the sliding contact along the bar changes the length and hence the resistance of the coiled wire through which current flows from terminal A to terminal B.

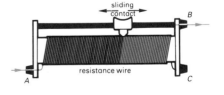

Figure 20.21 Varying resistance.

rheostat 可變電阻，變阻器　　potentiometer 分壓器

Resistors in series

Resistors or other circuit components may be joined together in a circuit in many different ways. The two resistors in Figure 20.22 are said to be connected **in series**. Measurements of the

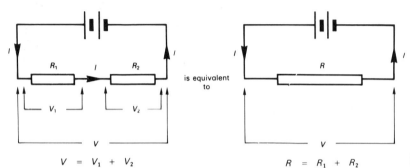

$$V = V_1 + V_2$$

$$R = R_1 + R_2$$

Figure 20.22   Resistors in series.

currents through the resistors and the p.d.s across them show the following basic rules about series circuits:

1. The current I is the same at all points throughout the circuit.

2. The total p.d. V across the resistors equals the sum of the p.d.s, V_1 and V_2, across each resistor, that is

$$V = V_1 + V_2 \ldots \ldots (a)$$

Applying Ohm's law,

$$V_1 = IR_1 \qquad \text{and} \qquad V_2 = IR_2 \ldots \ldots (b)$$

Combining (a) and (b),

$$V = V_1 + V_2 = IR_1 + IR_2$$

If R is the *equivalent* or total resistance, and $V = IR$,

$$IR = IR_1 + IR_2 = I(R_1 + R_2)$$

Hence, $R = R_1 + R_2$

Hence the equivalent resistance of two or more resistors connected in series is the sum of the individual resistances.

The equivalent resistance is always *higher* than the resistance of any one of the resistors by itself. The effect is the same as joining several short lengths of resistance wire together to form a longer length (Figure 20.23).

in series 串聯

Example 3

A 12 V battery is connected in series with a 8 Ω resistor and a 16 Ω resistor as in Figure 20.24. What is the p.d. across each resistor?

The 8 Ω and 16 Ω resistor are connected in series.
⇒ Equivalent resistance of the resistors in series
$= 8 \, Ω + 16 \, Ω = 24 \, Ω$

Applying Ohm's law, current $= \dfrac{12 \text{ V}}{24 \, Ω} = 0.5 \text{ A}$ ($I = \dfrac{V}{R}$)   **Figure 20.24**

A current of 0.5 A flows through each resistor.

Applying Ohm's law again, this time to each resistor in turn,

p.d. across the 8 Ω resistor
$= 0.5 \text{ A} \times 8 \, Ω = 4 \text{ V}$ ($V = IR$)

p.d. across the 16 Ω resistor
$= 0.5 \text{ A} \times 16 \, Ω = 8 \text{ V}$

Resistors in parallel

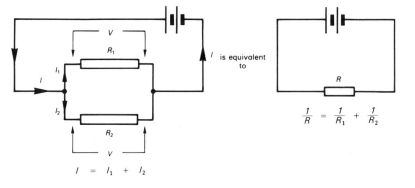

Figure 20.25   Resistors in parallel.

The two resistors in Figure 20.25 are connected **in parallel**. Measurements of p.d. and current show the following basic rules about parallel circuits:

1. The p.d. is the same across each parallel branch.

2. The sum of the currents through the different branches equals the current in the main circuit, that is

$$I = I_1 + I_2 \dots \dots \text{(c)}$$

Applying Ohm's law,

$$I_1 = \frac{V}{R_1} \quad \text{and} \quad I_2 = \frac{V}{R_2} \quad \dots\dots (d)$$

If R is the equivalent resistance of the resistors in parallel,

$$I = \frac{V}{R}$$

$$\frac{V}{R} = \frac{V}{R_1} + \frac{V}{R_2}$$

$$\Rightarrow \quad \boxed{\frac{1}{R} = \frac{1}{R_1} + \frac{1}{R_2}}$$

The equivalent resistance of resistors in parallel is always *less* than the resistance of any one of the resistors by itself. The effect is the same as bundling several resistance wires together to have a wider conducting path than before (Figure 20.26).

Figure 20.26 Bundling resistance wires together gives a wider conducting path and lower the resistance.

Example 4

A p.d. of 12 V from a battery is applied across a parallel connection of a 8 Ω and 16 Ω resistor (Figure 20.27). What is the current drawn from the battery?

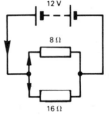

Figure 20.27

Let R be the equivalent resistance of the parallel resistors.

$$\frac{1}{R} = \frac{1}{8} + \frac{1}{16} = \frac{3}{16} \qquad\qquad (\frac{1}{R} = \frac{1}{R_1} + \frac{1}{R_2})$$

$$\Rightarrow R = \frac{16}{3}\ \Omega$$

$\Rightarrow$ Current drawn from the battery

$$= \frac{12\text{ V}}{\frac{16}{3}\ \Omega} = \frac{12 \times 3\text{ V}}{16\ \Omega} = 2.25\text{ A} \qquad (I = \frac{V}{R})$$

Alternative method

The p.d. across the resistor in each branch is 12 V.
Apply Ohm's law to each resistor in turn.

Current through the 8 Ω resistor

$$= \frac{12\text{ V}}{8\ \Omega} = 1.5\text{ A} \qquad\qquad (I = \frac{V}{R})$$

Current through the 16 Ω resistor
$$= \frac{12 \text{ V}}{16 \text{ Ω}} = 0.75 \text{ A}$$

⇒ Current in the main circuit
$$= 1.5 \text{ A} + 0.75 \text{ A} = 2.25 \text{ A}$$

Example 5

A p.d. of 12 V is applied to the network of resistors connected up as in Figure 20.28).
(a) What is the total resistance of the network?
(b) What is the current through the 8 Ω resistor?
(c) What is the p.d. across the 8 Ω resistor?
(d) What is the p.d. across the parallel combination of the 6 Ω and the 12 Ω resistor?
(e) What is the current through the resistor of each of the parallel branches?

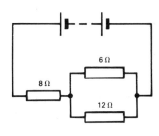

Figure 20.28

(a) Let R be the equivalent resistance of the resistors in parallel.

$$\frac{1}{R} = \frac{1}{6} + \frac{1}{12} = \frac{3}{12} = \frac{1}{4} \qquad (\frac{1}{R} = \frac{1}{R_1} + \frac{1}{R_2})$$

⇒ $R = 4 \text{ Ω}$

This combined resistance of 4 Ω is in series with the 8 Ω resistor. This circuit is equivalent to Figure 20.29.

⇒ Total resistance of the circuit
$$= 4 \text{ Ω} + 8 \text{ Ω} = 12 \text{ Ω} \qquad (R = R_1 + R_2)$$

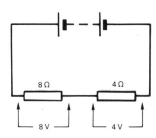

Figure 20.29

(b) Applying Ohm's law to the whole network, current in the main circuit
$$= \frac{12 \text{ V}}{12 \text{ Ω}} = 1 \text{ A} \qquad (I = \frac{V}{R})$$

Current through the 8 Ω resistor
= current in the main circuit = 1 A

(c) Applying Ohm's law,

p.d. across 8 Ω resistor $\qquad\qquad (V = IR)$
= 1 A × 8 Ω
= 8 V

(d) p.d. across the parallel combination of resistors + p.d. across 8 Ω resistor = 12 V

⇒ p.d. across the parallel combination of resistors
= 12 V − 8 V
= 4 V

(e) p.d. across the parallel combination of resistors
= p.d. across the 12 Ω resistor
= p.d. across the 6 Ω resistor
= 4 V

125

⇒ Current through the 6 Ω resistor
$$= \frac{4\text{ V}}{6\ \Omega} = 0.67\text{ A}$$

⇒ Current through the 12 Ω resistor
$$= \frac{4\text{ V}}{12\ \Omega} = 0.33\text{ A}$$

SHORT CIRCUIT

If a short length of copper wire is connected across a battery (Figure 20.30), the lamp goes out and the copper wire becomes very hot. As the wire has a very low resistance (virtually zero) it draws a large current through it. The wire acts as a **short-circuit**, providing an easy path for the current. A short circuit is to be avoided; in this case it causes the battery to go 'flat' almost immediately. Shorting a mains circuit overheats the connecting wires and may cause a fire.

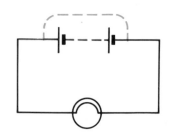

Figure 20.30　Short circuit.

CELLS IN SERIES AND IN PARALLEL

A group of cells connected together forms a battery. Figure 20.31 shows a battery made up of 3 cells, each of 1.5 V, joined *in series*. Each coulomb of charge flowing through the circuit has to pass through all 3 cells and so gains electrical potential energy from each of them. Hence the total e.m.f. of the battery is the sum of the e.m.f.s of all 3 cells, which is 4.5 V.

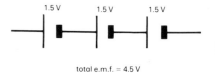

1.5 V　　1.5 V　　1.5 V

total e.m.f. = 4.5 V

Figure 20.31　Cells in series give larger e.m.f.

In Figure 20.32, the 3 cells are connected *in parallel*. The total e.m.f. of the 3 cells is still 1.5 V, since each coulomb of charge flowing through the circuit can pass through only one cell but not all 3. However, such parallel arrangement of cells has the advantages that (i) it can supply a larger current than a single cell, and (ii) it lasts longer before going 'flat'.

INTERNAL RESISTANCE OF A CELL

In Figure 20.33a, the voltmeter reads 3 V when it is connected across the battery. However, when a lamp is connected and draws a current from the battery (Figure 20.33b), the voltmeter reading drops, typically to 2.5 V. The 'lost volt' is due to the **internal resistance** of the battery which also requires a p.d. to drive a current through it. There is now a p.d. of 2.5 V across the lamp and a p.d. of 0.5 V across the internal resistance of the battery, the former being measured by the voltmeter (Figure 20.34).

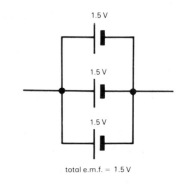

1.5 V

1.5 V

1.5 V

total e.m.f. = 1.5 V

Figure 20.32　Cells in parallel give the same e.m.f. but supply larger current.

short circuit 短路　　internal resistance 內電阻

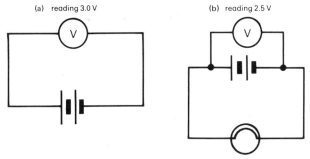

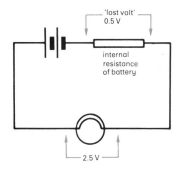

Figure 20.33 Voltmeter reading drops when lamp draws current from battery.

Figure 20.34 The 'lost volt' is due to internal resistance of battery.

POWER IN ELECTRIC CIRCUITS

Power is the rate at which energy is transferred from one form to another.

$$\text{Power} = \frac{\text{energy transfer}}{\text{time taken}}$$

Power is measured in watts (W) where 1 watt is 1 joule per second ($1\ \text{W} = 1\ \text{J s}^{-1}$).

In the circuit in Figure 20.35, a current of 2 A flows through the ray-box lamp when a p.d. of 12 V is applied across the lamp.

A p.d. of 12 V means that each coulomb of charge passing the lamp transfers to the lamp 12 J of electrical energy to light and internal energy.

A current of 2 A means that 2 C of charge passes the lamp per second.

Hence the energy transfer per second $= 12\ \text{J C}^{-1} \times 2\ \text{C s}^{-1}$
$= 24\ \text{J s}^{-1}$
$= 24\ \text{W}$

This illustrates a general rule for calculating electrical power.

$$\text{Power} = \text{p.d.} \times \text{current} \qquad \text{or} \qquad P = VI$$

Power is again measured in watts (W) if p.d. is measured in volts (V) and current in amperes (A), that is:

$$1\ \text{watt} = 1\ \text{volt ampere} \qquad (1\ \text{W} = 1\ \text{V A})$$

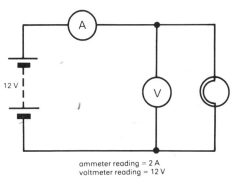

Figure 20.35 Investigating power consumed by ray-box lamp.

For a resistor of resistance R, Ohm's law applies.

$$P = VI = IR \times I = I^2 R$$

$$P = VI = V \times \frac{V}{R} = \frac{V^2}{R}$$

This gives alternative equations for calculating the power dissipated in a resistor:

$$P = VI = I^2 R = \frac{V^2}{R}$$

Example 6

Calculate the power dissipated in a 10 Ω resistor when the current through the resistor is (a) 2 A, (b) 4 A.

Apply $P = I^2 R$

(a) $P = 2^2 \times 10 = 40$ W

When the current is 2 A, the power dissipated is 40 W.

(b) $P = 4^2 \times 10 = 160$ W

When the current is 4 A, the power dissipated is 160 W.

Hence doubling the current increases the power dissipated in the resistor to 4 times.

Filament lamp

The filament of an electric lamp (Figure 20.36) is a small, coiled coil of tungsten which becomes white hot when a suitable current passes through it. Tungsten is used because of its high melting point (3400°C). Most lamps are filled with nitrogen or argon gas, rather than air, to reduce the evaporation of tungsten which would otherwise condense on the bulb and blacken it.

A filament lamp changes only about 10% of the input power into visible light; the other 90% is changed into internal energy used in heating up the filament. A fluorescent lamp is more efficient and can provide the same level of illumination with about one third of the input power.

Heating elements

In domestic appliances, such as electric fires, cookers, kettles and irons, the heating element is made from lengths of

filament

Figure 20.36 Coiled tungsten filament does not melt even when white hot (3000°C).

nichrome resistance wire, coiled to take up less space (Figure 20.37). The nichrome wire becomes red hot when a suitable current passes through it. Nichrome, an alloy of nickel and chromium, is used because it does not oxidize or become brittle when red hot.

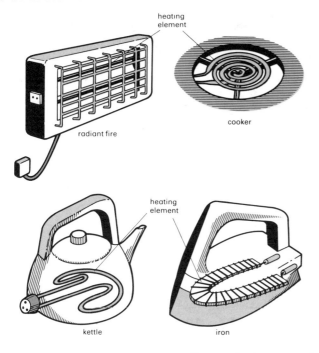

radiant fire

heating element

cooker

heating element

kettle

iron

Figure 20.37 Nichrome wire in heating elements does not melt even when red hot (900°C).

Voltage and power ratings are usually marked on an electrical appliance. An electric lamp rated at 200 V 100 W will change 100 J of electrical energy to internal energy per second when used with a 200 V mains supply.

Example 7

What is the resistance of the tungsten filament of a 200 V 100 W lamp?

Apply $\quad P = \dfrac{V^2}{R}$

$P = 100$ W, $\quad V = 200$ V

$R = \dfrac{V^2}{P} = \dfrac{(200)^2}{100} = 400\ \Omega$

The tungsten filament of a 200 V 100 W lamp has a resistance of 400 Ω.

SUMMARY

Current and charge

An electric current is the rate of flow of charge through a circuit.

$$\text{Current} = \frac{\text{charge}}{\text{time}} \quad (I = \frac{Q}{t})$$

Current is measured in amperes (A).
Charge is measured in coulombs (C).
1 coulomb = 1 ampere-second (1 C = 1 A s)

Electromotive force (e.m.f.) and potential difference (p.d.)

The e.m.f. of a battery indicates the electrical potential energy transferred to 1 coulomb of charge within the battery.

$$\text{e.m.f.} = \frac{\text{energy}}{\text{charge}}$$

The p.d. between two points indicates the electrical potential energy transferred when 1 C of charge passes between the points.

$$\text{p.d.} = \frac{\text{energy}}{\text{charge}}$$

E.m.f. and p.d. are both measured in volts (V).

Ohm's law

Ohm's law states that the p.d. across the ends of a conductor is directly proportional to the current flowing through it, provided that the temperature and other physical conditions are constant.

p.d. $\propto$ current

p.d. = constant $\times$ current

$V = RI$

$R = \dfrac{V}{I}$ (resistance $= \dfrac{\text{p.d.}}{\text{current}}$)

Resistance is measured in ohms.
A conductor has a resistance of 1 ohm if a current of 1 ampere flows through it when a p.d. of 1 volt is applied across its ends.

Not all conductors obey Ohm's law.

Resistance of a wire

The resistance R of a wire depends on its length (l), cross-sectional area (A) and the material from which it is made.

$R \propto l$ for the same A and material

$R \propto \dfrac{1}{A}$ for the same l and material.

The resistance of a metal increases with temperature.

Measuring resistance (Voltmeter-ammeter method)

Applying ohm's law ($R = \dfrac{V}{I}$), the resistance of a conductor can be found with the following circuit.

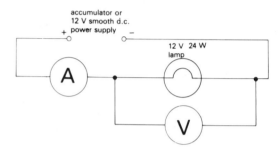

Combining resistors

In series: $R = R_1 + R_2 + \ldots \ldots$

In parallel: $\dfrac{1}{R} = \dfrac{1}{R_1} + \dfrac{1}{R_2} \ldots \ldots$

Combining cells

In series: $E = E_1 + E_2 + \ldots \ldots$

In parellel: If the cells are identical
total e.m.f. = e.m.f. of one cell

Cells connected in series give a larger e.m.f. and there is a large internal resistance.

Cells connected in parallel can provide a larger current than a single cell and last longer before becoming 'flat'.

Electrical power

$$P = VI$$

or

$$P = I^2 R$$

or

$$P = \frac{V^2}{R}$$

PROBLEMS

1. How much charge passes a point in a circuit when a steady current of 5 A flows for 1 minutes?

2. A battery of e.m.f. 12 V drives a current of 2 A through a lamp bulb connected across its terminals.
   (a) How much charge leaves the battery every second?
   (b) How much electrical potential energy is given to each coulomb of charge leaving the battery?
   (c) How much electrical potential energy is transferred by the battery in 1 s?
   (d) How long does it take the battery to supply 360 J of energy to the lamp bulb?

3. A charge of 15 C flows out from a battery in 5 s and, as a result, 90 J of energy is supplied to a lamp bulb connected across the battery. Calculate
   (a) the current through the lamp bulb,
   (b) the p.d. across the lamp bulb.

4. An experiment is carried out to investigate how the p.d. across a filament lamp is related to the current through the lamp.
   (a) Draw a circuit diagram showing how the p.d. and the current are measured and how to obtain various sets of readings.
   (b) The following results are obtained;

p.d./V	2	4	6	8	10
Current/A	0.12	0.2	0.25	0.28	0.29

   Calculate the values of the resistance of the lamp filament when the lamp is operated at (i) 2 V, (ii) 10 V.
   (c) Plot a graph of p.d. against current. In what way does the shape of the graph differ from the law connecting p.d. and current? Explain this difference.

5. A student performed an experiment to investigate Ohm's law using the circuit in Figure 20.38a. The results are shown in the graph in Figure 20.38b.

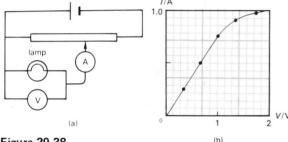

Figure 20.38

(a) What is the range of voltages in which Ohm's law is obeyed? $0 < x < 1$
(b) Suggest a reason why Ohm's law is not obeyed outside this range. temperature increase

(HKCEE 1980)

6. A current of 0.5 A flows through a length of resistance wire when the p.d. across the wire is 6 V.
   (a) What is the resistance of the wire?
   (b) What would be the current through the wire if the p.d. across the wire is increased to 9 V?

7. Calculate the equivalent resistance across XY in each of the cases in Figure 20.39.

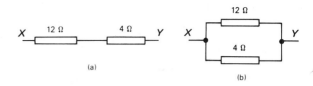

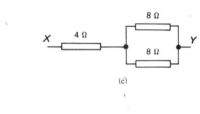

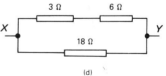

Figure 20.39

8. 3 resistors, of 3 Ω, 4 Ω and 12 Ω, are connected as in Figure 20.40 to a 6 V battery.
   Calculate
   (a) the equivalent resistance of the network of resistors,
   (b) the current through each of the 3 resistors,
   (c) the p.d. across each of the 3 resistors.

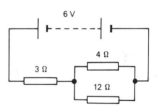

Figure 20.40

131

9. Two resistors, R_1 and R_2, are connected up in a circuit as in Figure 20.41. When the switch S is open, the ammeter reads 1 A and the voltmeter reads 8 V. When the switch S is closed, the ammeter reads 1.5 A and the voltmeter reads 6 V. Calculate the values of R_1 and R_2.

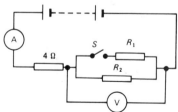

Figure 20.41

10. Two resistors, of 2 Ω and 6 Ω, are be connected to a 6 V battery. Calculate the current through each resistor when they are connected (a) in series, (b) in parallel.

11. A kettle is rated at 200 V 2000 W. Calculate the resistance of its heating element and the current through it when it is operated at its rated voltage.

12. Two lamps, marked 12 V 24 W and 12 V 36 W respectively, are connected in parallel across a 12 V supply (Figure 20.42).

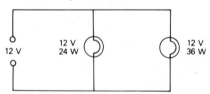

Figure 20.42

(a) Calculate the current drawn from the 12 V supply.
(b) Calculate the resistance of each lamp.
(c) If the lamps are connected in series across the 12 V supply, estimate the current drawn from the supply. What will be the effect on the lamp of such a connection?

13. A 6 V 12 W lamp has to be operated from a 12 V supply. What is the resistance of the resistor R which must be connected in series with the lamp (Figure 20.43) to allow it to operate at its rated voltage and power?

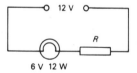

Figure 20.43

14. The two lamps, X and Y, are connected to a 12 V battery as in Figure 20.44. The value of the resistor R is so chosen that the two lamps are operated at their rated voltage and power. Lamp X is rated 6 V 12 W; lamp Y is rated 6 V 24 W. Calculate
(a) the current through lamp X, 2 A
(b) the current through lamp Y, 4 A
(c) the current through resistor R, 6 A
(d) the p.d. across R, 6 V
(e) the resistance of R. 1 Ω.

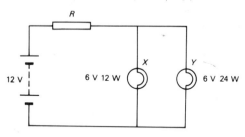

Figure 20.44

15. A set of Christmas tree lights, designed to operate from the 200 V mains, consists of twenty 10 V 2 W lamps.
(a) Calculate
(i) the current through the set of lamps,
(ii) the total resistance of the set of lamps.
(b) What would happen if one of the lamps burns out?
(c) To avoid failure, each lamp is so designed that if the filament burns out it becomes short-circuited. Suppose 4 lamps are burnt out at the same time, what is the p.d. across each of the remaining lamps?
(d) If the resistance of each lamp remains unchanged, what would be the current flowing through the remaining 16 lamps? In practice, the actual current is less than the calculated value. Explain why.

16. An immersion heater is rated at 220 V 440 W.
(a) When the heater is operated at its rated voltage and power, calculate
(i) the resistance of the heating element, 110 Ω
(ii) the current through the heater. 2 A
(b) Suppose the heater is now operated from a 200 V supply. Calculate
(i) the new current through the heater, 1.8
(ii) the power output of the heater. 363.6
Assume that the resistance of the heating element remains unchanged.
(c) What is the percentage loss of power when the heater is operated at 200 V rather than 220 V? 16.4.

17. Two resistors, of 2 Ω and 4 Ω, are connected in series to a 12 V battery. Calculate
    (a) the power dissipated in the 2 Ω resistor,
    (b) the power dissipated in the 4 Ω resistor,
    (c) the power output of the battery.

18. A student is given the following: an unknown resistor R, a battery, a voltmeter with internal resistance 1000 Ω and an ammeter with internal resistance 1 Ω. He finds that he can make up two different circuits (Figure 20.45 and Figure 20.46) to measure the resistance of R.

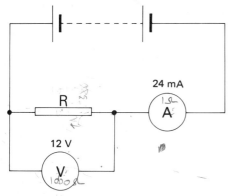

Figure 20.45

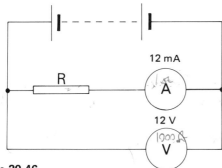

Figure 20.46

(a) The student obtains a voltmeter reading of 12 V, a milliammeter reading of 24 mA with the circuit in Figure 20.45, but meter readings of 12 V and 12 mA with that in Figure 20.46. Calculate the resistance of R from the results in each circuit and account for the difference. Which circuit gives the correct resistance of R? Explain.
(b) If the student is now given another resistor of the order of 10 Ω, which circuit, Figure 20.45 or Figure 20.46, would give better results? Why?

19. Figure 20.47 shows a circuit diagram. A_1, A_2, A_3 and A_4 are ammeters of negligible internal resistance. P, Q and R are resistance wires of the same material. Q is short and thick, while R is long and thin when compared with P.

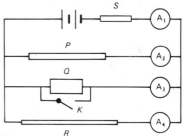

Figure 20.47

(a) The readings of the ammeters A_1, A_2, A_3 and A_4 are respectively a_1, a_2, a_3 and a_4. Arrange these readings in ascending order of magnitude.
(b) If the lengths of P and R are in the ratio of 3 : 4 and their cross-sectional areas are in the ratio of 2 : 1, calculate the ratio of
    (i) the resistance of P to that of R, and
    (ii) the rate of heat produced in P to that produced in R in the above circuit.
(c) What will happen to the ammeter readings when K is closed? Which ammeter/s would be ruined on closing switch K if the resistance S were absent?

(HKCEE 1978)

20. The circuit (Figure 20.48) shows a battery, a motor/generator, a two-way switch and three lamps connected in parallel. The motor drives a massive flywheel (Figure 20.49).

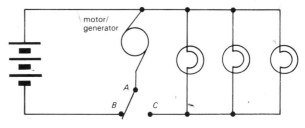

Figure 20.48

Figure 20.49

When the switch connects A to B, the motor drives the flywheel from rest to a steady speed. The switch is then changed so that it connects A to C. All three lamps are seen to light.

(a) Describe the energy changes which occur from the time the motor is switched on until the flywheel is rotating at full speed.

(b) Describe the energy changes which occur after the switch is changed over and the three lamps light.

After the flywheel has stopped rotating, the whole sequence is repeated, but with only one lamp in the circuit.

(c) What difference(s) will this make when the switch is changed over? Explain in terms of energy.

A small electric motor operates at 6 V and takes a current of 0.25 A as it lifts a 0.5 kg mass through 1.2 m in a time of 6 seconds.

(d) What is the power supplied to the motor?

(e) What power is needed to lift the mass at this rate?

(f) Explain the difference between your answers to (d) and (e).

(g) Could this motor lift a mass of 1 kg through 1.2 m in 6 seconds whilst still taking a current of 0.25 A? Explain your answer.

(h) Estimate the current which would be required if this motor were to succeed in lifting the 1 kg mass through 1.2 m in 6 seconds, assuming that the energy losses did not change.

(O&C Nov 1981)

21. Figure 20.50 shows an electrical circuit in which a current is passed through a resistor R. The supply voltage E can be altered, and the voltmeter has a high resistance.

Readings of the current and potential difference are recorded for different supply voltages.

Current/A	0.10	0.20	0.30	0.40	0.50	0.60	0.70
p.d./V	0.6	1.2	1.8	2.5	3.5	5.0	7.0

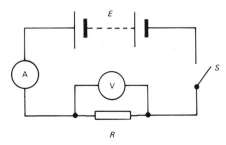

Figure 20.50

(a) Plot a graph of potential difference (along the y-axis) against current (along the x-axis).

(b) What is the resistance of R when the current is
  (i) 0.25 A,
  (ii) 0.60 A?

(c) Give one possible reason for the difference in these resistances.

(d) Calculate the power being transformed by the resistor when the current is 0.60 A.

(e) The resistor is placed in an aluminium block of mass 0.5 kg and connected to a potential difference of 5 V. If no heat is lost, calculate the rise in temperature of the aluminium block after 10 minutes. The specific heat capacity of aluminium is 900 J kg^{-1} °C^{-1}.

(f) Would the temperature rise be more or less if the heater were placed in a similar mass of water, all other conditions being the same? Explain your answer.

(O&C June 1978)

22. (a) When an ammeter is connected in series with a cell of negligible internal resistance and a lamp, the current reading is 0.2 A. A voltmeter connected across the terminals of the cell reads 1.5 V. Similar cells and similar lamps are used in the circuit shown below.

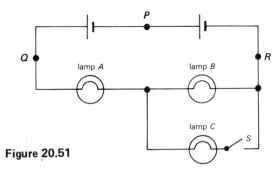

Figure 20.51

(i) What would you expect the current to be at point P, at point Q and at point R when the switch S is open?

(ii) Comment on the brightness of lamps A, B and C when the switch S is closed.

(iii) With switch S open, what would the voltmeter read if connected between Q and R?

(iv) The switch S is then closed. Would the reading of the voltmeter connected between Q and R increase, decrease or remain the same?

(b) A mains lamp is marked '240 V 60 W' and a car headlamp '12 V 60 W'.

(i) When the mains lamp is connected to a 240 V supply, what current will flow?

(ii) What is the resistance of the mains lamp?

(iii) How much energy is transformed when the mains lamp is operated for one hour?

(iv) How does the energy transformed by the car headlamp compare with that transformed by the mains lamp in the same time?

(v) What is likely to happen if the mains lamp and the car headlamp are connected in series across the 240 V supply? Explain your answer.

(O&C June 1976)

23. Figure 20.52 shows a circuit diagram to measure an unknown resistance R. Figure 20.53 shows the components used in the circuit.

(a) You are given 8 pieces of conducting wire. Draw in Figure 20.53 the wires connecting the terminals of the components to complete the circuit represented in Figure 20.52.

(b) State where you should set the slider of the rheostat at the beginning of the experiment. State the reason for your choice.

(c) If the resistor were connected in the reverse direction, how would the readings of the ammeter and the voltmeter be affected?

(d) Using the same components provided, draw a circuit diagram you would use to measure a resistance comparable to that of the voltmeter.

(HKCEE 1984)

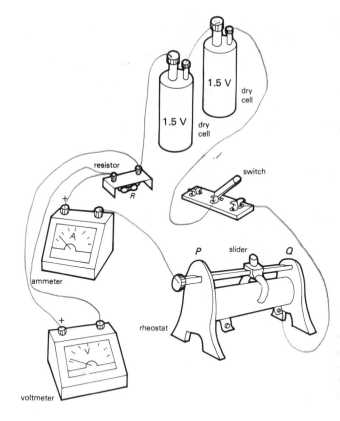

Figure 20.53

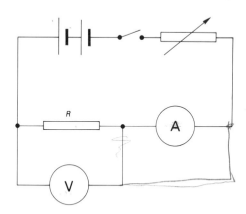

Figure 20.52

24. Figure 24.54 shows an experimental set-up to measure the resistance of a light bulb.

(a) Draw a circuit diagram for the experiment. Indicate on your diagram the positive terminals of the ammeter and voltmeter with '+' signs.

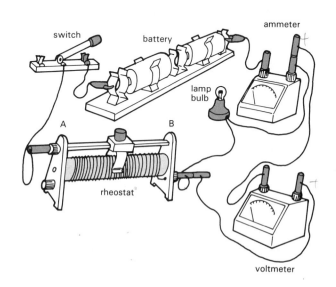

Figure 20.54

135

(b) If the slider in the rheostat moves from *A* to *B*, how does the reading of the ammeter change?

(c) Figure 24.55 shows the voltmeter and the ammeter used in the experiment. What is
   (i) the ammeter reading, and
   (ii) the voltmeter reading
   as indicated in the diagram? Hence calculate the resistance of the light bulb at this moment.

(d) (i) When the current increases, how does
       (1) the temperature, and
       (2) the resistance
       of the light bulb change?
   (ii) Make a rough sketch of the potential difference across the light bulb against the current.

(HKCEE 1987)

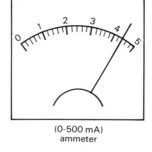
(0-500 mA)
ammeter

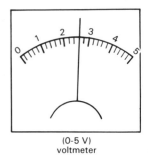
(0-5 V)
voltmeter

Figure 20.55

Domestic Electricity 21

Electric household appliances are operated from the mains supply. The cost of running them can be calculated from their power ratings. A number of devices has been built into the appliances and the mains circuit to ensure the safe use of electricity.

ELECTRICAL ENERGY

An electric appliance usually has a power rating marked on it. For example, a kettle may be marked 1000 W and this indicates that it changes 1000 J of electrical energy per second into internal energy of the water in it when operated at a suitable voltage. Table 21.1 lists the typical power ratings of some common household appliances.

Appliance	Power rating/W
Fan	150
Iron	1000
Kettle	2000
Lamps	40, 60, 100
Oven	1500
Oven (microwave)	600
Radio	70
Refrigerator	400 − 600
Rice cooker	500
Room air-conditioner	
1 horsepower	1000
1.5 horsepower	1200
2 horsepower	1400
3 horsepower	2300
Stereo amplifier	150
Television	
colour	100
black & white	85
Toaster	1100
Washing machine	500
Water heater	3000 − 4000
Vacuum cleaner	600

Table 21.1

Given the power rating, the electrical energy supplied to the appliance can be calculated.

$$\text{Energy} = \text{power} \times \text{time} \qquad \text{or} \qquad E = Pt$$

The power of an appliance can be expressed in terms of its resistance, the p.d. across it and the current flowing through it:

$$P = VI = I^2 R = \frac{V^2}{R}$$

Hence the electrical energy supplied to the appliance in time t is given by

$$E = VIt = I^2 Rt = \frac{V^2 t}{R}$$

Example 1

A kettle is plugged into the mains supply of 200 V. If the heating element has a resistance of 20 Ω, how much electrical energy is supplied to the kettle in 3 minutes?

Applying $\quad E = \dfrac{V^2 t}{R}$

$V = 200$ V, $\quad R = 20\ \Omega$, $\quad t = 3 \times 60$ s $= 180$ s

$E = \dfrac{(200)^2 \times 180}{20} = 360\,000$ J $= 3.6 \times 10^5$ J

Hence 3.6×10^5 J of electrical energy is supplied to the kettle in 3 minutes.

CALCULATING COST OF ELECTRICITY

The total electrical energy supplied to a household is measured by a **kilowatt-hour meter** (Figure 21.1). From the reading on the meter, the electric company calculates the electricity bill. The energy supplied is measured in **kilowatt hours (kW h)** rather than in joules.

One kilowatt hour, or one unit, is the energy supplied in 1 hour to an appliance whose power is 1 kW.

The kilowatt hour is a much larger unit than the joule.

Energy = power × time

$\Rightarrow \quad$ 1 kW h = 1 kW × 1 h

$\qquad\qquad$ = 1000 W × 60 × 60 s

$\qquad\qquad$ = 3 600 000 J

$\qquad\qquad$ = 3.6 × 10⁶ J

Figure 21.1 Kilowatt-hour meter.

kilowatt hour 千瓦時   kilowatt-hour meter 電錶，千瓦時計

Example 2

If electrical energy costs $0.60 per unit, what is the cost of using 5 lamps, connected in parallel (Figure 21.2), each rated at 100 W, for 8 hours?

Each lamp is rated at 100 W.
Total power of 5 lamps is 500 W or 0.5 kW.

$\Rightarrow$ Energy supplied in 8 hours $= $ power $\times$ time
$$= 0.5 \text{ kW} \times 8 \text{ h}$$
$$= 4 \text{ kW h}$$

Each kilowatt hour costs $0.60.

$\Rightarrow$ Total cost $= \$0.60 \times 4 = \$2.40$

Electric lamps are of low power rating and so are not expensive to run. However the electricity bill for the thousands of lamps used in the Christmas and Lunar New Year decorations (Figure 21.3) can amount to a huge sum of money.

Air-conditioners and room heaters are by far the most expensive appliances to run, not only because they are of very high power rating, but also because they are usually switched on for long periods of time.

MAINS CIRCUIT

When an appliance is plugged into the mains socket, electrical energy is supplied from the power station. Unlike the one-way current from a battery, the mains current flows backwards and forwards through the circuit 50 times per second. This current is known as **alternating current** or **a.c.** Power stations supply a.c. because it is easier to generate and transmit to the consumers than one-way **direct current** (d.c.). In Hong Kong the mains electricity is supplied at 200 V a.c. 50 Hz.

Figure 21.4 shows a simple a.c. mains circuit formed when an iron is plugged into a mains socket. The cable connecting the iron to the socket contains three insulated wires; they are called the **live**, the **neutral** and the **earth** wire (Figure 21.5). They are connected as shown.

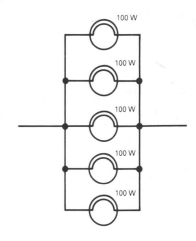

Figure 21.2 Find the power consumed by five 100 W lamps in 8 hours.

Figure 21.3 Merry Christmas and Happy New Year!

Figure 21.4 A simple a.c. mains circuit.

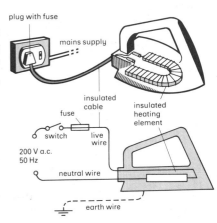

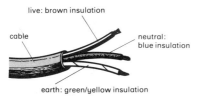

Figure 21.5 Wires inside cable are colour coded.

direct current 直流電   alternating current 交流電   live wire 活線，火線   neutral wire 中線

earth wire 地線   mains circuit 市電電路

The potential of the **live wire** is alternating between positive and negative, making the current flow backwards and forwards through the circuit.

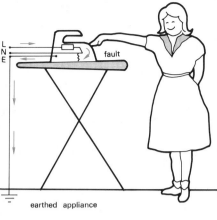

The **neutral wire** provides the 'return path' to the mains socket. It is earthed at the local substation of the electric company and so is at zero potential. Although current passes through the wire, there is no danger of an electric shock if it is touched accidentally.

The **earth wire** is a safety device which connects the metal body of the iron to the earth. If a fault develops, resulting in the live wire touching the body of the iron (Figure 21.6), a large current flows to the earth, since there is no resistance in the conducting path to the earth. If there were no earth wire, the body of the iron would become live and anyone who happened to touch it could receive a fatal electric shock.

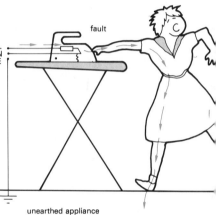

The **fuse** (Fgiure 21.7) is another safety device in the circuit. It is a short length of thin wire which overheats and melts when the current rises above a specified value. It is usually in the form of a cartridge fitted in the live wire either inside the plug or in the appliance. If a fault develops and a large current flows as described above, the fuse 'blows' and breaks the circuit before the cable can overheat and catch fire. The fuse also blows when a short circuit develops.

Like the fuse the **switch** is also fitted in the live wire. It would work equally well in the neutral wire, but then the iron and the cable would still be live when the switch was turned off. This would be dangerous if a fault developed or if the cable were broken accidentally.

Figure 21.6 Earthed appliance is much safer than unearthed appliance.

Three-pin plugs

Plugs provide a convenient and safe way of connecting different appliances to the mains. Some appliances are supplied with a plug moulded onto the end of the cable, but if not, a plug has to be connected. When wiring a plug it is important to check that the three wires are connected to the pins of the plug correctly (Figure 21.8). The **cable colour codes** are:

Live (L)	: brown
Neutral (N):	blue
Earth (E)	: yellow and green

Some cables still use the old colour codes of red for live, black for neutral and green for earth.

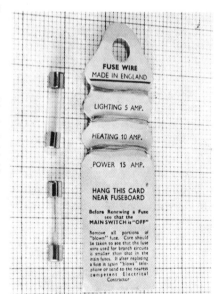

Figure 21.7 Cartridge fuse and fuse wire.

fuse 保險絲   switch 開關   plug 插頭   socket 插座

Fuse value

The fuse value used in an appliance indicates the maximum current which may flow without causing damage to the appliance and/or overheating of the cable. The correct fuse value can be easily calculated from the voltage and power rating marked on the appliance. The fuse value chosen should be slightly larger than the normal current.

Example 3

What is the suitable fuse value to protect a microwave oven rated at 200 V 600 W? Choose either 5 A or 15 A.

Applying $P = VI$

$$P = 600 \text{ W} \quad \text{and} \quad V = 200 \text{ V},$$

$$\Rightarrow \qquad I = \frac{600 \text{ W}}{200 \text{ V}} = 3 \text{ A}$$

The microwave oven should be fitted with a 5 A fuse.

DOMESTIC CIRCUITS

Figure 21.9 shows a typical household electric wiring plan. Electricity is supplied by an underground cable which contains

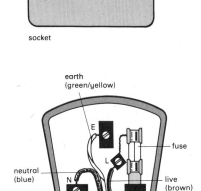

Figure 21.8 Three-pin plug and socket must be correctly wired.

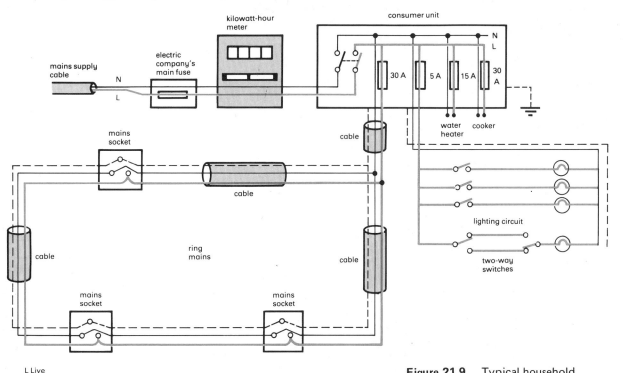

L Live
N neutral

Figure 21.9 Typical household electrical wiring.

141

a live and a neutral wire. These wires are connected to the **consumer unit**, or fuse box, via a kilowatt-hour meter. At the consumer unit, the wires branch out into several parallel circuits which normally include **lighting circuits**, **power circuits** for mains sockets, as well as separate circuits for water heater, cooker, etc. The cable of each circuit contains an earth wire in addition to the live and neutral. All earth wires of the various circuits are joined together and connected to an **earthing electrode** (Figure 21.10) which is buried underground for effective earthing.

Each circuit is fitted, in the consumer unit, with either a fuse or the more modern **circuit breaker** (Figure 21.11). A circuit breaker is an automatic switch which springs up and opens when the current rises above the specified value, but it can be closed again by depressing it. This is more convenient than replacing blown fuse wires.

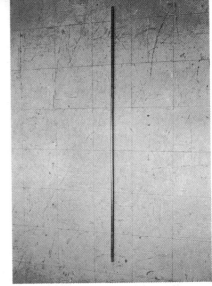

Figure 21.10 All earth wires of flats in a building are connected to the earthing electrode.

Figure 21.11 Circuit breaker of consumer unit.

The lighting circuit consists of a number of lamps connected in parallel. The cable is designed to carry a maximum current of 5 A. To control a lamp on a staircase, **two-way switches** are connected as shown in Figure 21.12. The circuit is complete when the switches are either both up or both down, but is broken when the switches are in opposite positions. In this way, the lamp can be switched on at the bottom of the staircase and then switched off at the top, or vice versa.

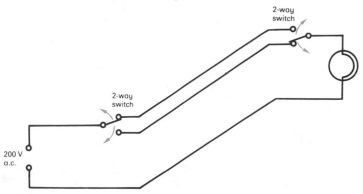

Figure 21.12 Two-way switch.

earthing electrode 接地電極   circuit breaker 斷路器   lighting circuit 照明電路   power circuit 電源電路

The power circuit consists of a cable which is looped round the house; this is called the **ring main**. Each of the live, neutral and earth wire of the cable forms a complete 'ring' and the mains sockets are tapped off from them. An advantage of the ring main is that the current to each socket flows through two paths (Figure 21.13) and so thinner cables can be used. The ring main can supply a maximum current of 30 A although the cables used are rated at 15 A. Many sockets can be tapped off from the ring main provided the total current does not exceed 30 A.

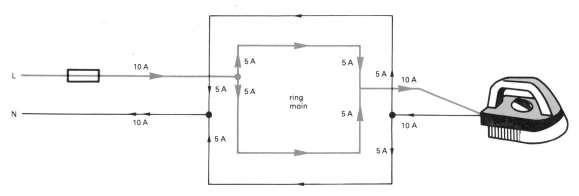

Figure 21.13   Current flows to iron by two paths.

ELECTRICAL SAFETY

All mains electric apparatus is potentially dangerous if not handled properly. Possible dangers include electric shocks, burns and fire.

A current as low as 1 mA through the human body can produce an unpleasant electric shock. If the current exceeds 15 mA, it is often not possible to let go of the supply. Any current higher than 25 mA is likely to be fatal. The passage of an electric current through the human body depends on the body resistance. This can vary from a few hundred ohms to several tens of kilohms, depending on whether the skin is moist or dry and on other body conditions. With a body resistance of for example 10 kΩ, a 200 V supply results in a current of 20 mA which could be fatal. To save a person from electrocution, first disconnect the supply and then apply artificial respiration. Do *not* touch the person until the supply has been disconnected, otherwise the current will also pass through you.

In some cases, a part of the body, for example a finger or a hand, may short-circuit a faulty appliance. This produces a less severe electric shock, but may lead to electrical burns.

ring main 環形幹線

The following are a few general rules about safety in using electricity.

1. Correctly wire the terminals of a three-pin plug to the live, neutral and earth wire. Check that non-moulded plugs have been correctly wired by electrical suppliers.

2. Ensure that the appliance and the circuit are properly earthed.

3. Use correct fuse values or circuit breakers. When a fuse blows, do not replace it until the fault has been traced and put right.

4. Never touch an appliance when the body is wet or when standing on a wet floor.

5. Do not operate too many appliances at one time on the same circuit (Figure 21.14). Overloading a mains socket may cause fire.

6. Inspect cables and plugs regularly and replace those that are worn.

7. Keep cables away from water and heating devices.

8. Do not pull the cable to remove the plug from the socket; pull the plug itself.

9. Keep combustible materials, for example, clothing and paper, away from lamps or heating devices.

10. Service appliances regularly to ensure that they are working correctly and safely.

Figure 21.14 Don't overload a socket.

Faulty wires start fires

SUMMARY

Power rating of an electric appliance

This indicates the electrical energy supplied to the appliance per second when it is operated at the correct voltage.

The electrical energy supplied to an appliance (or conductor) is

$$E = VIt = I^2Rt = \frac{V^2t}{R}$$

Electricity at home

In Hong Kong the mains electricity is supplied at 200 V a.c. 50 Hz.

The electric company measures the electrical energy supplied to the consumer in units of kilowatt hour (kW h).

One kilowatt hour (kW h) is the energy supplied in one hour to an appliance whose power is 1 kW.
1 kW h = 3.6 × 10⁶ J

Electric wiring

A mains cable contains a live, a neutral and an earth wire. The colour codes of the wires are:

Live (L)   : brown
Neutral (N) : blue
Earth (E)   : yellow and green

Safety and electricity

A fuse overheats and melts when the current in the circuit rises above the specified value. It is used to prevent too large a current flowing through the circuit and damaging the appliance or causing a fire.

Fuses and switches are connected in the live wire of a mains circuit.

Safety rules should be observed when using mains-operated electric appliances. Electrical hazards include electric shocks, burns and fire. Electricity may kill (electrocution).

PROBLEMS

1. A room heater is rated at 3000 W. How much electrical energy is supplied to the heater in 1 hour?

2. A current of 5 A flows through a resistor of 20 Ω. How much internal energy is transferred in 10 minutes?

3. How long does it take an immersion heater rated at 2000 W to heat up 1 kg of water from 20°C to boiling? The specific heat capacity of water is 4200 J kg⁻¹ C⁻¹.

4. If electrical energy costs $0.70 per kW h, calculate the cost of using
   (a) a 100 W colour TV for 5 hours,
   (b) a 2.5 horsepower air-conditioner of average power rating 2000 W for 10 hours,
   (c) a 150 W electric fan for 10 hours.

5. In a mains circuit why are the fuses and switches fitted in the live wire rather than the neutral wire? Why is the earth wire connected to the metal body of an electrical appliance?

6. A rice cooker is rated at 200 V 500 W. If fuses of 1 A, 3 A and 5 A are available, which one is most suitable for protecting the cooker?

7. An electric lamp is rated at 200 V 60 W.
   (a) Calculate
       (i) the lamp resistance when in normal use,
       (ii) the current flowing through the lamp.
   (b) How many such lamps can be connected in parallel to the 200 V mains which is protected by a 5 A fuse?

8. (a) Figure 21.15 shows the incomplete wiring of power supply in a room. The wiring of the

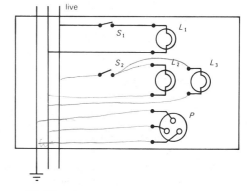

Figure 21.15

lamp L_1 is already completed. S_2 is the switch for both of the lamps L_2 and L_3, and P is a power socket. Copy Figure 21.5 and complete the wiring
  (i) for the lamps L_2 and L_3,
  (ii) for the power socket P.
(b) A 1.5 kW air conditioner operates 10 hours a day in summer time. If electrical energy is charged at the rate of 20 cents per kWh, find the cost in operating the air conditioner for 30 days.

(HKCEE 1979)

9. Figure 21.16 shows a 200 V supply socket, a 3-pin plug, and an electric kettle with a rating: '200 V 1.5 kW'. The kettle has 3 wires A, B, C leading from it. Wire A is joined through a switch S to the heating element H of the kettle; wire B completes the circuit of the kettle; wire C is joined to the metal case of the kettle.

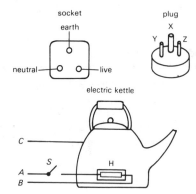

Figure 21.16

(a) (i) To which of the pins X, Y, Z of the plug should each of the wires A, B, C of the kettle be connected?
   (ii) What is the function of the 'earth' terminal in the socket?
(b) (i) A 15 A fuse is connected to the socket. On which of the three lines: earth, neutral and live, should the fuse the placed?
   (ii) What is the maximum number of these kettles that can be joined in parallel to the socket without blowing the 15 A fuse?
(c) (i) If the efficiency of the kettle is 80%, how long will it take to heat 1 kg of water from $20°C$ to $100°C$? (Specific heat capacity of water $= 4\,200$ J kg^{-1} K^{-1})
   (ii) If the cost of electricity is 40 ¢ per kW h, how much does this heating process cost?

(HKCEE 1981)

10. (a) Figure 21.17 shows the type of 3-pin electrical plug with the cover removed used in the United Kingdom. The electric cable connected to the plug contains three wires with colour-coded insulation, namely brown, blue and green/yellow stripe. Identify each of the colour-coded wires by stating to which of the terminals A, B or C in the diagram they should be connected.

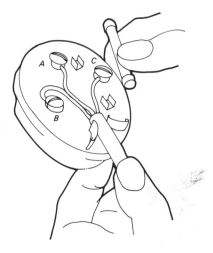

Figure 21.17

Identify the terminal through which no current passes in normal circumstances. What is the purpose of the wire connecting this terminal to an electrical appliance such as an electric fire? Describe how it works.
What is the purpose of the device, held above C in the diagram, that is about to be inserted into the plug? Describe how it works.
(b) An electric cooker has the following specification:

	No. of items	Power of item /W
Ceramic hob, *small* heating area	2	1250
Ceramic hob, *large* heating area	2	1500
Grill	1	2000
Oven	1	2500

Calculate how much energy (in kW h) the cooker will use in 30 minutes when all the items are used simultaneously.
How much will it cost to run the cooker during this time if electrical energy costs approximately $0.60 for 1 kW h?
Calculate the maximum current that will be carried by the cable connecting this cooker to a 250 V mains supply.

(London June 1982)

11. A household electric circuit consists of a heating unit (200 V, 1000 W) and a lighting unit (200 V, 200 W) connected in parallel to the mains of 200 V as shown in Figure 21.18.

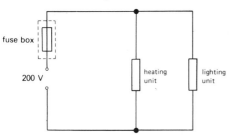

Figure 21.18

(a) Find the maximum current drawn from the mains.

(b) Is a 5 A fuse suitable for use in the fuse box? Explain briefly.

(c) If electricity costs 60 ¢ per kW h and the whole system is switched on for 150 hours, what will be the cost of the electricity used?

(HKCEE 1983)

12. The circuit diagrams X, Y and Z (Figure 21.19) show an electric heater connected in three different ways to a 240 V a.c. supply. The heater has two similar heating elements, A and B, each with a resistance of 60 ohms. There are three settings of the heater: low, medium and high.

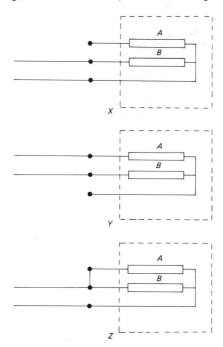

Figure 21.19

(a) Calculate the current drawn from the supply in each of the circuits X, Y and Z.

(b) Which circuit corresponds to the *high* setting and which corresponds to the *low*?

(c) Calculate the power in circuit X.

(d) If electrical energy costs approximately $0.60 per kW h, calculate the cost of using the heater when connected as in X for 30 minutes.

The heater with its three settings is connected to the supply by a 3-pin plug which has a fuse inside it.

(e) (i) What is the purpose of the fuse?
    (ii) How does it work?

(f) Fuses marked 3 A, 5 A, 10 A and 13 A are available. Which would be the most appropriate one to use? Explain your choice.

(g) Element A burns out. Discuss whether the heater would operate on each of the settings.

(h) If in circuit X the voltage supply were halved, what effect would this have on the power?

(O&C June 1983)

13. Figure 21.20 shows a simplified system of a 200 V domestic circuit. N and L denote the neutral and live wires respectively.

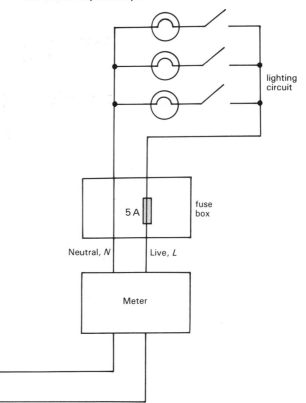

Figure 21.20

(a) Give a reason why the lamps are all connected in parallel instead of in series.

(b) The light bulbs of the circuit shown in Figure 21.20 are all marked "60 W 200 V". Suppose that all the light bulbs are switched on.
   (i) What is the total resistance of the lighting circuit?
   (ii) What is the total current drawn from the power supply?

(c) (i) Explain the use of the fuse in the circuit.
   (ii) Give one reason why the switches should be connected to the live wire L instead of to the neutral wire N.
   (iii) What physical quantity does the meter measure?

(d) Someone suggests changing the household voltage supply in Hong Kong from 200 V a.c. to 220 V a.c. Give one reason to support this suggestion.

(HKCEE 1986)

Electromagnetism

The discovery of the magnetic effect of a current by Oersted in 1819 began the study of electromagnetism, which has brought about, among other things, the electric motor, the dynamo, the telephone, the loudspeaker and the microphone.

MAGNETS

For a long time, **lodestone**, a naturally occurring mineral ore, has been known to attract iron objects and to always lie pointing in a north-south direction when freely suspended. This direction seeking property of lodestone was used to make the compass which is essential for navigation. Historians have now established that it was the Chinese who first invented the compass. Figure 22.1 shows a south-pointing magnetic spoon constructed from descriptions found in literature of the late Han Dynasty (around 100 A.D.). When rotated on the copper plate, the spoon always comes to rest pointing south. The compass, together with printing techniques and gunpowder, have been hailed as the three most important inventions of mankind.

Figure 22.1   Model of compass found in China, circa 100 A.D.

Metals like iron, steel, cobalt and nickel are attracted to a magnet; these materials are called **magnetic**. When a bar magnet is dipped into some paper clips, the clips cling to it, particularly around its two ends (Figure 22.2). The two ends to which magnetic materials are attracted are called the **poles** of the magnet.

If a magnet is suspended at its centre by a piece of thread (Figure 22.3), it will swing round and settle down in a north-south direction. The pole of the magnet which points north is called the **north-seeking pole** or **N-pole** for short; that which points south is called the **south-seeking pole** or **S-pole**.

Figure 22.2   Paper clips are attracted towards poles of magnet.

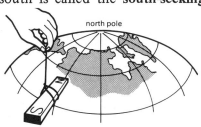

north pole

Figure 22.3   Freely suspended magnet always points north-south.

electromagnetism 電磁學   lodestone 磁石   compass 羅盤   magnetic pole 磁極   **149**

If two magnets are brought near each other, each magnet exerts a force on the other. A N-pole repels another N-pole but attracts a S-pole (Figure 22.4), whereas a S-pole repels another S-pole but attracts a N-pole. To sum up,

like poles repel each other; unlike poles attract each other

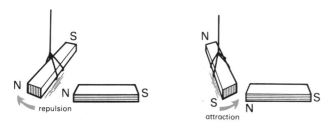

Figure 22.4   Like poles repel; unlike poles attract.

MAGNETIC FIELDS

Magnetic force is strongest near the poles of a magnet and in fact acts throughout the entire space around the magnet. Figure 22.5 shows the effect of sprinkling iron filings on to a card placed over a bar magnet. The magnet exerts forces on the iron filings which settle into the pattern shown. A **magnetic field** is said to exist throughout where magnetic forces act.

The magnetic field pattern can also be obtained using a small plotting compass (Figure 22.6). This consists of a tiny magnetic needle supported by a spindle through its centre so that it can turn freely. The tip of the needle is the N-pole of the compass and the tail is the S-pole.

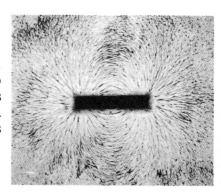

Figure 22.5   Demonstrating magnetic field lines.

Figure 22.6   Plotting compasses.

The compass is placed near, for example, the N-pole of a bar magnet which rests on a sheet of paper. Pencil dots are made on the paper to mark the positions of the tip and tail of the needle. The compass is then moved so that the tail is where the tip has been previously and the new position of the tip is marked (Figure 22.7). This process is continued until the compass ends up at the S-pole of the magnet. The line joining all the dots forms a **magnetic field line**. Other field lines are plotted by starting the compass at other positions

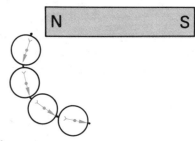

Figure 22.7   Tracing field lines around bar magnet with plotting compass.

magnetic field 磁場   magnetic field line 磁力線

and the complete pattern so obtained is shown in Figure 22.8. This is similar to the pattern obtained using iron filings.

The direction of the field lines is taken to be the direction in which the N-pole (tip) of the compass points. Where the field lines are closely spaced the magnetic field is strong; where they are widely spaced the field is weak.

When two bar magnets are placed close together, their magnetic fields interact. Figure 22.9 shows the combined field patterns between (a) two like poles and (b) two unlike poles. At a point mid-way between the like poles in Figure 22.9a, the field due to one pole exactly cancels out the field due to the other. This point is called a **neutral point**. Magnetic materials, such as iron filings, placed at this point experience no magnetic force.

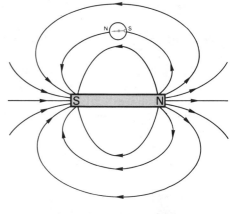

Figure 22.8   Magnetic field lines around bar magnet.

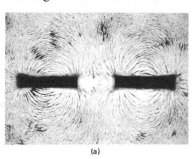
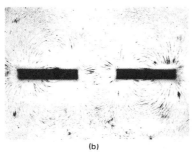

| (a) | (b) |

Figure 22.9   Combined field patterns between (a) two like poles and (b) two unlike poles. Note the neutral point mid-way between the magnets in (a).

Magnadur magnets are strong slab magnets which have poles on the large faces (Figure 22.10). Figure 22.11 shows the magnetic field pattern due to two magnadur magnets placed on an iron yoke, with unlike poles facing each other. The field lines are closely but evenly spaced showing that the magnetic field is strong and of uniform strength.

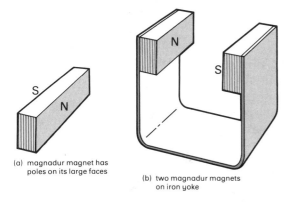

(a) magnadur magnet has poles on its large faces

(b) two magnadur magnets on iron yoke

Figure 22.10   Magnadur magnet.

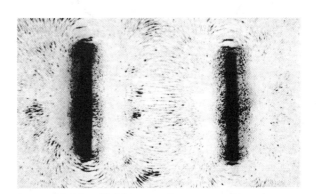

Figure 22.11   Field pattern between unlike poles of two magnadur magnets.

MAGNETIC EFFECT OF CURRENT

A current through a wire produces similar effects on iron filings or a nearby compass. This was accidentally discovered in 1819 by Oersted in Denmark while he was giving a physics lecture on electric cells. During the lecture Oersted connected a battery to a length of wire which happened to be lying *parallel* to a nearby compass. To his surprise, and that of his students, the needle of the compass turned at once. He had done similar experiments before, but on all previous occasions he had placed the wire at right angles to the compass and no such effect was observed. Oersted's experiment can be repeated using the apparatus shown in Figure 22.12. A special low-voltage power supply, of 1 V d.c. or 1 or 2 V a.c. (Figure 22.13), is used to drive a large short-circuited current through the wire.

Figure 22.13 This low-voltage power supply supplies short-circuited currents of up to 8 A.

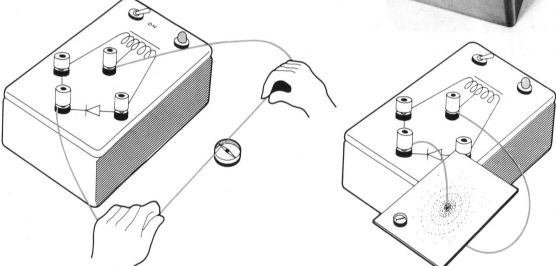

Figure 22.12 Oersted's experiment.

Figure 22.14 Investigating magnetic field due to current through straight wire.

Field due to current through straight wire

Figure 22.14 shows how the field due to a current through a wire can be investigated. The pattern of the iron filings on the card (Figure 22.15) shows that the field lines are circles centred about the wire. The density of the iron filings shows that the magnetic field is strongest near the wire but decreases in strength as the distance from the wire increases.

The plotting compass sets along the field line and shows the direction of the field at different points. If the current direction is reversed, the field direction is also reversed but the field pattern is otherwise unchanged. The field lines are

Figure 22.15 Field pattern around current-carrying wire.

clockwise (Figure 22.16) when the current flows 'down into the page' and counter-clockwise when the current flows up 'out of the page'. The symbols for the current directions are explained in Figure 22.17 — this is like looking at the tip and tail of an arrow.

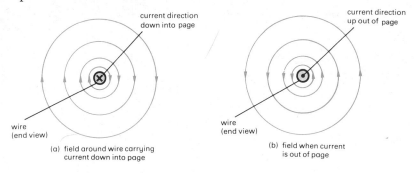

current direction down into page

wire (end view)

(a) field around wire carrying current down into page

current direction up out of page

wire (end view)

(b) field when current is out of page

Figure 22.16 (a) Field around wire carrying current down into page. (b) Field when current is out of page.

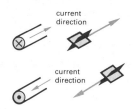

current direction

current direction

Figure 22.17 Symbols for current directions.

If the current direction is known, the direction of the field around a wire can be worked out using the so-called **right-hand grip rule** (Figure 22.18):

> **If the thumb of the right hand points in the direction of the current, the fingers grip in the direction of the field.**

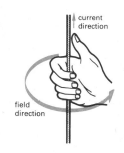

current direction

field direction

Figure 22.18 Right-hand grip rule for direction of field.

Field due to current in coil

Figure 22.19 shows the field pattern produced by a current flowing through a circular coil. At the centre of the coil the field lines are straight and at right angles to the plane of the coil; outside the coil they run in loops. The right-hand grip rule can be applied to find the field direction of any short section of the coil.

Field due to current in solenoid

A solenoid is a long coil made up of a number of turns of wire. When a current flows through a solenoid each turn acts as a single coil and produces a magnetic field. The field pattern shown in Figure 22.20 may be regarded as the combined field

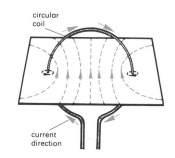

circular coil

current direction

Figure 22.19 Field due to current in coil.

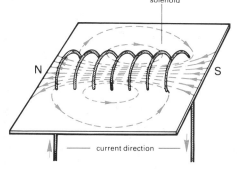

solenoid

N

S

current direction

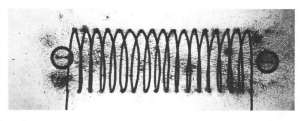

Figure 22.20 Field due to current in solenoid.

solenoid 螺線管

153

of all the turns. Inside the solenoid the field lines are straight and evenly spaced indicating that the field is of uniform strength. Outside the solenoid the pattern is similar to that around a bar magnet, with one end of the solenoid behaving like a N-pole and the other end like a S-pole. The polarity can be worked out by applying the **right-hand grip rule for solenoid** (Figure 22.21):

> If the fingers of the right hand grip the solenoid in the direction of the current, the thumb points to the N-pole.

The strength of the magnetic field of a solenoid can be increased by (a) increasing the current and (b) increasing the number of turns.

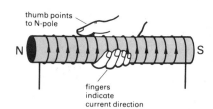

Figure 22.21   Right-hand grip rule for solenoid.

ELECTROMAGNET

The magnetic field around a solenoid becomes very much stronger if the solenoid has a soft-iron core. Solenoids of this type are called **electromagnets**. Unlike a permanent magnet, the magnetism of an electromagnet is temporary and can be switched on and off. A simple electromagnet (Figure 22.22) can be formed by winding about 20 turns of PVC-covered wire round one arm of a soft-iron C-core.

Figure 22.23   Gantry crane handling heavy steel castings by electromagnets.

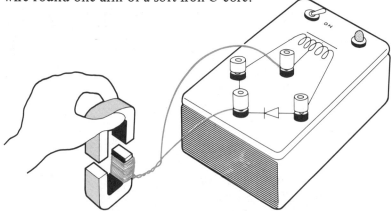

Figure 22.22   Simple electromagnet.

Large electromagnets are used in cranes for lifting heavy iron objects (Figure 22.23). Small ones are used in various electrical devices.

Electric bell and buzzer

An electric bell (Figure 22.24) contains an electromagnet which is switched on and off very rapidly by a 'contact-breaker'. When the bell switch is pressed, current flows through the electromagnet which becomes magnetized and pulls the hammer

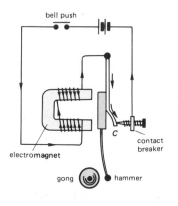

Figure 22.24   An electric bell.

soft iron core 軟鐵芯   electromagnet 電磁體

across to strike the gong. The movement breaks the contact and switches off the current. The hammer springs back, closes the contact, and current starts flowing in the electromagnet once again. The process is repeated while the switch is pressed and therefore the electric bell keeps on ringing.

A buzzer (Figure 22.25) is very similar to an electric bell, except that instead of the hammer, a rapidly vibrating metal strip is made to strike a metal or plastic plate. This gives the buzzing sound when the switch is pressed.

Figure 22.25   A buzzer.

Telephone

Figure 22.26 shows a simple telephone system. When someone speaks into the mouthpiece of the telephone, sound waves cause the aluminium diaphragm to vibrate. When the diaghragm moves inwards, the carbon granules are squeezed closer together and their electrical resistance decreases. When the diaphragm moves outwards, the carbon granules spread out and their resistance increases. The variations in the resistance of the carbon granules, due to sound wave variations, produce similar variations in the current in the telephone cable.

In the earpiece, this varying current flows through the coils of an electromagnet. This pulls the iron diaphragm towards the electromagnet, the distance moved varying with the current. As a result, the diaphragm vibrates and produces sound waves which are a copy of those that enter the mouthpiece.

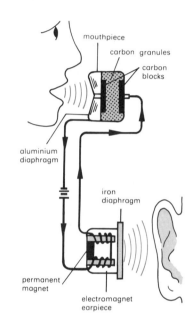

Figure 22.26   A simple telephone system.

FORCE ON CURRENT-CARRYING CONDUCTOR

When a wire carrying a current is placed in a magnetic field, it experiences a force. Figure 22.27 shows a flexible length of wire placed at right angles to the strong magnetic field of a U-shaped magnet. When the current is switched on, the wire moves upwards indicating that there is an upward force acting on it. If the direction of either the current or the magnetic field is reversed, the wire moves downwards. In both cases, the directions of the force (F), the magnetic field (B) and the current (I) are at right angles to one another.

If the current and the field direction are not at right angles, the force is smaller. If the current is parallel to the field, no force is produced no matter how strong the field or how large the current is.

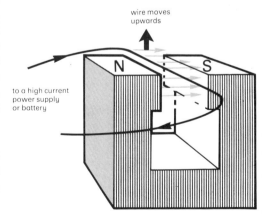

Figure 22.27   A current-carrying wire in a magnetic field experiences a force.

Knowing the directions of the current and of the field, the direction of the force can be found by applying **Fleming's left hand rule** (Figure 22.28):

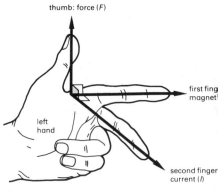

thumb: force (F)

first finger
magnet

left
hand

second finger
current (I)

> **If the thumb and the first two fingers of the left hand are held at right angles to one another,**
>
> **with the first finger pointing in the direction of the field *(B)***
>
> **and the second finger in the direction of the current *(I)*,**
>
> **then the thumb points in the direction of the force *(F)*.**

The force acting on a current-carrying conductor can be increased by:

Figure 22.28 The Fleming's left-hand rule.

1. increasing the strength of the magnetic field,

2. increasing the size of the current,

3. increasing the length of the conductor.

Catapult field

The force acting on a current-carrying conductor can be explained by considering the combined field due to the current and the magnet. The apparatus in Figure 22.29 can be used to show on an overhead projector,

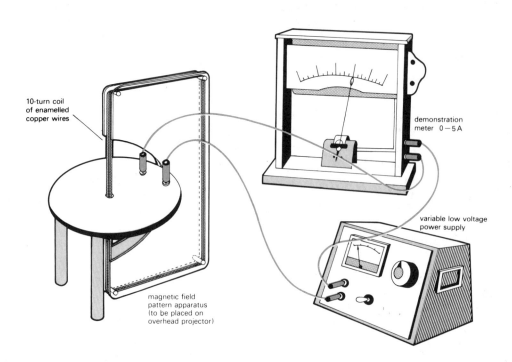

10-turn coil
of enamelled
copper wires

demonstration
meter 0 – 5 A

variable low voltage
power supply

magnetic field
pattern apparatus
(to be placed on
overhead projector)

Figure 22.29 Investigating the catapult field.

catapult field 彈場   catapult 彈弓

1. the circular field lines due to a large current flowing through the straight copper wires,

2. the straight field lines due to two magnadur magnets placed at some distance apart with unlike poles facing each other, and,

3. the combined field of (1) and (2), as shown in Figure 22.31.

The combined field may be regarded as the result of adding the fields of (1) and (2) together (Figure 22.31). From the pattern it appears as if the conductor is being 'catapulted' in the direction from the strong field region towards the weak field region. Hence it is named a catapult field.

Figure 22.30 A current-carrying conductor appears to be catapulted.

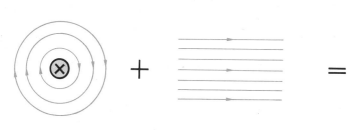 

Figure 22.31 Explaining the catapult field.

Moving-coil loudspeaker

A moving-coil loudspeaker makes use of the force acting on a current-carrying conductor in a magnetic field. It contains a short coil which is free to move inside a strong cylindrical permanent magnet (Figure 22.32). The magnet has a central

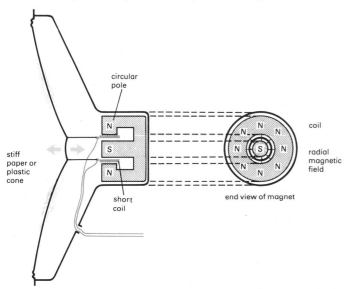

Figure 22.32 A moving-coil loudspeaker.

S-pole and a surrounding N-pole. The field lines are radial and at right angles to the turns of the coil. When a varying current flows through the coil, a force acts on the coil which, according to Fleming's left-hand rule, pushes it backwards and forwards. This makes the paper cone attached to the coil vibrate, setting up sound waves in the surrounding air. The nature of the sound waves depends on the frequency and amplitude of the varying current flowing through the coil. The current could come from a microphone, a radio, a record player, a signal generator, etc.

TURNING EFFECT ON COIL IN MAGNETIC FIELD

In Figure 22.33, a current flows through a rectangular coil of wire which is free to rotate between the poles of a magnet. From Fleming's left-hand rule, an upward force acts on the left side of the coil and a downward force acts on the right side. These two forces form a turning moment or **couple** which rotates the coil in the clockwise direction. A couple is a measure of the turning effect of two equal but opposite parallel forces. It is equal to the product of one of the forces and the perpendicular distance between them.

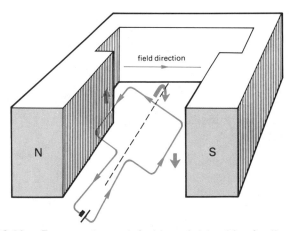

Figure 22.33   Forces acting on left side and right side of coil produce turning effect on coil.

When the coil lies with its face parallel to the field (Figure 22.34a), the couple is greatest. As the coil turns, the perpendicular distance between the two forces becomes smaller (Figure 22.34b) and so the couple decreases. When the face of the coil is at right angles to the field (Figure 22.34c), the couple is zero since the two equal but opposite forces act along the same line. If inertia makes the coil overshoot the vertical, the forces turn the coil back in the counter-clockwise direction (Figure 22.34d). The coil oscillates a few times before it finally comes to rest, lying at right angles to the field.

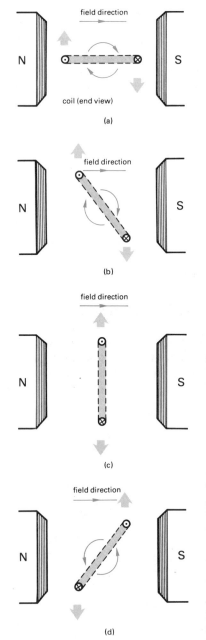

Figure 22.34   The rotation of a current-carrying coil in a magnetic field.

couple 力偶

The turning effect on the coil can be increased by:

1. increasing the current,
2. increasing the number of turns in the coil,
3. increasing the strength of the magnetic field,
4. increasing the area of the coil — lengthening the coil increases the forces acting on its sides; widening the coil increases the couple produced by the forces.

SIMPLE DC MOTOR

A simple d.c. motor, shown in Figure 22.35, contains a rectangular coil of wire of many turns mounted on an axle between the poles of a magnet. Current is passed through the coil via a pair of **carbon brushes** which are pushed against two copper half-rings, together called a **commutator**, by two small springs. The commutator is fixed to the coil and rotates with it.

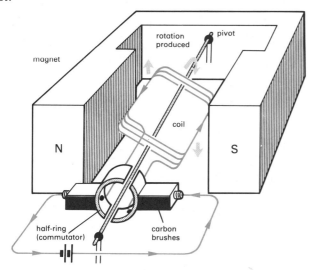

Figure 22.35 A simple d.c. motor.

When current flows through the coil as in Figure 22.36a, forces act on the coil, turning it in the clockwise direction. As the coil approaches the vertical (Figure 22.36b), the turning effect is about to become zero, but because of inertia, it overshoots the vertical. When the coil turns past the vertical (Figure 22.36c), the half-rings change contact from one brush to another. This reverses the current flowing through the coil and so also reverses the forces acting on its sides. The coil therefore carries on rotating in the same direction. As the coil rotates, each time it passes the vertical, the current and forces are reversed and so clockwise rotation is maintained.

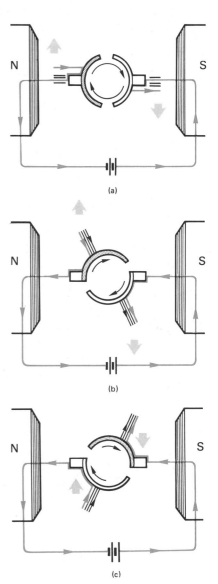

Figure 22.36 Commutator reverses the current direction in every half turn of the coil.

motor 電動機   brushes 電刷   commutator 換向器

A model electric motor can be constructed by winding a coil round a wooden block and mounting the block on an axle so that it can rotate freely (Figure 22.37). The wooden block is placed between two magnadur magnets on an iron yoke. The commutator consists simply of the two bare ends of the wire of the coil placed in contact with the wire from the power supply as shown.

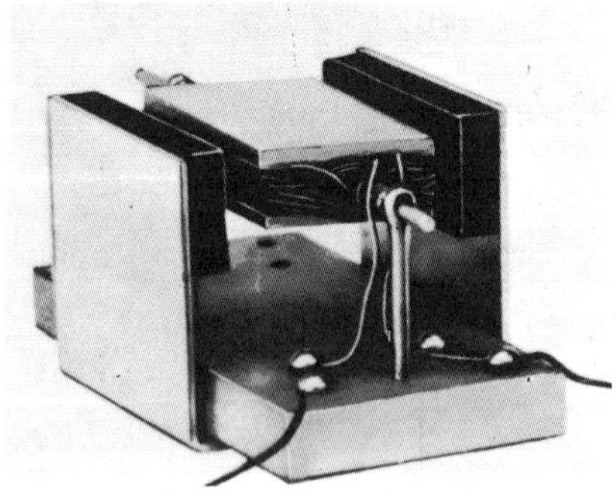

Practical motors

The simple motor described above provides too small a turning effect to have any practical use. Practical motors have the following features which give smoother action, higher speed and greater power:

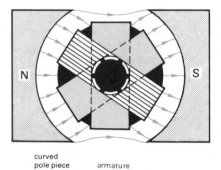

Figure 22.37   A model electric motor.

1. The coil consists of a large number of turns and is wound on a soft-iron core called an **armature** which becomes magnetized and increases the magnetic field strength of the coil.

2. The armature has several coils mounted on it, each having its own pair of commutator segments (Figure 22.38). This increases the turning effect and provides a smoother rotation.

3. Cylindrical magnets are used which, together with the soft-iron armature, provide a radial field. Each coil is then parallel to the field for its entire rotation and so the couple produced is more or less constant.

In some motors, the magnetic field is provided by an electromagnet rather than a permanent magnet (Figure 22.39). Such motors can be operated by a.c. as well as d.c. Although the alternating current through the coils keeps changing its direction, the magnetic field also changes direction to keep pace with it. As a result, the motor carries on rotating in the same direction.

curved
pole piece   armature

Figure 22.38   The interior of a practical motor.

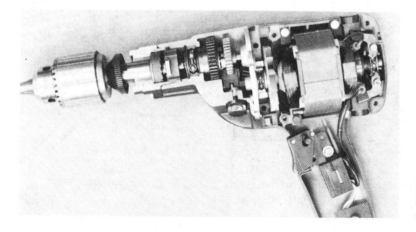

Figure 22.39   The magnetic field in the electric drill is provided by electromagnets.

armature 電樞，引鐵

MOVING-COIL GALVANOMETER

The moving-coil galvanometer is another device which makes use of the turning effect on a coil in a magnetic field. It is an electrical meter which detects very small current, usually of the order of milliamperes (10^{-3} A) or even microamperes (10^{-6} A). If it is calibrated accurately to read currents in milliamperes, it is then a **milliammeter**.

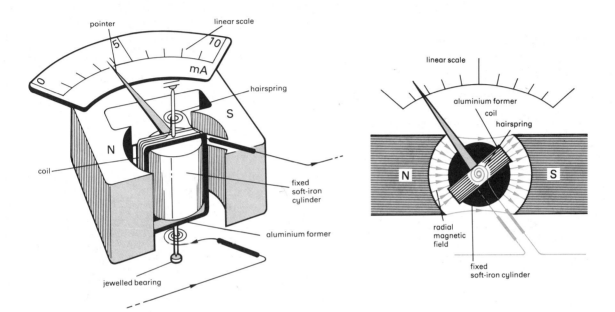

Figure 22.40   A moving-coil galvanometer.

A moving-coil galvanometer contains a rectangular coil pivoted on jewelled bearings between the poles of a cylindrical permanent magnet (Figure 22.40). The magnet, together with the *fixed* soft-iron cylinder in the middle of the coil, provides a radial field. Current is passed through the coil via a pair of spiral springs called hairsprings. When current flows, the coil rotates in the magnetic field and moves the pointer across the scale. The rotation of the coil is opposed by the hairsprings and the coil comes to rest when the couple turning it is balanced by the opposing couple from the springs. The higher the current the greater is the deflection of the coil which is shown by the movement of the pointer across the scale.

If the current flowing through the coil is reversed, the coil rotates in the opposite direction. The pointer movement is prevented by an end-stop, but even so the meter may be damaged. Hence a moving coil galvanometer is only used to measured d.c. If an a.c. is to be measured by a galvanometer, it must first be changed to d.c. by a rectifier (see p.213).

galvanometer 電流計   milliammeter 微安培計   hairsprings 游絲

A model moving-coil meter can be constructed as in Figure 22.41 using basically the same apparatus as the model motor, but each end of the coil on the wooden block is made into a loose spiral of several turns, to act as the hairsprings.

The current needed to deflect the pointer to the end of the scale is called the **full scale deflection (f.s.d.) current**. The smaller the f.s.d. current the more sensitive is the meter. The f.s.d. current of a sensitive moving-coil meter is typically around 100 microamperes (μA).

The sensitivity of a galvanometer can be increased by:

1. increasing the number of turns in the coil,
2. increasing the strength of the magnetic field,
3. increasing the area of the coil,
4. using weaker hairsprings.

A much more sensitive meter is the **light-beam galvanometer** in which the coil is suspended by a gold alloy wire, instead of being pivoted by jewelled bearings. A beam of light projected onto the scale replaces the pointer. The suspension wire is twisted as the coil is turned and this provides the opposing couple. The light-beam galvanometer shown in Figure 22.42 typically has a f.s.d. current of around 8 μA.

ADAPTING MILLIAMMETER TO MEASURE LARGE CURRENTS

If a resistor of low value is connected across the terminals of a milliammeter, some of the current bypasses the meter and flows through the resistor instead (Figure 22.43). A resistor used in this way is called a **shunt**. By using shunts of suitable resistance values, a milliammeter can be adapted to measure much larger currents.

Figure 22.41 A model moving-coil meter.

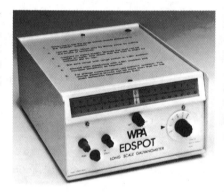

Figure 22.42 A light beam galvanometer.

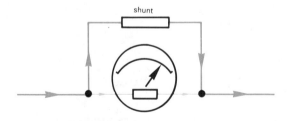

Figure 22.43 The current bypasses the meter and flows through the shunt.

If the f.s.d. current and resistance of a milliammeter are known, it is possible to calculate the shunt resistance needed to adapt the meter to measure currents up to any given value.

full scale deflection 滿標偏轉   shunt 分流器

Example 1

A milliammeter has a resistance of 10 Ω and a f.s.d. current of 10 mA. What is the value of the shunt resistance needed to convert the meter to measure currents up to 1 A? What is the resistance of the adapted meter?

Figure 22.44 shows a suitable shunt S connected across the milliammeter.

Since the meter can only take a maximum current of 10 mA (0.01 A), the rest of the current must bypass the meter through the shunt.

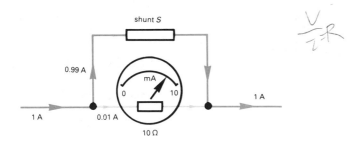

Figure 22.44 Determining resistance of shunt.

$\Rightarrow$ Current through the shunt $= 1 - 0.01 \text{ A} = 0.99 \text{ A}$

Since the meter and the shunt are connected in parallel,

$$\text{p.d. across the shunt} = \text{p.d. across the meter}$$

$$0.99 \times S = 0.01 \times 10$$

$$\Rightarrow \quad S = \frac{0.01}{0.99} \times 10 = \frac{10}{99} = 0.101$$

The shunt resistance is 0.101 Ω.

The resistance R of the adapted 0–1 A ammeter is the equivalent resistance of the meter and the shunt connected in parallel.

$$\frac{1}{R} = \frac{1}{10} + \frac{1}{\frac{10}{99}} = \frac{1}{10} + \frac{99}{10} = 10$$

$$\Rightarrow \quad R = 0.1$$

The resistance of the adapted meter is 0.1 Ω, much lower than that of the original meter.

The resistance of a shunted ammeter is very low. This is an advantage, since an ammeter is connected *in series* in a circuit and must have a *low resistance,* otherwise it changes the current to be measured.

ADAPTING MILLIAMMETER TO MEASURE VOLTAGES

A milliammeter can also function as a voltmeter. If the milliammeter in Example 1 is connected across part of a circuit which has a p.d. of 0.1 V, it draws a current of 10 mA (Figure 22.45). This gives a full scale deflection of the meter's pointer. 0.1 V is the **full scale deflection (f.s.d.) voltage** of the meter.

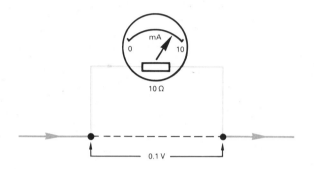

Figure 22.45   A 10 Ω, 0−10 mA meter gives a full scale deflection when connected across the p.d. of 0.1 V.

For a moving-coil meter,

> **f.s.d. voltage = f.s.d. current × resistance of meter**

The f.s.d. voltage of the milliammeter is very low, but it can be increased by connecting a high resistance in series with it as in Figure 22.46. The resistor, called a **multiplier**, takes a large share of the p.d. across the combination and limits the current through the meter to the allowed value.

If the f.s.d. current and resistance of a milliammeter are known, it is possible to calculate the multiplier resistance needed to adapt the meter to measure voltages up to any given value.

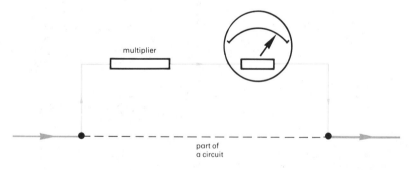

Figure 22.46   The multiplier takes a larger share of the p.d. and limits the current flowing through the meter.

Example 2
A milliammeter has a resistance of 10 Ω and a f.s.d. current of 10 mA. What is the value of the multiplier resistance needed to convert the meter to measure voltages up to 10 V? What is the resistance of the adapted meter?

multiplier 倍加器

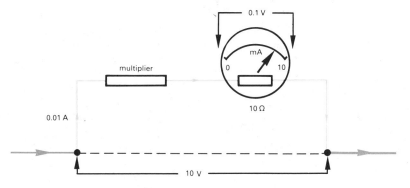

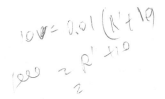

Figure 22.47 Determining the resistance of a multiplier.

Figure 22.47 shows a suitable multiplier R connected in series with the meter.

$$\text{f.s.d. voltage of meter} = 0.01 \text{ A} \times 10 \text{ }\Omega = 0.1 \text{ V}$$

When a current of 0.01 A flows, the p.d. across the meter is 0.1 V.

$$\Rightarrow \quad \text{Voltage across the multiplier} = 10 \text{ V} - 0.1 \text{ V} = 9.9 \text{ V}$$

Applying Ohm's law
$$V = IR$$
$$9.9 = 0.01 \times R$$
$$\Rightarrow \quad R = 990$$

The resistance of the multiplier is 990 Ω.
The resistance of the adapted meter is 990 Ω + 10 Ω or 1000 Ω.
This is much higher than the resistance of the milliammeter.

A voltmeter is connected *across* different parts of a circuit and must have a *high resistance* so that it only draws a small current from the main circuit. Ideally, the voltmeter should have an infinite resistance.

Most ammeters and voltmeters have shunts and multipliers connected inside the case. The basic meter shown in Figure 22.48a has many different plug-in shunts and multipliers for adapting it to measure various ranges of currents and voltages. A multimeter (Figure 22.48b) has a large number of built-in shunts and multipliers which can be selected by turning a dial.

Figure 22.48a Basic meters furnished with shunts and multipliers.

Figure 22.48b The multimeter contains built-in shunts and multipliers.

multimeter 萬用電錶

165

SUMMARY

Magnetic field around a magnet

A magnetic field is represented by field lines which go from a N-pole to a S-pole and indicate the direction of the magnetic field at various points. Where the field lines are closely spaced, the field is strong; where they are widely spaced, the field is weak.

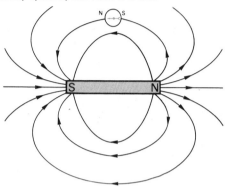

Magnetic field and electric current
Straight wire — circular field

The field lines around a straight current-carrying conductor are circular with the conductor as the centre. This direction of the field can be worked out using the right-hand grip rule:

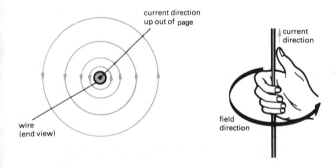

Solenoid — Uniform field lines inside

The magnetic field of a current-carrying solenoid is similar to that of a bar magnet. The N-pole of the solenoid can be worked out using the right-hand grip rule for solenoid:

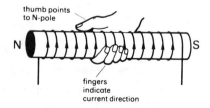

Electromagnet

An electromagnet is a solenoid with a soft-iron core. Electromagnets are used in the electric bell, and the telephone earpiece, among many other electrical devices.

Fleming's left hand rule

A current-carrying conductor experiences a force when it is placed in a magnetic field. The directions of the force (F), the magnetic field (B) and the current (I) are at right angles to one another. The direction of the force can be worked out using Fleming's left-hand rules:

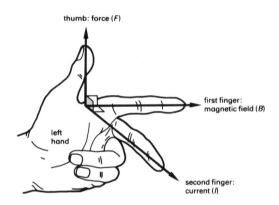

Electric motor

A current flowing through a coil in a magnetic field produces a turning effect on the coil.

This principle is made use of in the electric motor and the moving-coil galvanometer. Both contain a rectangular coil free to rotate between the poles of a magnet.

In a d.c. motor current is supplied via a half-ring commutator which reverses the current direction through the coil every half turn of the coil. This enables the coil to rotate continuously in the same direction.

Moving-coil galvanometer

In a moving-coil galvanometer, the rotation of the coil is opposed by a pair of hairsprings. The larger the current, the greater is the deflection of the coil.

Shunts

A moving-coil milliammeter can be adapted to measure larger current by connecting a shunt of a suitable resistance value across its terminals. Current bypasses the meter and flows through the shunt.

An ammeter should have a low resistance.

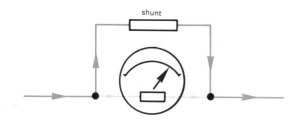

Multipliers

A moving-coil milliammeter can be adapted for use as a voltmeter by connecting a multiplier of a suitable resistance value in series with it. The high resistance multiplier takes a share of the p.d. across the meter.

A voltmeter should have a high resistance.

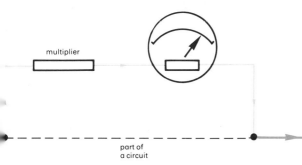

PROBLEMS

1. Two identical bar magnets are placed side by side as in Figure 22.49a. Copy the diagram and mark on it the position of any neutral point(s). Repeat for Figure 22.49b. Ignore the effect of the Earth's magnetic field.

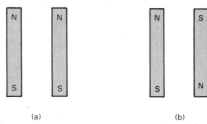

(a)   (b)

Figure 22.49

2. (a) Figure 22.50a shows the cross-section of a current-carrying wire. Copy the diagram and mark on it the magnetic field directions at P and at Q.
   (b) Figure 22.50b shows two parallel, straight wires carrying equal currents in the same direction. Copy the diagram and mark on it the magnetic field directions at X, at Y and at Z. Y is mid-way between the two wires.

(a)   (b)

Figure 22.50

3. Figure 22.51 shows a solenoid would on a lamp of cardboard tubing.

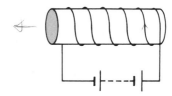

Figure 22.51

   (a) Draw magnetic field lines around the solenoid and mark the end of the solenoid which behaves in the same way as the N-pole of magnet.
   (b) Describe the effect on the magnetic field at any point if.
      (i) the number of turns is increased,
      (ii) the current is increased,
      (iii) a soft-iron core is placed inside the solenoid.

4. Two compasses are placed one at each end of a solenoid which is positioned along the east-west direction (Figure 22.52a). Initially, the compass needles point north.

   (a) Copy the diagram and draw how the compass needles deflect when a current flows through the solenoid in the direction shown.

   One compass is then moved to some distance away from the solenoid and the needle points north-east (Figure 22.52b).

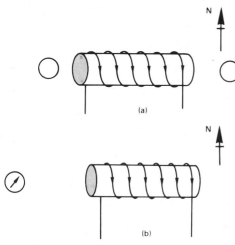

Figure 22.52

   (b) Explain why the compass needle points north-east.
   (c) Describe three ways in which the compass needle could be made to turn more towards the solenoid without bringing the compass and the solenoid closer together.

5. Figure 22.53 shows the end view of a current-carrying wire in a magnetic field. The current direction is out of the paper.

   (a) Copy the diagram and mark on it the direction of the force acting on the wire.
   (b) Describe the effect on the force if
      (i) the current is reversed,
      (ii) the magnetic field is reversed,
      (iii) both the current and the magnetic field are reversed.

Figure 22.53

6. Figure 22.54 shows the cross-section of two parallel straight wires carrying currents in the same direction.

Figure 22.54

   (a) Copy the diagram and draw a few magnetic field lines due to current flowing through wire A.
   (b) Mark on the diagram the magnetic field direction at wire B.
   (c) Hence deduce the direction of the force acting on wire B due to the magnetic field set up by current through wire A. Mark this direction on the diagram.
   (d) Similarly, deduce the direction of the force acting on wire A due to the magnetic field set up by current through wire B. Do the two wires attract or repel each other?

7. Figure 22.55 shows the end view of a coil which is free to rotate in a magnetic field.

Figure 22.55

   (a) If the current flows through the coil in the direction shown, what are the directions of the forces acting on the two sides of the coil? Copy the diagram and mark on it the direction of the forces.
   (b) Redraw the diagram to show the position of the coil in which the turning effect is (i) maximum, (ii) zero.
   (c) State four ways in which the turning effect on the coil could be increased.

8. Figure 22.56 is a sketch of a simple d.c. motor.

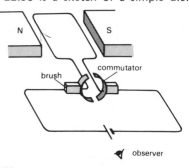

Figure 22.56

(a) What is the direction of rotation of the coil as seen by the observer?

(b) What will happen to the direction of rotation of the coil if the poles of the magnet and the polarities of the cell are reversed at the same time?

(c) Describe the motion of the coil if the two ends of coil are connected directly to a cell without using the commutator and the brush.
(HKCEE 1979)

. (a) Figure 22.57 shows two slab magnets. Copy the diagram and draw lines to represent the magnetic field between the magnets.

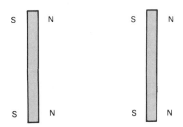

Figure 22.57

Figure 22.58

(b) Figure 22.58 represents a wire which is at right angles to the plane of the paper and in which there is an electric current. Copy the diagram and draw lines to represent the magnetic field due to this current.

(c) In Figure 22.59 the wire carrying the current is placed between the two slab magnets. Draw a sketch of the magnetic field in this case.

Figure 22.59

(d) This field is sometimes called *a catapult field*. Explain why this name has arisen.

Figure 22.60 shows a model d.c. electric motor.

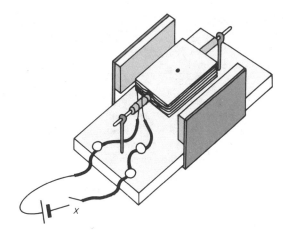

Figure 22.60

(e) When the switch X is closed momentarily the coil turns to a vertical plane. Explain why this happens.

(f) Switch X is then closed and left closed. The coil now rotates. State two changes in the construction of the motor which will cause the coil to rotate more quickly and explain in each case why the change will have this effect.

(g) Would this motor work on an a.c. supply? Explain your answer.

(h) The permanent magnets are replaced by electromagnets fed by the same a.c. supply as the coil. What might happen? Give your reasons.

(O&C June 1981)

10. A sensitive galvanometer has a full scale deflection current of 100 μA and internal resistance of 1000 Ω. Calculate

   (a) the shunt resistance required to adapt the galvanometer into an ammeter reading up to 100 mA.

   (b) the total resistance of the adapted ammeter in (a).

   (c) the multiplier resistance required to adapt the galvanometer into a voltmeter reading up to 1 V.

   (d) the total resistance of the adapted voltmeter in (c).

11. (a) Figure 22.61 shows the internal structure of a voltmeter with voltage ranges
   (i) 0–1 V at position 1, and
   (ii) 0–10 V at position 2.

   The ammeter A has a full scale deflection of 10 mA, and its internal resistance is 10 Ω. Calculate the resistances of R_1 and R_2.

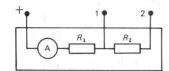

Figure 22.61

(b) The voltmeter in (a) is used to measure the potential difference between points P and Q in the circuit shown in Figure 22.62. Which position (1 or 2) of the voltmeter would you use to obtain a more *accurate* result? Explain briefly.

(HKCEE 1980)

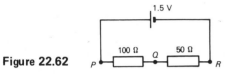

Figure 22.62

12. (a) A galvanometer G has a full scale deflection of 10 mA and a resistance of 36 Ω. It is used to construct an ammeter as shown in Figure 22.63. It is given that the resistance R is 24 Ω.

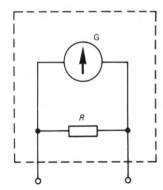

Figure 22.63

(i) Calculate the maximum current the ammeter can measure.
(ii) How would the maximum current be affected if the value of R increases? Explain briefly.

(b) Figure 22.64 shows a circuit containing a 500 Ω resistance S connected to a 6 V battery of negligible internal resistance.

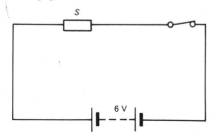

Figure 22.64

(i) What is the current through the resistance S?
(ii) If the ammeter in (a) is used to find the current in Figure 22.64, what would be the current measured?
(iii) Account briefly for the difference of values of (i) and (ii).

(HKCEE 1982)

13. Figure 22.65 shows a moving-coil loudspeaker. Copy the shaded part and indicate on your sketch the position and nature of any magnetic poles.

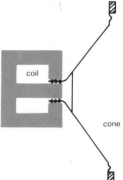

Figure 22.65

(a) Why is the area of the cone large?
Describe and explain what happens to the coil and what is heard when
(i) a dry cell is attached to the terminals of the loudspeaker and the current is switched on and then off,
(ii) a 50 Hz alternating voltage is applied to the terminals.
When the loudspeaker is emitting a sound how does the movement of the coil alter if the sound becomes
(iii) louder,
(iv) of higher pitch?

(b) A galvanometer has a resistance of 40 Ω and gives a full scale reading when carrying a current of 2.0 mA.
(i) Calculate the value of the resistor which must be added to the galvanometer in order that it shall give a full scale reading when a potential difference of 10 V is applied.
(ii) Draw a diagram showing how the resistor is connected to the galvanometer.
(iii) Draw a second diagram showing your resistor and galvanometer connected to measure the potential difference across a lamp which is connected to a cell.

(London June 1979)

14. Figure 22.66 shows a simple experimental set-up to study the motion of a motor. *AB* and *CD* are solenoids connected to a battery *E*. *F* and *G* are connected to an external voltage supply. Its variation with time is as shown in Figure 22.67. (Positive voltage indicates that the potential at *F* is higher than that at *G*.)
    (a) What is the polarity of the solenoids
        (i) at *B*,
        (ii) at *C*?
    (b) What is the direction of rotation of the coil *PQRS*
        (i)   in the first minute,
        (ii) in the second minute, and
        (iii) in the third minute?
    (c) What would happen to the rotation of the coil *PQRS* if the input voltage supply reversed at a high frequency (e.g. 50 Hz)?
    (d) Suppose that instead of being connected to the battery *E*, the terminal of the solenoid at *A* is connected to *F* and the terminal of the solenoid at *D* is connected to *G*. *F* and *G* remain connected to the external voltage supply indicated in Figure 22.67.
        (i) What is the direction of rotation of the coil *PQRS*
            (1) in the first minute,
            (2) in the second minute, and
            (3) in the third minute?
        (ii) What would happen to the rotation of the coil *PQRS* if the input voltage supply reversed at high frequency (e.g. 50 Hz)?
    (e) State three methods to increase the turning speed of this motor.

(HKCEE 1984)

15. A galvanometer has a resistance of 1000 Ω and measures currents ranging from 0 to 100 μA.
    (i) Draw a circuit diagram to illustrate how the galvanometer can be used to measure currents from 0 to 100 mA, making use of a resistor.
    (ii) Find the resistance of the above resistor. (1 μA = 10^{-6} A, 1 mA = 10^{-3} A)

(HKCEE 1985)

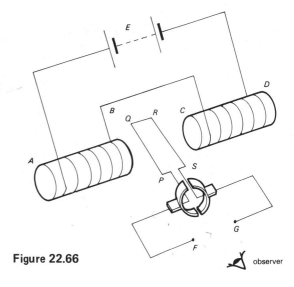

Figure 22.66

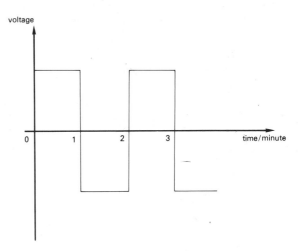

Figure 22.67

Electromagnetic Induction 23

In 1831, Michael Faraday (Figure 23.1) discovered electromagnetic induction – the production of a current in a conductor moving in a magnetic field.

INDUCED EMF AND CURRENT

When a bar magnet is pushed into a coil as in Figure 23.2, the light-spot of the galvanometer is deflected to one side. It returns to the centre zero when the magnet is stationary inside the coil, but is deflected to the other side when the magnet is withdrawn. The same results are obtained if the coil is moved instead of the magnet. In other words, an e.m.f. is *induced* in a conductor when there is a *relative motion* between the conductor and a magnetic field. If a conductor forms part of a complete circuit as in this case, an induced current flows through the conductor.

Figure 23.1   Michael Faraday 1791–1867.

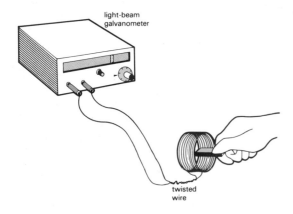

Figure 23.2   When magnet is moving towards or away from coil, e.m.f. is induced in coil.

Further experiments show that the induced e.m.f., and hence the induced current, can be increased by:

1. moving the magnet or coil at a higher speed,

2. increasing the number of turns in the coil,

3. using a stronger magnet.

An e.m.f. can also be induced in a wire by moving it across a magnetic field as in Figure 23.3a. The light-spot of the galvanometer is deflected backwards and forwards as the wire is moving upwards and downwards across the field. There is no deflection when the wire is held still or when it is moved parallel to the field (Figure 23.3b). If the length of the wire in the magnetic field is increased by looping several turns of wire into a coil round the magnet as in Figure 23.3c, the induced e.m.f. will be increased.

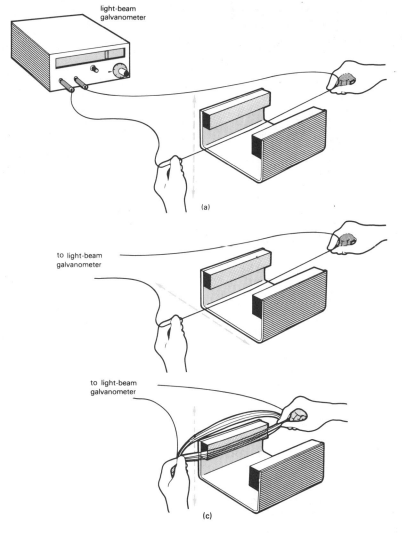

Figure 23.3 Any induced e.m.f.? (a) Wire moved at right angles across magnetic field. (b) Wire moved parallel to magnetic field. (c) Length of wire in field increased.

From such results, Faraday concluded that an e.m.f. is induced in a conductor whenever it 'cuts' through magnetic field lines. He summed up his findings in **Faraday's law of electromagnetic induction**:

The e.m.f. induced in a conductor is directly proportional to the rate at which the conductor cuts through the magnetic field lines.

induced e.m.f. 感生電動勢

Direction of induced current

The direction of the induced current can be worked out using **Lenz's law**, discovered by the Russian scientist, Heinrich Lenz, in 1834:

> **An induced current always flows in a direction such that it opposes the change producing it.**

In Figure 23.4a, the N-pole of the magnet is pushed into the coil. The induced current flowing through the coil turns the coil into a weak electromagnet with a N-pole at the end facing the N-pole of the magnet. The magnet is repelled and its motion is thus opposed.

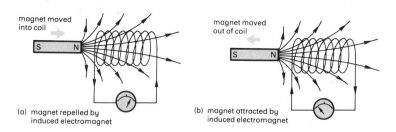

(a) magnet repelled by induced electromagnet

(b) magnet attracted by induced electromagnet

Figure 23.4   Lenz's law.

When the magnet is pulled out of the coil (Figure 23.4b), the induced current turns the end of the coil facing the N-pole of the magnet into a S-pole. The magnet is attracted and its removal from the coil is hindered. The direction of the induced current is therefore opposite to that obtained when the magnet approaches the coil.

If the polarities of the ends of the coil are known, the direction of the induced current can be found using the right-hand grip rule given on p.154.

Lenz's law can in fact be deduced from a conservation-of-energy point of view. In the above example, the motion producing the induced current is opposed so that work has to be done by the applied force which causes the motion: mechanical energy is transferred to electrical energy. If the induced current turned the coil into a S-pole when a N-pole was approaching, the N-pole would be pulled towards the coil. We would need to give only a slight push to start the process, the action would then be self-perpetuating.

Fleming's right hand rule

It is possible to use Lenz's law to find the direction of the induced current in a wire moving across a magnetic field. In Figure 23.5, the wire is moving upwards and this causes an induced current to flow. This current is in a magnetic field,

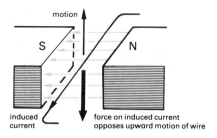

Figure 23.5   Determining direction of induced current.

so there is a force acting on it whose direction is given by Fleming's left-hand rule. The direction of the induced current must be such that the force opposes the upward motion of the wire.

A more direct method to find the direction of the induced current is to use **Fleming's right-hand rule** (Figure 23.6):

> If the thumb and the first two fingers of the right hand are held at right angles to one another, with
>
> the thumb pointing in the direction of the motion or force (*F*)
>
> the first finger in the direction of the magnetic field (*B*) then
>
> the second finger points in the direction of the induced current (*I*).

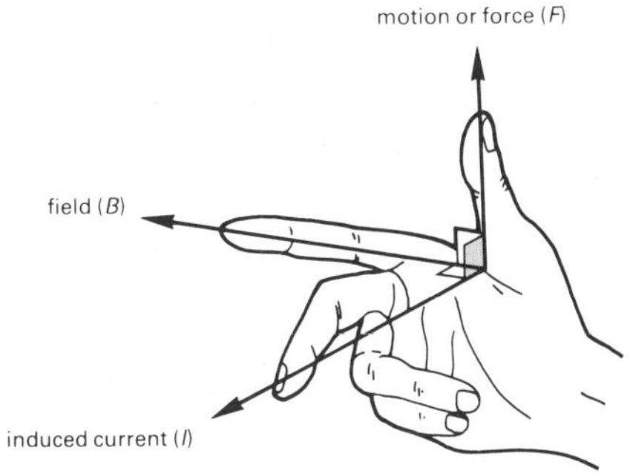

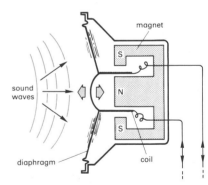

Figure 23.6 Fleming's right-hand rule.

The right-hand rule should not be confused with the left-hand rule given on p.156. The left-hand rule applies when a current produces motion, whereas the right-hand rule applies when motion induces the flow of a current.

Moving-coil microphone

A moving-coil microphone (Figure 23.7) is similar in construction to a moving-coil loudspeaker. It consists of a small coil which is attached to a diaphragm and is free to move inside a cylindrical permanent magnet. When sound waves set the diaphragm vibrating, the coil is made to vibrate in the magnetic field. When the coil is moving forwards it produces an induced current in one direction, and when it is moving backwards it produces an induced current in the opposite direction. The output current of the microphone is therefore an alternating current (a.c.) with the same frequency as the sound waves. This current is the signal which is amplified and played through a loudspeaker.

Figure 23.7 Moving-coil microphone.

The apparatus in Figure 23.8 illustrates the working principle of a microphone. A vibrating, magnetized tuning fork is brought near a soft-iron C-core into which a 2400-turn coil is inserted.

Figure 23.8 Vibrating magnet induces an a.c. in coil.

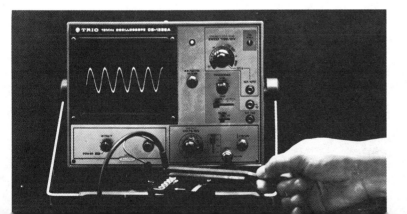

An a.c. is induced in the coil and this is displayed on the CRO. The frequency of the a.c. is the same as that of the tuning fork. Whereas in a microphone a vibrating coil in a magnetic field produces the induced a.c., in this set-up it is the magnetic field that vibrates; but both produce the same effects.

Record player pick-up

A magnetic pick-up consists of a stylus (needle) which is attached to a small coil positioned near a permanent magnet (Figure 23.9). The pick-up converts signals recorded in the grooves of a record into electrical signals. When the stylus runs along a groove it vibrates, causing the coil to vibrate in the magnetic field with the same frequency. A small a.c. signal is therefore induced in the coil and is amplified and played through the loudspeaker.

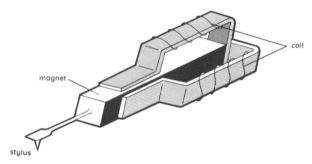

coil

magnet

stylus

Figure 23.9   Record player pick-up.

To produce 'stereo' sound, two separate signals are recorded in a single groove on a record. This groove makes the stylus vibrate in two perpendicular directions, and two coils are used to pick up the signals from the two vibrations. The two signals are amplified and played through two separate loudspeakers, giving a sense of 'breadth' to the sound.

Magnetic tape recording and playback

Magnetic tape is used for recording and reproducing sound (audio) as well as vision (video) signals (Figure 23.10). It is also used for storing information in computers. It is a plastic tape coated with a layer of very fine magnetic powder of iron(III) or chromium oxide. Both recording and playback

Figure 23.10   Audio and video signals recorded on magnetic tapes can be played back on video recorder.

pick-up 拾音器   stylus 唱針

are carried out by a pick-up head which is a specially shaped iron core having a coil round it (Figure 23.11). When recording, an amplified signal is passed through the coil in the pick-up head. The varying current in the coil magnetizes the powder on the tape as the tape is moved past the head at a constant speed.

In playback, the tape is moved past the head at the same constant speed and the recorded variations in the magnetic powder on the tape produce a *varying* magnetic field in the iron core. The varying magnetic field induces a varying current in the coil and the signal is amplified and reproduced.

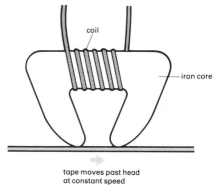

Figure 23.11   Pick-up head for magnetic tapes.

INDUCED EMF AND CURRENT IN ROTATING COIL

If a rectangular coil is rotated in a magnetic field, it cuts the field lines and an e.m.f. is induced in it. As a result, an induced current flows through the coil and the outside circuit.

Figure 23.12a shows the rotating coil as it passes the horizontal position. One side of the coil is moving upwards and the other side downwards through the magnetic field. An induced current flows and its direction is given by applying Fleming's right-hand rule to the sides of the coil.

Figure 23.12b shows the coil one quarter of a turn later as it passes through the vertical position. The two sides of the coil are now moving *parallel* to the magnetic field and so no field lines are cut. The induced e.m.f. and current therefore drop to zero.

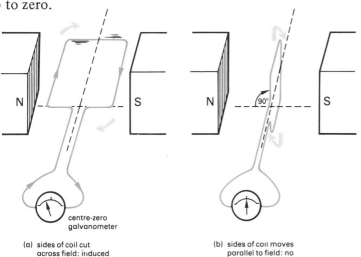
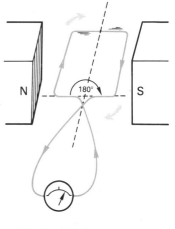

(a) sides of coil cut across field: induced current flows

(b) sides of coil moves parallel to field: no induced current flows

(c) coil makes half a turn: induced current flows in opposite direction

Figure 23.12   Induced current in coil rotating in magnetic field.

Another quarter of a turn later, the coil is horizontal (Figure 23.12c). An induced current flows, but its direction in the outside circuit is now opposite to that in Figure 23.12a. This is because the side of the coil which has been moving upwards is now moving downwards, and vice versa.

When the coil completes three quarters of a turn, it is again vertical and the induced e.m.f. and current again drop to zero. On completing one revolution, the situation is the same as in Figure 23.12a. For each half rotation of the coil, the current reverses its direction of flow; thus continued rotation produces an alternating current (a.c.).

Simple a.c. generator

A simple a.c. generator or **alternator**, shown in Figure 23.13, consists of a rectangular coil of many turns mounted on an axle between the poles of a magnet. The ends of the coil are fixed to two copper **slip rings** which rotate with the coil. Two **carbon brushes** press against the slip rings linking them with the outside circuit. When the coil is rotated, an alternating e.m.f. is induced in the coil which causes an a.c. to flow through the cutside circuit.

Figure 23.13   Simple a.c. generator.

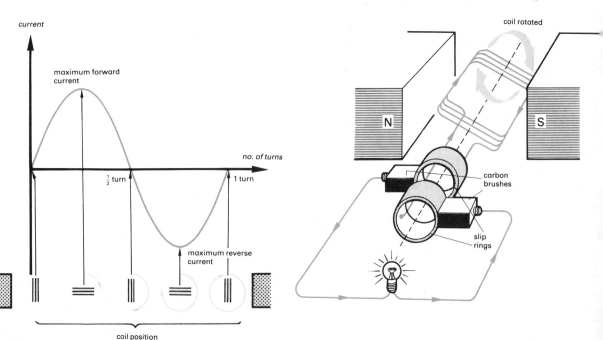

Figure 23.14   Current output of a.c. generator.

Figure 23.14 is a graph showing how the current in the outside circuit varies during one complete rotation of the coil, starting with the coil vertical. The current is taken as positive in one direction and negative in the other direction. It is greatest

alternator 交流發電機   slip rings 滙電環

when the coil is horizontal and cutting through the field lines most rapidly. It is zero and on the point of changing direction when the coil is vertical.

The induced e.m.f., and hence the induced current, can be increased by:

1. using a stronger magnet,

2. increasing the number of turns in the coil,

3. winding the coil on a soft-iron armature,

4. rotating the coil at a higher speed.

Increasing the speed of rotation of the coil also increases the frequency of the a.c. generated.

Simple d.c. generator

An a.c. generator becomes a d.c. generator or **dynamo** if the slip rings are replaced by a pair of half-rings or commutator (Figure 23.15) like that found on a simple d.c. motor. The commutator reverses the connections of the coil with the outside circuit every time the coil passes through the vertical, and so the current in the outside circuit always flows in the same direction. Figure 23.16 is a graph showing how the current generated varies during one complete rotation of the coil. Although varying in value, the current never changes its direction – it is therefore a direct current (d.c.).

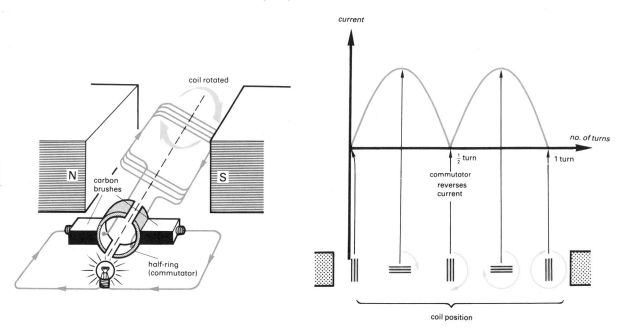

Figure 23.15 Simple d.c. generator.

Figure 23.16 Current output of d.c. generator.

dynamo 發電機

The simple d.c. generator is exactly the same in construction as a simple d.c. motor and in fact one can be used as the other. When the model electric motor is rotated as in Figure 23.17, the meter pointer is deflected to one side only, showing that a d.c. is being generated.

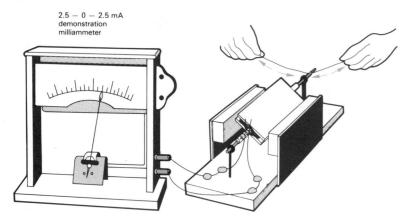

Figure 23.17 Model electric motor converted to d.c. generator.

Practical generators

Practical generators vary greatly in size, from small bicycle dynamos used for lighting lamps to huge a.c. generators in power stations which supply electricity to a large territory.

Figure 23.18 shows the essential parts of a **bicycle dynamo (a.c.).** The dynamo has a cylindrical permanent magnet which rotates between the arms of a soft-iron C-core, inducing an e.m.f. in the coil. When the bicycle dynamo is rotated slowly as in Figure 23.19, the meter pointer is deflected to and fro, showing that an a.c. is produced. When the waveform of the

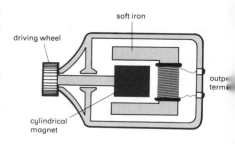

Figure 23.18 Bicycle dynamo.

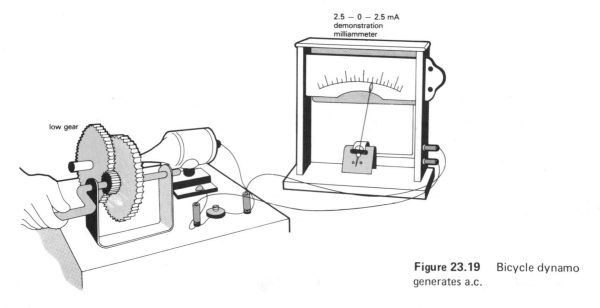

Figure 23.19 Bicycle dynamo generates a.c.

a.c. is displayed on a CRO, it is a somewhat distorted sine wave. The dynamo was designed to light small lamps efficiently, not to produce good sine-wave waveforms.

Practical d.c. dynamos are similar in design to practical d.c. motors. They may be installed in motor cars for charging the battery. The dynamo is coupled to the engine by a rubber belt and is rotated by it. Some cars use alternators (Figure 23.20), but the a.c. generated has to be converted to d.c. by a rectifier before being used.

Huge alternators (Figure 23.21) are used in power stations. Unlike the simple a.c. generator, the alternator has a stationary set of coils (the **stator**) arranged around a rotating electro-magnet (the **rotor**). The advantage of this arrangement is that only a small fraction of the generated current is fed through the rotating slip-rings and brushes to power the electromagnet, whilst the much larger current generated in the stator is led away through stationary cables. The rotor is usually driven by a steam turbine (Figure 23.22). The steam is produced in a number of ways depending on whether the power station is powered by coal, oil or a nuclear reactor.

Figure 23.20   Alternator installed in motor car engine.

Figure 23.21   A 120 MW generator being overhauled at Tsing Yi Power Station.

Figure 23.22   Steam turbine being installed at Castle Peak Power Station.

EDDY CURRENTS

If a fan-shaped aluminium sheet is set swinging, it may swing for some time before frictional force brings it to rest. If, however, the sheet is swung between the poles of a strong magnet as in Figure 23.23a, it will stop swinging almost immediately. The motion in a magnetic field induces an e.m.f. in the aluminium sheet. Being a solid conductor, it allows these

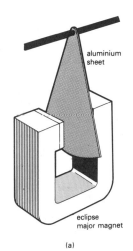

aluminium sheet

eclipse major magnet

(a)

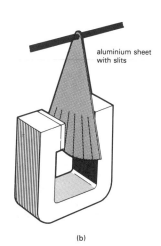

aluminium sheet with slits

(b)

Figure 23.23   Damping effect of eddy currents.

stator 定子   rotor 轉子   turbine 渦輪

induced currents to flow in closed paths inside itself. These currents are called **eddy currents**. By Lenz's law, they must flow in a direction that *opposes* the motion. If the aluminium sheet has slots as in Figure 23.23b, it will oscillate a few more times before coming to rest. This is because the slots offer more resistance to the flow of eddy currents inside the sheet and so the motion is damped less.

The coil of a moving-coil galvanometer is usually wound onto an aluminium frame. If the galvanometer detects a current, the coil and the frame rotate in the radial field inside the galvanometer. Eddy currents are induced in the frame as it turns through the magnetic field. The damping effect of eddy currents brings the coil quickly to a steady reading.

Eddy currents also occur in a stationary conductor placed in a *changing* magnetic field. In Figure 23.24a, an aluminium ring rests on a coil which is looped through a retort stand. When an a.c. is passed through the coil, the changing magnetic field causes eddy currents to be induced in the ring. The changing magnetic field due to eddy currents in the ring is, by Lenz's law, always opposite in direction to that due to the coil. As a result, the ring is repelled by the coil and 'floats' in mid-air. No such effect is produced if the aluminium ring has a slot in it.

If the aluminium ring is held in position resting on the coil, it will get warm very rapidly. Eddy currents flowing inside the ring heat it up. This is called **induction heating** and is used in industry for melting metal ores. The ores are surrounded by a coil carrying a high frequency a.c. The rapidly changing magnetic field induces large eddy currents in the conducting parts of the ores, and as a result the ores melt. Induction heating is also used in cooking. Figure 23.24b shows an induction cooker which heats up the food by producing large eddy currents in the metal cooking pot (Figure 23.24c). The cooker is not hot to touch since eddy current cannot be induced in the hand.

MUTUAL INDUCTANCE

Two soft-iron C-cores are clipped together as in Figure 23.25 and each has a coil wound round it. One coil, the **primary coil**,

Figure 23.24a   Eddy current effect: aluminium ring made to float in mid-air.

Figure 23.24b   The induction cooker cooks food by induction heating.

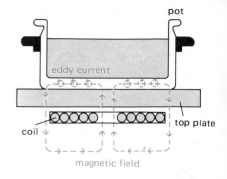

Figure 23.24c   A high frequency a.c. through the coil produces large eddy currents in the metal cooking pot and this heats up the food.

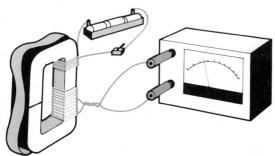

Figure 23.25   Current is induced in secondary coil at make as well as break of primary circuit.

eddy currents 渦電流   primary coil 原線圈

is connected to a battery and a switch, and the other, the **secondary coil** is connected to a centre-zero galvanometer. When the switch in the primary coil is closed, the galvanometer gives a momentary deflection. When the switch is opened, the galvanometer again gives a momentary deflection, but in the opposite direction. There is no deflection when the switch is left closed or open. This is a case of induced e.m.f. which is *not* produced by the relative motion between a conductor and a magnetic field.

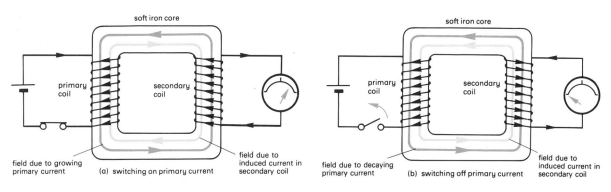

soft iron core

primary coil   secondary coil

field due to growing primary current   (a) switching on primary current   field due to induced current in secondary coil

soft iron core

primary coil   secondary coil

field due to decaying primary current   (b) switching off primary current   field due to induced current in secondary coil

Figure 23.26   Mutual inductance.

This induced e.m.f. can be explained by referring to Figure 23.26. When the switch is closed (Figure 23.26a), the primary current increases from zero to its maximum value in a fraction of a second. This produces a rapid build-up of magnetic field lines through the primary coil. These growing field lines go round the C-cores and 'cut' through the secondary coil. An e.m.f. is induced in the secondary coil and an induced current flows through it. According to Lenz's law, the induced current must flow in such a direction as to oppose the build-up of the magnetic field lines. When the current reaches its maximum value, the magnetic field becomes steady, and no e.m.f. is induced.

On opening the switch (Figure 23.26b), the primary current decreases to zero causing a rapid collapse of the magnetic field lines in the C-cores. An e.m.f. is again induced in the secondary coil, but now the induced current flows in a direction so as to oppose the collapse of the field lines.

In the above experiment, an e.m.f. is induced in a coil when current through a stationary, neighbouring coil is switched on and off or *changed*. This effect is called **mutual inductance** and was discovered in 1831 by Faraday. Figure 23.27 shows the original iron ring used by Faraday for winding the primary coil and the secondary coil for the experiment.

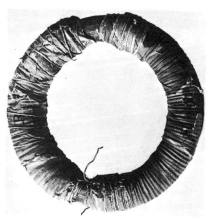

Figure 23.27   Faraday's iron ring — the first transformer.

secondary coil 副線圈   mutual inductance 互感

SIMPLE TRANSFORMER

If the current in the primary coil in Figure 23.25 is switched on and off repeatedly, an induced current flows in alternate directions in the secondary coil. However, a more convenient way to produce the same effect is to pass an alternating current through the primary.

An alternating current is changing all the time. When it is passed through the primary coil as in Figure 23.28, it sets up an alternating magnetic field in the core. This changing field induces an alternating e.m.f. and current of the *same frequency* in the secondary coil.

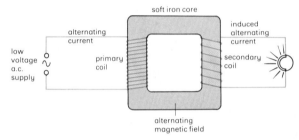

Figure 23.28 Simple transformer.

The primary and the secondary coil together with the core in Figure 23.28 form a simple **transformer**. When an a.c. is passed through the primary, electrical energy is continuously being transferred from the primary to the secondary circuit and so the lamp lights.

Voltages in transformer

Figure 23.29 shows a simple transformer made by winding a 10-turn coil round one C-core and a 25-turn coil round another, and clipping the two C-cores together. The 10-turn primary coil is connected to a 1 V a.c. supply and a small lamp and the 25-turn secondary coil is connected to an identical lamp. When the supply is switched on, both lamps light, but the seondary lamp is much brighter than the primary lamp. This shows that the voltage across the secondary (V_s) is higher than that across the primary (V_p).

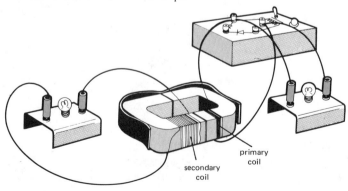

Figure 23.29 Voltage across 25-turn coil is higher than that across 10-turn coil.

transformer 變壓器

If the primary and the secondary voltage are measured, using a CRO connected across each coil in turn, it will be found that the ratio of the voltages is equal to the ratio of the numbers of turns of the coils, that is:

$$\frac{\text{secondary voltage}}{\text{primary voltage}} = \frac{\text{number of turns in secondary}}{\text{number of turns in primary}}$$

$$\frac{V_s}{V_p} = \frac{N_s}{N_p}$$

Strictly speaking, this equation is true only for an ideal transformer in which no energy is lost while being transferred from the primary to the secondary. However, it is a good enough approximation for most practical purposes.

Hence by choosing suitable numbers of turns for the coils of a transformer, the a.c. voltage in the secondary can be made greater or smaller than that in the primary. In other words, a transformer can be used to change or *transform* an a.c. voltage from one value to another.

A **step-up** transformer has more turns in the secondary than in the primary and the secondary voltage is greater than the primary voltage. On the other hand, a **step-down** transformer has fewer secondary turns than primary turns and the secondary voltage is less than the primary voltage. Figure 23.30 shows the circuit symbols for step-up and step-down transformers.

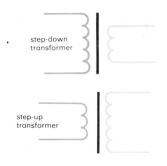

Figure 23.30 Circuit symbols for transformer.

Currents in transformer

If no energy is lost in a transformer, all the power supplied to the primary will be delivered by the secondary. That is:

$$\text{power input} = \text{power output}$$

$$\begin{array}{c}\text{primary} \\ \text{voltage}\end{array} \times \begin{array}{c}\text{primary} \\ \text{current}\end{array} = \begin{array}{c}\text{secondary} \\ \text{voltage}\end{array} \times \begin{array}{c}\text{secondary} \\ \text{current}\end{array}$$

Using symbols, $V_p \times I_p = V_s \times I_s$

$\Rightarrow$ $\dfrac{V_s}{V_p} = \dfrac{I_p}{I_s}$

From $\dfrac{V_s}{V_p} = \dfrac{N_s}{N_p}$

$$\frac{I_p}{I_s} = \frac{N_s}{N_p}$$

step-up transformer 升壓器   step-down transformer 降壓器   185

Therefore, if the secondary voltage is step-up, the secondary current will be step-down, and vice versa. Figure 23.31 shows a step-down transformer with a turns ratio of 20 : 1. The voltage is reduced from 200 V to 10 V but the current is increased from 0.5 A to 10 A in the same proportion and the power remains the same.

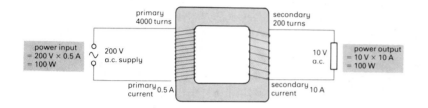

Figure 23.31   Stepping down the voltage steps up the current.

Example 1
A transformer has 3000 turns in its primary coil and is used to operate a 12 V 24 W lamp from the 200 V a.c. mains (Figure 23.32). Assuming that there is no energy loss in the transformer and that the lamp is operated at the correct rating, find
(a)   the number of turns in the secondary coil,
(b)   the current in the secondary coil,
(c)   the current in the primary coil.

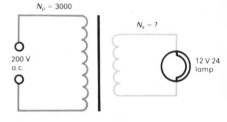

Figure 23.32

(a)   Applying the transformer equation,

$$\frac{V_s}{V_p} = \frac{N_s}{N_p}$$

$$\Rightarrow \quad N_s = \frac{V_s}{V_p} \times N_p = \frac{12 \text{ V}}{200 \text{ V}} \times 3000 = 180$$

The secondary coil has 180 turns.

(b)   The correct rating of the lamp is 12 V and 24 W.

$$P = VI$$

$$\Rightarrow \quad I = \frac{P}{V} = \frac{24 \text{ W}}{12 \text{ V}} = 2 \text{ A}$$

The current taken by the lamp is 2 A and so the secondary current is 2 A.

(c)   Assuming that there is no energy loss in the transformer,

power input = power output

$$V_s \times I_s = V_p \times I_p$$

$$\Rightarrow \quad I_p = \frac{12 \text{ V}}{200 \text{ V}} \times 2 \text{ A} = 0.12 \text{ A}$$

The primary current is 0.12 A.

Practical transformers

Practical transformers have primary and secondary coils wound next to one another round a complete soft iron core as in Figure 23.33. This ensures that the field lines are trapped in closed loops in the core, and that all the field lines from the primary pass through the secondary.

In all practical transformers there are some energy losses, which means that the power output is less than the power input. Energy losses are due mainly to three factors:

1. *Resistance of coils.* As the coils have some resistance they are heated up by currents flowing through them. Coil resistance is reduced by making the coils from thick copper wires.

2. *Eddy currents in the core.* As the core is in a changing magnetic field, eddy currents are induced in it and as a result the core heats up. Eddy currents are reduced by using a *laminated* core (Figure 23.34) made from thin sheets of soft iron, insulated from each other so that they have a high resistance.

3. *Magnetization and demagnetization of the core.* The alternating current flowing through the transformer continually magnetizes and demagnetizes the core. Work has to be done to change the magnitude and direction of the magnetic field and this is transferred as internal energy. This energy loss is reduced by making the core from soft iron, a material which can be magnetized and demagnetized easily.

The transformer is a very efficient device. Well designed transformers can have an efficiency rating as high as 99%.

Figure 23.33   Practical transformer.

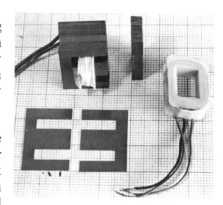

Figure 23.34   Laminated soft-iron core of transformer.

Use of transformers

The most important use of transformers is to efficiently provide any required alternating voltage for operating electrical appliances. The transformer in Example 1 steps down the mains voltage of 200 V a.c. to 12 V a.c. to operate a 12 V 24 W lamp. The next example shows the insufficiency of using a resistor, connected in series, to take up 188 V from the mains leaving 12 V for the lamp.

Example 2

A 12 V 24 W lamp is connected in series with a resistor to a 200 V a.c. mains (Figure 23.35). If the resistor is of such a value that the lamp is operated at the correct rating, find

magnetization 起磁   demagnetization 去磁，消磁

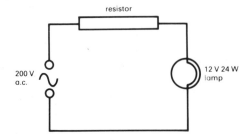

resistor

200 V
a.c.

12 V 24 W
lamp

Figure 23.35

(a) the current through the lamp,
(b) the value of the resistor used,
(c) the power supplied by the mains,
(d) the efficiency of the circuit in supplying power to the lamp.

(a) The ratings of the lamp are 12 V and 24 W.

Applying $P = VI$

current through the lamp $= \dfrac{P}{V} = \dfrac{24 \text{ W}}{12 \text{ V}} = 2 \text{ A}$

(b) The resistor must take up 188 V from the mains leaving 12 V for the lamp.

Applying Ohm's law $\quad R = \dfrac{188 \text{ V}}{2 \text{ A}} \qquad (R = \dfrac{V}{I})$

$\qquad\qquad\qquad = 94 \ \Omega$

(c) Power supplied by the mains = power input

$\qquad\qquad\qquad\qquad = 200 \text{ V} \times 2 \text{ A}$

$\qquad\qquad\qquad\qquad = 400 \text{ W}$

(d) Power delivered to the lamp = power output

$\qquad\qquad\qquad\qquad = 24 \text{ W}$

$\qquad\text{Efficiency} = \dfrac{\text{power output}}{\text{power input}} \times 100\%$

$\qquad\qquad\qquad = \dfrac{24 \text{ W}}{400 \text{ W}} \times 100\%$

$\qquad\qquad\qquad = 6\%$

Only 6% of the energy supplied per second by the mains is used for lighting up the lamp, the remaining 94% being changed into internal energy of the resistor. This is extremely wasteful.

An appliance such as a television set has many components which operate at different voltages ranging from several volts to a few kilovolts. The television is operated from a 200 V a.c.

mains and it uses a single transformer to provide the required voltages. The secondary coil of the transformer is tapped at different points so that the mains voltage is stepped up or down for the different components. The low voltage power supply used in school laboratories also has a multi-tapped transformer (Figure 23.36). The required voltage can be obtained by connecting the zero voltage terminal and the appropriate terminal.

Figure 23.36   Circuit of multi-tapped transformer.

TRANSMISSION OF ELECTRICAL POWER

Electrical power generated in power stations usually has to be transmitted over great distances by overhead cables to the consumers (Figure 23.37). The resistance of the cables is kept as low as possible, but is still significant. This gives rise to power loss due to the heating of the cables.

Figure 23.38 shows a **model power line** in which a d.c. power supply represents a power station and two lengths of resistance wire represent the transmission cables. When the supply is switched on, the lamp at the 'station' is lighted up brightly but that at the consumer end only glows dimly due to power loss in the cables.

Figure 23.37   Overhead transmission cables serving Castle Peak Power Station.

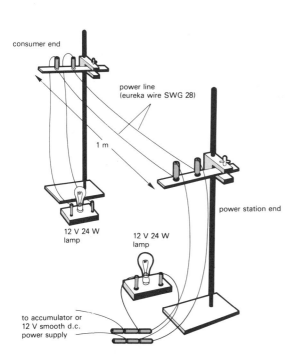

Figure 23.38   Demonstrating power loss in d.c. model power line.

power line 輸電線

189

The power loss in the 'cables' can be measured by disconnecting the 'station' lamp and connecting an ammeter and two voltmeters to the circuit as in Figure 23.39. The following is a set of typical results:

Current $I = 1.1$ A

Voltage at the 'power station' $V_p = 12$ V

Voltage at the consumer end $V_c = 6.6$ V

Power supplied by 'station' $V_p \times I = 13.2$ W

Power delivered to the consumer $V_c \times I = 7.3$ W

$\Rightarrow$ Power loss in the cables $= 5.9$ W

The power loss in the cable is about 45% of the power supplied.

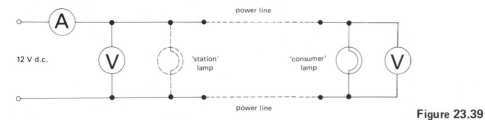

Figure 23.39 Measuring power loss in d.c. model power line.

If the d.c. power supply is replaced by a 12 V a.c. supply, the lamp at the consumer end is still dimly lit. However, if the 12 V a.c. is stepped up at the 'station' with a 1 : 20 transformer and then stepped down at the consumer with a 20 : 1 transformer as in Figure 23.40, the consumer lamp becomes almost as bright as the 'station' lamp. In stepping up the voltage the transformer steps down the current through the 'cables' and so the power loss in the cable is reduced.

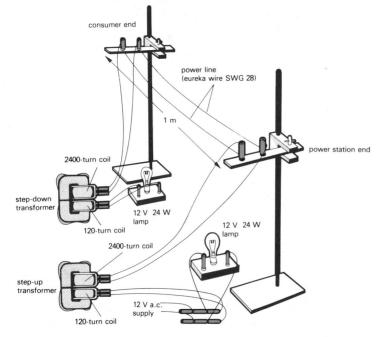

Figure 23.40 Model power line: transmission by high voltage a.c. reduces power loss.

The above experiment demonstrates why a.c., rather than d.c., is used for long distance power transmission. It is because a.c. voltages can be changed easily and without much loss of power by transformers; while d.c. voltages can also be changed but the process is rather inefficient, especially for high power.

Example 3

4 kW of power are supplied at the end of power cables of total resistance 5 Ω. Calculate the power loss in the cables if power is transmitted (a) at 200 V, (b) at 4000 V.

(a) Power transmitted at 200 V:

Applying $P = VI$,

current through cables $= \dfrac{4000 \text{ W}}{200 \text{ V}} = 20 \text{ A}$

$\Rightarrow$ Power loss in cables $= I^2 R = (20)^2 \times 5 \text{ W}$

$= 2000 \text{ W}$

(b) Power transmitted at 4000 V:

Current through cables $= \dfrac{4000 \text{ W}}{4000 \text{ V}} = 1 \text{ A}$

$\Rightarrow$ Power loss in cables $= (1)^2 \times 5 \text{ W} = 5 \text{ W}$

The power loss in the cables is much reduced by transmitting the power at a higher voltage.

Example 4

Figure 23.41 shows a model electrical transmission system. The power line has a total resistance of 5 Ω. If the transformers are considered as ideal, and the 12 V 24 W lamp is operated at its correct ratings, calculate:
(a) the current through the lamp,
(b) the current through the 'transmission cables',
(c) the current drawn from the supply,
(d) the power loss in the 'cables',
(e) the power output of the supply,
(f) the supply voltage.

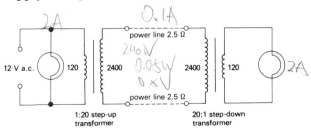

1:20 step-up transformer   20:1 step-down transformer

Figure 23.41

(a) Current through the lamp $= \dfrac{24 \text{ W}}{12 \text{ V}} = 2 \text{ A}$ $\left(I = \dfrac{P}{V}\right)$

(b) Turns ratio of the step-down transformer

$$= 2400 : 120 \; = 20 : 1$$

This transformer steps up the current to 2 A.

$$\Rightarrow \text{Current through the 'cables'} \; = \frac{2 \text{ A} \times 1}{20} = 0.1 \text{ A}$$

(c) Turns ratio of the step-up transformer

$$= 120 : 2400 \; = 1 : 20$$

This transformer steps down the current to 0.1 A.

$$\Rightarrow \text{Current drawn from the supply} = 0.1 \text{ A} \times 20 \; = 2 \text{ A}$$

(d) Power loss in the 'cables'

$$= I^2 R \; = (0.1)^2 \times 5 \text{ W} \; = 0.05 \text{ W}$$

(e) Power output of the supply

$$= \text{power supplied to lamp} + \text{power loss in 'cables'}$$
$$= 24 \text{ W} + 0.05 \text{ W} \; = 24.05 \text{ W}$$

(f) Voltage across the primary of the step-down transformer

$$= 12 \text{ V} \times 20 = 240 \text{ V}$$

Voltage across the 'transmission cable' of resistance 5 Ω

$$= 0.1 \text{ A} \times 5 \; = 0.5 \text{ V}$$

$\Rightarrow$ Voltage across the secondary of the step-up transformer

$$= 240 \text{ V} + 0.5 \text{ V} \; = \; 240.5 \text{ V}$$

$\Rightarrow$ Voltage of the supply

$$= \text{voltage across the primary of the step-up transformer}$$
$$= \frac{240.5 \times 1}{20} \; = 12.025 \text{ V}$$

Hence if the lamp at the consumer end is to be operated at exactly 12 V, the supply voltage should be 12.025 V.

POWER GENERATION, TRANSMISSION AND DISTRIBUTION IN HONG KONG

Power stations

There are two power companies in Hong Kong: the China Light & Power Company and the Hong Kong Electric Company.

Table 23.1 Power stations operated by China Light & Power Company.

Power station	Castle Peak (opened in 1982)			Tsing Yi (opened in 1969)		Hok Un (opened in 1920 and later redeveloped)	
	A		B Coal-fired	A Oil-fired	B Oil-fired	Oil-fired	Gas turbine
	Coal/ oil-fired	Gas turbine					
Generating capacity/MW	1400	240	2033 +678*	720	800	480	284

*will be completed in 1990

Table 23.2 Power stations operated by Hong Kong Electric Co.

Power station	Lamma (opened in 1982)			Ap Lei Chu (opened in 1968)
	Phase I Coal/oil-fired	Phase II Coal-fired	Gas turbine	Oil-fired
Generating capacity/MW	750	700 + 350*	55	600†

* under construction

† will be phased out in the 1990

The former supplies electricity to Kowloon and the New Territories, including Lantau, Cheung Chau and a number of other outlying islands, while the latter provides supplies to Hong Kong Island and the neighbouring islands of Ap Lei Chau and Lamma. Tables 23.1 and 23.2 give information on the power stations operated by the two power companies. The old stations are all oil-fired, but the newly built Castle Peak 'A' station (Figure 23.42) and the Lamma Phase I station can use either coal or oil as fuel. Coal is being used because it is cheaper than oil. The planned expansion of both stations will have only coal-fired generators.

Power transmission

China Light & Power Company transmits electricity at 400 kV, 132 kV and 66 kV. Electricity generated at the power station is stepped up to one of these voltages (Figure 23.43) and transmitted to the various substations in Kowloon and the New Territories where it is stepped down and distributed to the consumers. The 400 kV system, now being built in stages, transmits power from the new Castle Peak Station. It is being developed to reinforce the existing 132 kV system which

Figure 23.42 Turbine Hall of Castle Peak Power Station 'A'.

power transmission 輸電

transmits power from the Tsing Yi and Hok Un stations. The 400 kV network, when completed, will comprise 90 km of overhead lines encircling the New Territories and 14 km of underground cables in Kowloon (Figure 23.44). Figure 23.45 shows the Tsz Wan Shan Substation to which power is transmitted from the Castle Peak Station by a 400 kV overhead line.

Hong Kong Electric Company's transmission system operates at 275 kV, 132 kV and 66 kV. Power from the Lamma and Ap Lei Chau stations is transmitted at 275 kV by submarine cables to the Wong Nei Chong Gap Switching Substation. From there power is supplied by a 132 kV network, mostly of

Figure 23.43   Transformer at power station.

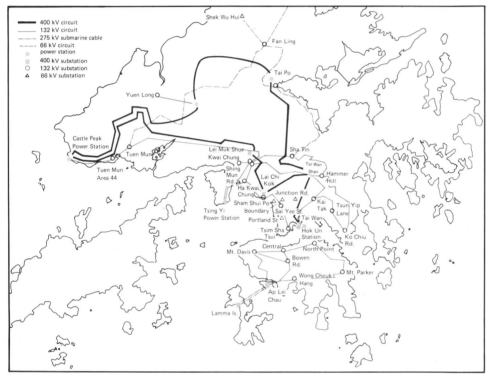

Figure 23.44   Transmission network in Kowloon and New Territories.

overhead lines, round Hong Kong Island to major load centres at Wong Cheuk Hang, Mount Davis, Bowen Road, Central, North Point and Mount Butler. From these major load centres power is transmitted at 66 kV to the various substations by underground cables.

Power distribution

At the China Light & Power Company, power is distributed at three main voltages: 33 kV for heavy industry, for example the Mass Transit Railway, 11 kV for factories, offices and large residential buildings (Figure 23.46), and 346 V for homes and farms. Supply is 50 Hz alternating current at 200 V.

Figure 23.45   Tsz Wan Shan Substation.

The Hong Kong Electric Company distributes power mainly at 11 kV and 346 V. Supply is also 50 Hz alternating current at 200 V.

Figure 23.47 shows a simplified diagram of the generation, transmission and distribution of electricity.

System Control Centre at Taipo

The demand for electricity varies from hour to hour during the day and from day to day. At the peak hours all generating units have to be operated, but at times of low demand some units may have to be shut down. It is important that the demand for electricity at different times can be predicted reasonably accurately so that the power generated meets but does not exceed the demand. This avoids wastage because 'excess' power cannot easily be stored. The matter is complicated by the fact that electricity generated by an oil-fired station is more costly than that generated by a coal-fired station. The System Control Centre (Figure 23.48) of the China Light & Power Company at Taipo monitors the demand for electricity and regulates power generation at the Castle Peak, Tsing Yi and Hok Un stations as required. Control and monitoring are carried out by a specially designed computer system. The Hong Kong Electric Company has a similar control system.

Figure 23.46 Transformer in large residential block.

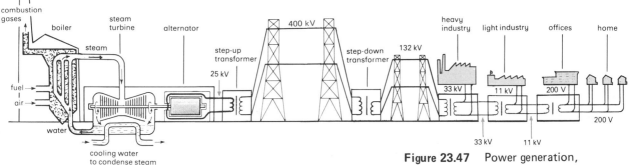

Figure 23.47 Power generation, transmission and distribution.

Figure 23.48 Control room at System Control Centre, Taipo.

195

SUMMARY

Induced e.m.f.

It can be demonstrated that the induced e.m.f. in a conductor moving in a magnetic field can be increased by increasing
1. the strength of the field,
2. the length of the conductor in the field,
3. the speed of the conductor.

Faraday's law and induced e.m.f.

From these results, Faraday concluded that the e.m.f. induced in a conductor is directly proportional to the rate at which the conductor cuts through the magnetic field lines.

Direction of induced e.m.f.
Lenz's law

Lenz's law states that an induced current always flows in a direction such that it opposes that change producing it.

Fleming right hand rule

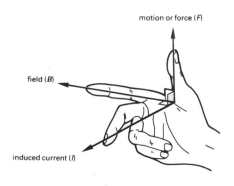

motion or force (F)

field (B)

induced current (I)

Generators — a.c. and d.c.

An alternating current is induced in a coil which is rotating in a magnetic field.

An **a.c. generator (alternator)** uses a pair of slip rings to pass the induced current in the rotating coil to the outside circuit.

A **d.c. generator (dynamo)** uses a pair of half-rings, the commutator instead. The commutator reverses the connection of the coil to the outside circuit every time the coil makes half a turn, and so a fluctuating d.c. flows in the outside circuit.

Eddy currents

Eddy currents flow inside a solid conductor lying in a changing magnetic field.

Effects:
1. Damping effect on the motion of the coil of a moving-coil galvanometer.
2. Induction heating.

Transformer

When an a.c. is passed through the primary coil of a transformer, electrical energy is continuously being transferred from the primary to the secondary circuit, that is, an a.c. then flows in the secondary coil.

The ratio of the voltages across the primary and the secondary of a transformer is equal to the turns ratio of the two coils:

$$\frac{V_s}{V_p} = \frac{N_s}{N_p}$$

A step-up transformer has more turns in the secondary than in the primary. It steps up the voltage, but steps down the current at the same time:

$$\frac{I_s}{I_p} = \frac{N_p}{N_s}$$

Energy losses in transformers

For an ideal transformer the power input to the primary is equal to the power output at the secondary. In a practical transformer there are power losses due to
1. the resistance of the coils,
2. eddy currents in the core,
3. the magnetization and demagnetization of the core.

These causes small amounts of the input energy to be changed into internal energy. Well-designed transformers can have an efficiency of 99%.

Transmission of electrical power

Power generated at the power station is stepped up to an extra high voltage for transmission over great distances and then stepped down before it reaches the consummers.

Stepping up the voltage steps down the current through the transmission cables and this reduces power loss in the cables.

An a.c. voltage can be stepped up or down easily without much loss of power using transformers.

PROBLEMS

1. The wire in Figure 23.49 is being moved downwards through the magnetic field.
   (a) Copy the diagram and mark on it the direction of the induced current.
   (b) Describe the effect on the induced current if
      (i) the wire is moved upwards rather than downwards,
      (ii) the wire is held still in the magnetic field,
      (iii) the wire is moved downwards at a higher speed,
      (iv) the wire is moved parallel to the magnetic field lines,
      (v) a stronger magnet is used.

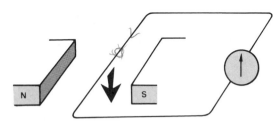

Figure 23.49

2. A bar magnet is pushed into a coil as in Figure 23.50.

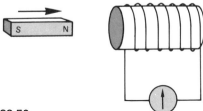

Figure 23.50

   (a) Copy the diagram and mark on it.
      (i) the end of the coil which becomes a N-pole and that which becomes a S-pole,
      (ii) the direction of the induced current in the coil.
   (b) State three ways in which the size of the induced current could be increased.

3. Figure 23.51 shows the end view of the coil of a simple a.c. generator. The coil is connected through brushes and slip rings to an outside circuit. It is rotated in the clockwise direction as shown.
   (a) Copy the diagram and indicate the direction of the induced current.

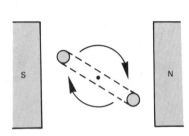

Figure 23.51

   (b) The induced current varies as the coil rotates. Redraw the diagram to show the position of the coil when the current is (i) maximum, (ii) zero.
   (c) State three ways in which the current can be increased.

4. A bar magnet is suspended by an elastic spring so that it can oscillate in and out of a coil (Figure 23.52). The coil is connected to a centre-zero galvanometer.
   (a) The magnet is set oscillating. Describe the resulting movement of the galvanometer pointer.

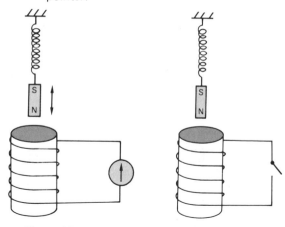

Figure 23.52

   (b) The galvanometer is now replaced by a switch. The magnet is again set oscillating. Describe the effect, if any, of closing the switch.

5. Figure 23.53 shows a solenoid with an iron core, a bar magnet and compasses A and B with needles pointing in the direction indicated. Neglect the effect of the earth's magnetic field.
   (a) Copy Figure 23.53 and sketch the magnetic field between X and Y. Indicate
      (i) the polarities of X and Y,
      (ii) the neutral point, and
      (iii) the direction of the current in the solenoid.

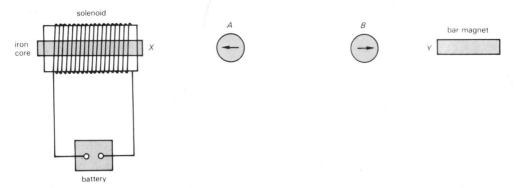

Figure 23.53

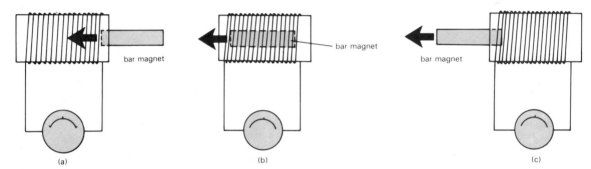

Figure 23.54

(b) What happens to the neutral point in each of the following cases:
 (i) the iron core is taken out of the solenoid at the left hand and,
 (ii) the battery is replaced by a centre-zero galvanometer?

(c) After the two changes described in (b) have been made, the bar magnet is moved towards the solenoid and passes through it. Indicate on Figure 23.54 the positions of the galvanometer pointer when
 (i) the magnet is just entering the solenoid (a),
 (ii) the magnet is inside the solenoid (b),
 (iii) the magnet is just leaving the solenoid (c).
(HKCEE 1982)

6. Figure 23.55 shows an alternating current generator.
 (a) Describe briefly with the aid of a diagram how the alternating current generator can be converted into a direct current generator.
 (b) Sketch a graph of the output voltage of the a.c. generator against time.
 Indicate on the time axis of your graph the times at which
 (i) the plane of the coil is parallel to the magnetic field (using the letter H), and

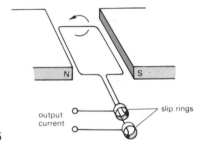

Figure 23.55

 (ii) the plane of the coil is perpendicular to the magnetic field (using the letter V).
 (c) Describe what happens to the output voltage if
 (i) the generator rotates at double its original speed.
 (ii) the generator rotates in the opposite direction.
 (iii) the number of turns of the coil is doubled.
(HKCEE 1983)

7. (a) Figure 23.56 shows a simple generator. Explain why an e.m.f. is produced between the ends of the coil when it is rotated.
 Answer (i), (ii) and (iii) by drawing three sketch graphs, one below the other on a sheet of graph paper.
 (i) Draw a sketch graph showing how the e.m.f. between the ends of the coil

varies with time over at least one revolution of the coil. Relate the positions of the coil to the values shown on your graph.

(ii) Draw a sketch graph showing what you would expect if the speed of rotation of the coil were doubled.

(iii) Draw a sketch graph showing what you would expect if in addition to rotating at twice the speed, the coil contained twice as many turns.

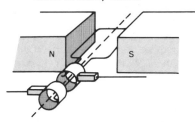

Figure 23.56

(b) A power station generator produces an e.m.f. of 33 000 V at a frequency 50 Hz. The domestic supply is approximately 250 V, 50 Hz. Explain how the output of the power station can be modified for use in the home.
(London January 1979)

8. The N-pole of a bar magnet Figure 23.57 is thrust into an aluminium ring which is freely suspended by a piece of thread. The ring moves to the right indicating that it behaves like a magnet.
Copy the diagram and mark on it

(a) the polarity of the face of the ring nearest the magnet,

(b) the direction in which the induced current flows in the ring.

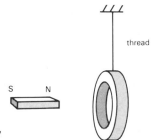

Figure 23.57

9. Two coils wrapped on paper cylinders are connected and arranged as shown in Figure 23.58. What will happen to the lamp

(a) at the moment when the switch is closed?

(b) when the switch remains closed?

(c) at the moment when the switch is re-opened?

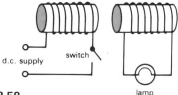

Figure 23.58

If the power supply is changed to a.c., and the above processes are repeated, what will happen to the lamp during these operations?
(HKCEE 1979)

10. Figure 23.59 represents a transformer with a primary coil of 400 turns and a secondary coil of 200 turns.

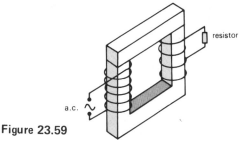

Figure 23.59

(a) If the primary coil is connected to the 240 V a.c. mains what will be the secondary voltage?

(b) Explain carefully how the transformer works.

(c) Calculate the efficiency of the transformer if the primary current is 3 A and the secondary current 5 A.

(d) Give reasons why you would expect this efficiency to be less than 100%.

(e) The secondary coil is removed and a small coil connected to a low voltage lamp is placed as shown.

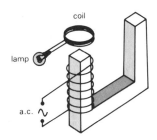

Figure 23.60

Explain the following observations:

(i) the lamp lights,

(ii) if the coil is moved upwards, the lamp gets dimmer,

(iii) if a soft iron rod is now placed through the coil, the lamp brightens again.

(iv) the lamp will not light if a d.c. supply is used instead of an a.c. one.
(London January 1978)

11. A transformer has 4000 turns in its primary coil and is used to operate a 6 V 24 W lamp from the 200 V a.c. mains. Assuming that the transformer is 100% efficient and that the lamp is operated at its correct rating, find
    (a) the number of turns in the secondary coil,
    (b) the current in the secondary coil,
    (c) the current in the primary coil.

12. (a) It is required to run a 6 V, 24 W lamp from a 240 V a.c. mains using a transformer as shown in Figure 23.61.

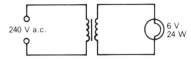

Figure 23.61

    (i) Calculate the current that would be taken by the lamp when operating normally.
    (ii) Calculate the turns ratio of the transformer you would use.
    (iii) Calculate the current taken by the primary coil of the transformer, assuming it to be 100% efficient.
    (iv) Why, in practice, is the efficiency of the transformer less than 100%?

  (b) Alternatively the 6 V, 24 W lamp can be operated normally from a 240 V d.c. supply using a suitable fixed resistor, R, as in Figure 23.62.

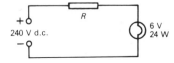

Figure 23.62

    (i) What is the resistance of the lamp?
    (ii) What is the p.d. across the resistor?
    (iii) What is the resistance of the resistor?
    (iv) How much energy is dissipated in the resistor in 1 s?

  (c) Why may the method used to light the lamp described in (a) be preferable to that described in (b)?

(London June 1980)

13. A 2 kW 200 V alternator delivers power to a transmission cable of total resistance 2 Ω.
    (a) Calculate the current flowing in the transmission cable and hence the power loss in the cable.
    (b) If now a transformer is used to step up the voltage to 2000 V, what is the current flowing in the cable? What is now the power loss in the cable?

14. A 12 V battery, with negligible internal resistance, is connected by two wires, each of resistance 1 ohm, to a resistor R.
    (a) Calculate the power transformed in R if its resistance is (i) 1 ohm, (ii) 2 ohms.
    Tables 23.3 shows the power P transformed in R for three more values of resistance.

R/Ω	3	4	5
P/W	17.3	16.0	14.7

Table 23.3

  (b) Plot a graph of power P (y-axis) against resistance of R (x-axis), including the two values which you calculated in part (a).
  (c) Comment on the shape of the graph and say, without detailed calculation, what you think the power would be if R had
    (i) a large resistance, e.g. more than 100 ohms,
    (ii) a small resistance, e.g. less than 0.01 ohms.
  (d) In order to light correctly a lamp labelled 12 V 24 W at a greater distance, wires ten times as long and a different battery are required.
    (i) What is the current flowing through the wires?
    (ii) What is the p.d. across each wire?
    (iii) What is the voltage of the battery required? (Assume it has no internal resistance.)
    (iv) What is the power wasted in the wires?
To waste less power, someone suggests that an a.c. supply should be used instead, together with two transformers.
  (e) Draw the circuit diagram for such an arrangement and explain why your circuit ensures that the power wastage in the wires is now smaller.
  (f) In what other ways might energy be wasted in your circuit?

(O&C June 1980)

15. An overhead electrical transmission line consists of a pair of cables which have a potential difference of 132 000 V applied across them at the power station. The cables have a resistance of 0.165 ohm/km and each of the two cables is 10 km long. The current flowing in the cables is 400 A.
    (a) What is the total resistance of the 20 km of cable?
    (b) What is the voltage drop along the transmission line?
    (c) What is the power input to the line at the power station?

(d) How much power is 'lost' in the line?

(e) What happens to this 'lost' energy?

The power station also serves a nearby transformer which is used to reduce the potential difference to 240 V so that electrical energy can be supplied to houses and factories.

(f) Which of the transformer's coils will have the larger number of turns? How many times more?

(g) Calculate the current flowing in the secondary coil of this transformer when the system is working at a rate of 1440 kW.

(h) Explain why the potential difference at the generator (132 000 V) is too high to be used in factories and homes.

(i) What are the advantages and disadvantages of using high voltage alternating current for the transmission of electrical energy?

(O&C Nov 1980)

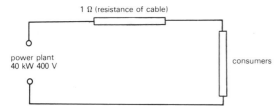

Figure 23.63

16. (a) Figure 23.63 shows a crude arrangement for the transmission of electrical energy from a power plant to the consumers. The resistance of the cable is 1 Ω.
Calculate
   (i) the current in the cable,
   (ii) the power loss in the cable, and
   (iii) the power loss in the cable if the output voltage is changed to 4000 V, while the power output remains at 40 kW.

(b) Explain why it is more practical for electrical energy to be transmitted by a.c.

(c) Draw a simple circuit diagram to illustrate how in practice electrical energy is transmitted by a.c. from the power plant to the consumers.

(HKCEE 1978)

17. Figure 23.64 shows a model electrical transmission system. KL and MN each represents a length of power 'cable', each having a resistance of 5 Ω. Assume that the transformers are ideal, that is, they deliver the same power as they receive, and that the lamp is operated at its correct ratings.
Calculate

(a) the current flowing through the lamp,

(b) the current through the transmission cable,

(c) the power loss in the transmission cable,

(d) the power output of the supply,

(e) the voltages across LN, KL, MN and KM,

(f) the supply voltage across PQ.

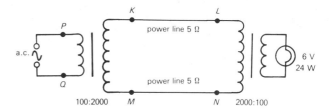

Figure 23.64

18. Figure 23.65 shows a piece of apparatus built in a school laboratory.

The two ends of the wires, A and B, shown in Figure 23.65 are connected to a galvanometer.

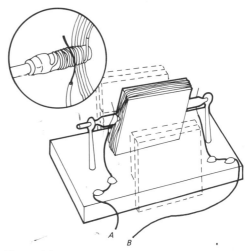

Figure 23.65

(a) Describe the movement of the galvanometer needle when the coil is turned slowly by hand.

(b) It is said that this movement of the galvanometer is due to 'electromagnetic induction'. Explain what this means.

(c) Suggest two changes in the construction of the apparatus which will result in a greater deflection of the galvanometer needle. Explain.

(d) Suggest what will happen to the movement of the needle if the speed of rotation is made greater and greater.

(e) The two leads are now connected to a CRO in place of the galvanometer and the coil is rotated. Describe what would be observed

(i) if the time base were off,

(ii) if the time base were on.

A student claims that the apparatus can also be used as a motor.

(f) What will happen if it is connected to a d.c. supply? Explain.

(g) What will happen if it is connected to an a.c. supply? Explain.

(h) Explain what might happen in (f) and (g) if the coil were rewound with a greater length of thinner wire.

(O&C Nov 1982)

19. (a) Graph A in Figure 23.66 shows how the e.m.f. produced by a simple dynamo varies with time.

Graphs B and C show how the e.m.f. produced by the same dynamo varies with time after certain alterations and modifications have been made.

(i) How many revolutions has the coil of the dynamo made in the time interval OT on graph A?

(ii) What is the frequency of the alternating e.m.f. as shown by graph A?

(iii) Which letters on graph A correspond to the plane of coil of the dynamo being parallel to the magnetic field?

(iv) Explain why the e.m.f. at Q is zero.

(v) What alteration has been made for the dynamo to produce the e.m.f. represented by graph B?

(vi) What modification has been made to the dynamo for it to produce the e.m.f. represented by graph C? Illustrate your answer with sketches showing the original and the modified arrangements.

(b) A dynamo is driven by a 5 kg mass which falls at a steady speed of 0.8 m s. The current produced is supplied to a 12 W lamp which glows with normal brightness. Calculate the efficiency of this arrangement.

(London Jan 1982)

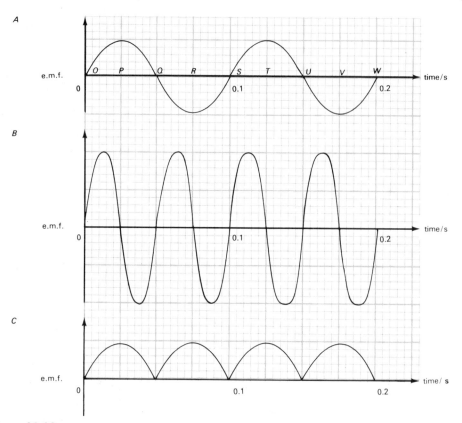

Figure 23.66

202

20. Figure 23.67 shows a simple experimental set-up to study the induced current in a wire moving in a magnetic field.
    (a) Draw a diagram to indicate the directions of motion of the wire, of the magnetic field and of the induced current (if any)
        (i) if the wire is moving quickly upwards.
        (ii) if the wire is moving quickly sideways towards the north pole.
        Describe briefly what happens to the galvanometer pointer in each case.
    (b) State THREE methods of increasing the induced current in the experiment.
                                                 (HKCEE 1985)

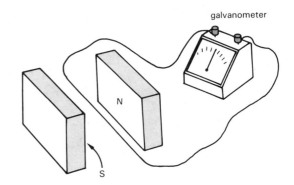

Figure 23.67

21. A lamp X marked '12 V 24 W' and a switch S are connected with long conducting wires to a 12 V battery with negligible internal resistance when it is used in a lighting system as shown in Figure 23.68. The total resistance of the conducting wires is 1.2 Ω.
    (a) Find the resistance of lamp X.
    (b) Draw a circuit diagram representing the lighting system shown in Figure 23.68.
    (c) Find
        (i) the current passing through lamp X, and
        (ii) the power dissipated by lamp X.
        Explain briefly why the power dissipated is not equal to 24 W as marked on the lamp.
    (d) If lamp X is replaced by another lamp Y marked '200 V 24 W' and the battery is replaced by a 200 V supply, would lamp Y become brighter than lamp X? Explain briefly.
                                                 (HKCEE 1985)

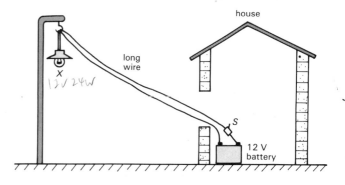

Figure 23.68

22. Figure 23.69 shows an arrangement to study the input and output characteristics of a transformer. The readings of the ammeters and voltmeters are as follows:
    Reading of A_1 = 2.5 A
    Reading of A_2 = 1.8 A.
    Reading of V_1 = 12 V.
    Reading of V_2 = 2 V.
    (a) Calculate
        (i) the power input,
        (ii) the power output, and
        (iii) the efficiency
        of the transformer.

    (b) If R is replaced by another resistor of higher resistance, how would the reading of the ammeter
        (i) A_1, and
        (ii) A_2
        change?
    (c) Suggest TWO changes in the transformer which will improve its efficiency. In each case, give ONE reason to support your suggestion.
                                                 (HKCEE 1987)

Figure 23.69

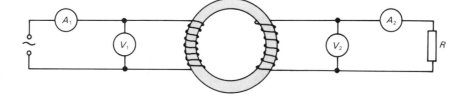

Electronics  **24**

Electronics has become an important part of modern life and everyone should know something about it, even only at an elementary level. We shall first study the cathode ray oscilloscope and the TV. We shall then look at a number of simple electronic devices and logic gates and find out how these can be put together to do useful jobs.

THE ELECTRON

Discovery of the electron

Towards the end of last century, experiments were carried out to study the conduction of electricity through a gas at a very low pressure. It was found that when an extra high voltage was applied across two electrodes in a tube in which air had been removed (Figure 24.1), the cathode (negative electrode) seemed to emit rays. These rays caused a green fluorescence where they struck the glass wall. The rays were then called **cathode rays**. Later, however, through a series of experiments, it was established that cathode rays were in fact streams of fast-moving negatively charged particles. These particles were considered to be present in all atoms and were called **electrons**. The discovery of the electron marked a turning point in physics and led to great technological advances.

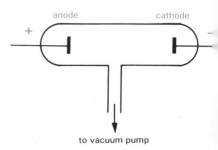

Figure 24.1 A discharge tube: cathode rays are emitted from the cathode when an extra-high voltage is applied across the electrodes and air has been removed from the tube.

Thermionic emission

Nowadays, electrons are usually produced by passing a current through a tungsten filament in a vacuum, heating it to white hot. Electrons are emitted from the tungsten surface as they gain enough energy to escape to the surrounding space. This is called **thermionic emission**.

Figure 24.2 shows a **diode tube** for demonstrating thermionic emission. The tube contains two electrodes each in the form of a small metal disc. The anode is connected to the positive terminal of a 400 V d.c. power supply via a milliammeter and the cathode is connected to the negative terminal. The cathode has a tungsten filament which is heated by a 6 V d.c. supply. Air has been removed from the tube so that the electrons emitted are free to move without colliding with air molecules.

diode 二極管   thermionic emission 熱離子發射

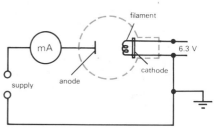

Figure 24.2 A thermionic diode tube.

When the diode tube is connected up as shown and the filament is heated, a small current flows through the circuit. The white hot filament emits electrons which are attracted towards the anode (Figure 24.3) and so bridge the gap between the anode and the cathode in the tube.

If the filament is not heated, no current flows through the circuit. If the filament is heated but the connections to the supply are reversed to make the anode negative, again no current flows. This is because the emitted electrons are now repelled by the anode and so cannot reach it. Hence, a diode tube can conduct only in one direction.

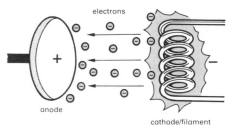

Figure 24.3 Electrons emitted by the white hot filament are attracted towards the anode.

Electron beam in magnetic and electric fields

An electron beam can be made to pass through a magnetic and an electric field to find out the effects on it. Figure 24.4a shows a **Maltese cross tube** in which a wide beam of electrons casts a shadow of a cross on a fluorescent screen. When a magnet is brought near the tube, the shadow changes position (Figure 24.4b). This shows that an electron beam can be deflected

Figure 24.4
(a) The shadow of Maltese cross on the screen.
(b) The electron beam deflected by a magnetic field.

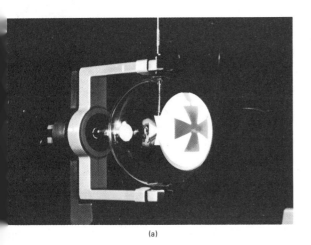

(a)

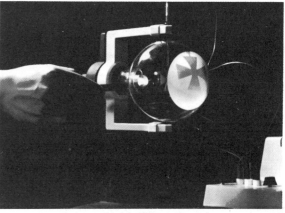

(b)

Maltese cross tube 馬爾塔十字管

by a magnetic field. The direction of deflection indicates that the electron carries a negative charge. Figure 24.5 shows a **deflection tube** in which a fine electron beam is bent as it passes through an electric field. This shows that an electron beam can also be deflected by an electric field.

The property that an electron beam can readily be deflected by a magnetic and an electric field is used in the cathode ray oscilloscope and the TV.

CATHODE RAY OSCILLOSCOPE

The cathode ray oscillocope (Figure 24.6) or CRO for short, is a very useful instrument for studying electric and electronic circuits. It consists of a **cathode ray tube** and some complex electronic circuits which control the movement and brightness of an electron beam inside the tube.

The cathode ray tube (Figure 24.7) has three main parts:

(a) *Electron gun.* This produces a fine electron beam which appears as a bright spot on the screen. It consists of a filament, a cathode, two anodes and another electrode called the grid. The grid is kept at a negative potential which can be varied by the **intensity** control on the front panel of the CRO. It controls the number of electrons passing through it and so changes the brightness of the spot on the screen.

The two anodes are kept at different positive potentials. When the **focus** control is varied, the p.d. between the anodes is changed and this brings the electron beam to a sharp focus on the screen.

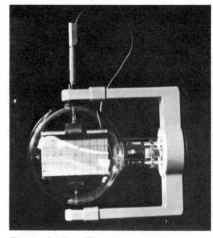

Figure 24.5 The electron beam deflected by an electric field.

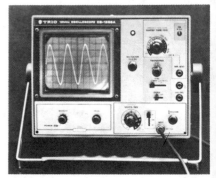

Figure 24.6 A cathode ray oscilloscope (CRO).

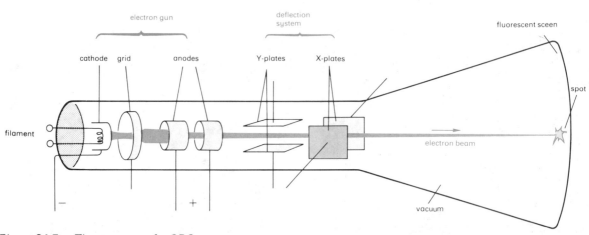

Figure 24.7 The structure of a CRO.

deflection tube 偏轉管   cathode ray 陰極射線   cathode ray oscilloscope 示波器   focus 聚焦   intensity 亮度

(b) *Deflection system.* This consists of two sets of parallel plates which deflect the electron beam when a voltage is applied across them. The **Y-plates** deflects the beam vertically whereas the **X-plates** deflects it horizontally.

(c) *Fluorescent screen.* This is at the wide end of the tube and is coated with a fluorescent material on the inside glass surface. The screen glows where an electron beam strikes it.

Vertical deflection

Figure 24.8 shows how the spot on the screen of the CRO is affected when different voltages are applied to the Y-plates (with zero voltage across the X-plates).

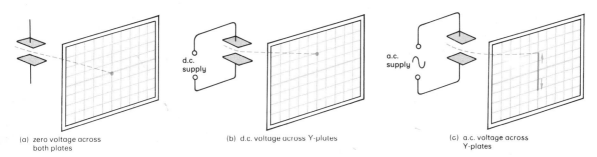

(a) zero voltage across both plates

(b) d.c. voltage across Y-plates

(c) a.c. voltage across Y-plates

Figure 24.8 Applying various voltages across the Y-plates.

With zero voltage across the Y-plates (Figure 24.8a), the spot is at the centre of the screen. When a steady d.c. voltage is applied as in Figure 24.8b, the electron beam is deflected upwards towards the positive plate, and as a result the spot moves upwards on the screen. Reversing the connections of the voltage source to the Y-plates produces a downward deflection. The magnitude of the deflection of the spot is directly proportional to the applied voltage.

When an a.c. voltage of frequency 50 Hz is applied to the Y-plates (Figure 24.8c), the spot oscillates up and down 50 times per second. The oscillation is so rapid that a continuous vertical line appears on the screen.

Voltages are normally applied to the Y-plates via a built-in amplifier in the CRO. This allows the voltage to be amplified to a level which will produce a suitable deflection on the screen. The **gain control** on the front panel can be set to provide different degrees of amplification to the input voltage.

The gain control is usually calibrated in V/cm or mV/cm. A gain of, for example, 2 V/cm means that for every 2 volts applied across the input terminal of the CRO, a 1 cm vertical deflection is produced.

Y-plates Y-板   X-plates X-板   gain control 增益控制

Horizontal deflection: time base

A varying voltage from a built-in circuit, called the **time base**, is normally applied to the X-plates of the CRO. This makes the spot move across the screen from left to right at a steady speed (Figure 24.9), then 'fly back' very rapidly to its starting point and repeat the sweep motion. Figure 24.10 shows how this applied voltage varies with time.

An a.c. voltage applied to the Y-plates makes the spot oscillate up and down. If the time base voltage is also applied to the X-plates, the spot is, at the same time, made to sweep steadily across the screen. The combined effect of the two motions produces a *waveform* of the applied a.c. voltage as shown in Figure 24.11. If a pencil is moved up and down on a piece of paper, pulling the pencil across the paper at the same time will produce a similar waveform (Figure 24.12).

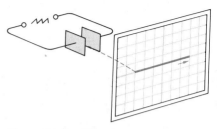

Figure 24.9 Time base sweeps spots steadily across the screen.

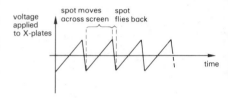

Figure 24.10 How the time base voltage varies with time.

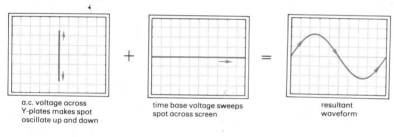

Figure 24.11 How a wave form is displayed on a CRO.

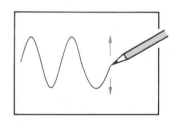

Figure 24.12 Moving a pencil up and down while pulling it sideways produces a similar waveform.

A waveform is traced as the spot sweeps across the screen. The spot flies back to its starting point and traces a new waveform, and the process is repeated, often hundreds or thousands of times per second. The new waveform must be adjusted so that it *exactly* overlaps the previous one, otherwise the image on the screen will not be stationary. The adjustment is often carried out automatically by setting an appropriate sweep speed using the **time base control**.

The time base control is normally calibrated in s/cm, ms/cm or μs/cm. This gives the time required for the spot to sweep 1 cm horizontally across the screen.

USE OF CRO

Waveform display

CROs are widely used for displaying waveforms of alternating voltages to show how they vary with time. Sound waveforms can be displayed by connecting a microphone to the input

time base 時基

terminal of the CRO. The waveform of the **body pick-up** is shown if the CRO input cable is held in the hand (Figure 24.13). This is a distorted sine wave due to an alternating voltage of frequency 50 Hz induced in the human body by the mains electricity. The waveform disappears if the other hand touches the earth plug or the metal case of the CRO.

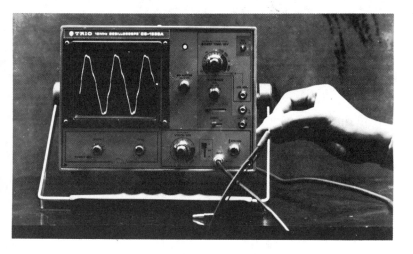

Figure 24.13 Displaying body pick-up on a CRO.

Measuring voltage

As the deflection of the spot is directly proportional to the voltage applied to the input terminals, a CRO can be used as a voltmeter. In fact, it is a very good voltmeter because it has a very high internal resistance, usually of the order of megaohms.

To measure a steady d.c. voltage, the time base is usually switched off, and so it is the spot which is deflected (Figure 24.14a). Or the time base may be switched on to *any* high sweep speed to obtain a horizontal line (Figure 24.14b) and the d.c. voltage is then used to deflect this line rather than the spot. The latter method is preferred because it avoids the concentration of the electron beam to a point which, after a prolonged period of time, may wear off the fluorescent material on the screen.

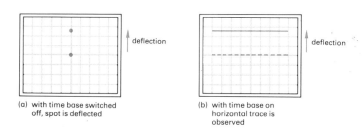

(a) with time base switched off, spot is deflected

(b) with time base on horizontal trace is observed

Figure 24.14 Measuring the d.c. voltage with a CRO.

To measure an a.c. voltage, the time base is switched off so that the displayed waveform is turned into a vertical line (Figure 24.15). The amplitude of the waveform can then be measured readily from the scales on the screen and the **peak voltage** can be calculated from this amplitude.

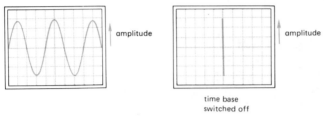

amplitude

amplitude

time base
switched off

Figure 24.15 Measuring the a.c. voltage with a CRO.

Example 1

The CRO gain control is set at 2 V/cm. If the horizontal trace is deflected upwards by 3 cm (Figure 24.16), what is the unknown voltage applied to the input terminals of the CRO?

> Gain control setting is 2 V/cm. This means for every 2 V applied, the trace is deflected vertically by 1 cm.

⇒ Unknown voltage = 3 cm × 2 V/cm = 6 V

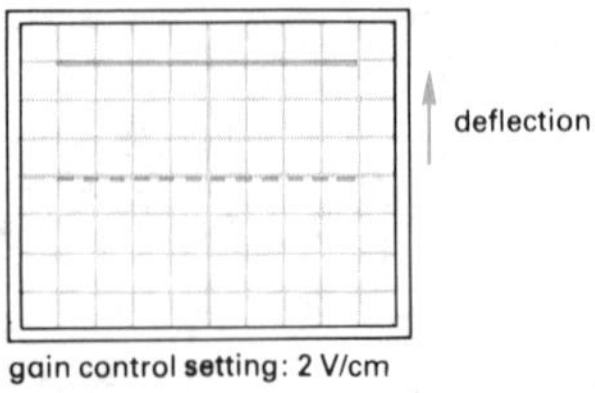

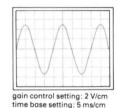

deflection

gain control setting: 2 V/cm

Figure 24.16

Example 2

Figure 24.17 shows the waveform produced on the CRO screen when an a.c. supply is connected to the input terminals. If the gain control is set to 2 V/cm, calculate the peak voltage of the a.c. supply.

> Amplitude of the waveform = 2.5 cm

⇒ Peak voltage   = 2.5 cm × 2 V/cm = 5 V

> The a.c. supply has a peak voltage of 5 V.

gain control setting: 2 V/cm
time base setting: 5 ms/cm

Figure 24.17

Measuring frequency

The frequency of an a.c. voltage can be found by measuring the horizontal distance occupied by the waveform on the CRO screen.

Example 3

If the time base control of the CRO in Figure 24.17 is set to 5 ms/cm, calculate the frequency of the a.c. supply. How is the waveform affected if the time base is set to a higher sweep speed, 2 ms/cm? Sketch the new waveform.

> Time base control is set to 5 ms/cm. This means the spot sweeps 1 cm horizontally in 5 ms.

> On the screen,

> width of 2.5 complete waves = 10 cm

peak voltage 峯值電壓

⇒ Width of 1 complete wave = 4 cm

⇒ Time taken to trace out 1 complete wave

$$= \text{period of the wave}$$
$$= 4 \text{ cm} \times 5 \text{ ms/cm} = 20 \text{ ms}$$
$$= 0.02 \text{ s}$$

⇒ Frequency of the wave $= \dfrac{1}{\text{period}} = \dfrac{1}{0.02 \text{ s}} = 50 \text{ Hz}$

The frequency of the a.c. supply is 50 Hz.

Time base setting is changed to 2 ms/cm.

Time taken to trace out 1 complete wave is 20 ms (from above).

⇒ Horizontal distance occupied by 1 complete wave in the new time base setting

$$= \dfrac{20 \text{ ms}}{2 \text{ ms/cm}} = 10 \text{ cm}$$

Hence 1 wave occupies the full width of the screen. The new waveform is shown in Figure 24.18.

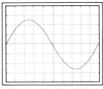

gain control setting: 2 V/cm
time base setting: 2 ms/cm

Figure 24.18

TELEVISION

A television receiver is basically a modified form of CRO, but it uses magnetic coils rather than parallel metal plates to deflect the electron beam and has two time base circuits. The horizontal or **line** time base sweeps the spot across the screen; the vertical or **frame** time base moves it down the screen at a much slower speed. The spot therefore 'draws' a series of horizontal lines (Figure 24.19) which cover the screen (625 lines in the Hong Kong system). For a black and white television set, the spot varies in brightness from white through grey to black as it travels over the screen, and this produces the picture (Figure 24.20). The brightness of the spot is controlled by the incoming signals from the aerial. The screen displays 25 still pictures per second which, due to persistence of vision, appear as a series of progressing animated pictures.

A colour television tube has three electron guns each producing an electron beam which scans the screen. The screen is coated with many tens of thousands of phosphor strips as shown in Figure 24.21 and these emit red or green or blue light when struck by an electron beam. A perforated metal plate called a **shadow mask** is accurately positioned behind the screen so that each electron beam is allowed to strike strips of one colour only. That is, one beam strikes only the red strips, another only the green strips and the third one only the blue strips. As a

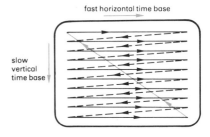

fast horizontal time base

slow vertical time base

Figure 24.19 The spot 'draws' 625 lines on the TV screen.

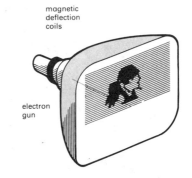

magnetic deflection coils

electron gun

Figure 24.20 As the spot sweeps the TV screen, it varies its brightness from white through grey to black.

result, separate red, green and blue pictures are produced which overlap, one on top of the other, and give a full colour picture.

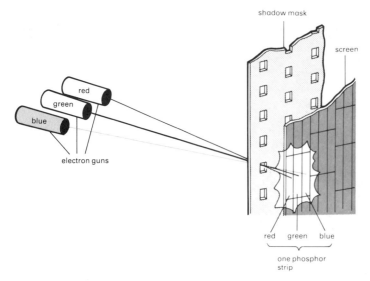

shadow mask

screen

red

green

blue

electron guns

red   green   blue

one phosphor strip

Figure 24.21   A full-colour picture on the TV screen is formed by the overlapping of separate red, green and blue pictures.

The **full-colour outdoor video display system** installed at the Happy Valley Race Course (Figure 24.22) works on a different principle and does not use an electron beam to scan the screen. The screen (Figure 24.23), which is 7.2 m high and 19.5 m wide, the largest of its type in the world, consists of an array of 28 000 separate red, green and blue cathode ray tubes. One red, one blue and two green tubes together form a display point on the screen. Two green tubes are used so as to enable the screen image to be seen clearly in full daylight. When the video display system accepts signals from, for example, a video camera, a computer controls and adjusts the brightness of the different colour tubes which together produce a colour image on the screen. The system can provide live broadcast of the race, instant replays, close-ups of actions and many other special features.

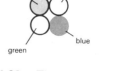

19.5 m

red

green

green

blue

Figure 24.23   The screen is made up of 28 000 red, green and blue cathode ray tubes.

Figure 24.22   The race as seen on the full colour outdoor video display system at the Happy Valley Race Course.

SOME USEFUL ELECTRONIC DEVICES

The electronic devices considered below are all treated as 'black-boxes'. It is not necessary to understand details of their internal construction but we should know something about their behaviour and how they can be put to useful applications.

Semiconductor diode

Previously, diodes were mainly of the thermionic type, but now they are mostly made from semiconducting materials of silicon or germanium. Figure 24.24 shows several semiconductor diodes and the circuit symbol. They have advantages over the thermionic diodes in that they are small in size and do not consume much energy.

If a diode is connected up in the *forward* direction in a circuit, a current flows (Figure 24.25a); if it is in the *reverse* direction, no current flows (Figure 24.25b). The arrowhead of the symbol for diode indicates the direction of the conventional current. A diode can be built into, for example, a moving-coil meter, to allow current to flow in one direction only through the meter but not the other. This protects the meter from damage by wrong connection.

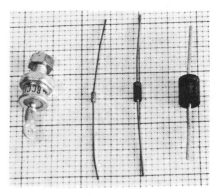

Figure 24.24a   Some semiconductor diodes.

Figure 24.24b   The circuit symbol of a diode.

Figure 24.25   A diode conducts only when it is connected in the forward direction.

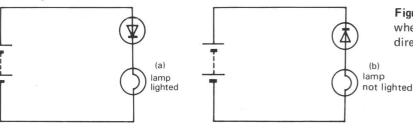

(a) lamp lighted

(b) lamp not lighted

Converting a.c. to d.c.

The one-way conducting property of the diode can be used for converting an a.c. to a d.c., a process called **rectification**. Figure 24.26 shows how a diode is used as a **rectifier**. The resistor represents a load to which a d.c. has to be supplied. The output waveform across the load is <u>the *positive* half cycles of</u> the input a.c. waveform <u>and represents a *varying d.c.* This is because the</u> <u>negative half cycles of the a.c. cannot pass through the diode</u>. This is called **half-wave** rectification.

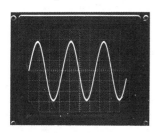
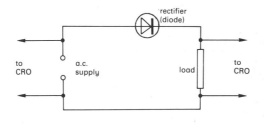
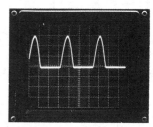

rectifier (diode)

to CRO

a.c. supply

load

to CRO

Figure 24.26   The half-wave rectification.

semiconductor diode 半導體二極管   rectifier 整流器   half-wave rectification 半波整流

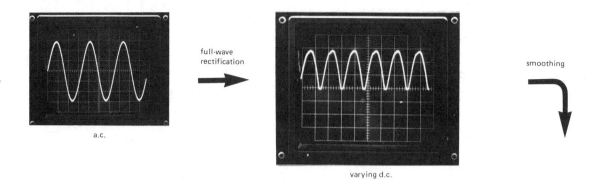

a.c.   full-wave rectification   varying d.c.   smoothing

steady d.c.

Figure 24.27   The full-wave rectification and smoothing of current.

Half-wave rectification is wasteful of electrical power and circuits can be designed to provide **full-wave** rectification (Figure 24.27). After the rectification, the *varying d.c.* is usually further changed to a *steady d.c.,* like that from a battery, before it is supplied to an electrical appliance. This is called **smoothing**. Full-wave rectification and smoothing are too difficult to be explained here.

Use of rectifiers

Electrical appliances such as electronic calculators, radios, hi-fi sets, etc., are designed to operate from a d.c. supply. If they are to be used on the mains, an a.c. adaptor (Figure 24.28) has to be used. This a.c. adaptor steps down the a.c. mains to the appropriate voltage, rectifies and smooths it before supplying to the appliance.

Figure 24.28   An a.c. adaptor used for an electronic calculator.

The traction motors on a MTR train are d.c. motors which operate at 1 500 V d.c. The MTR takes power from the power companies at 33 kV a.c. and redistributes it at 11 kV a.c.

full-wave rectification 全波整流   smoothing 濾波

Transformer/rectifier substations (Figure 24.29) are built at various points along the MTR line for converting the 11 kV a.c. to 1 500 V d.c. This is transmitted via overhead cables to the trains to power the traction motors. Each substation supplies power to a section of the MTR line to minimize power loss in transmission by d.c. On the train, there is an alternator coupled to the tractor motor. This supplies 240 V a.c. for lighting and 440 V a.c. for air-conditioning on the train.

Figure 24.29 The rectifiers at MTRC Kowloon Bay Station.

Figure 24.30 The overhead cables transmit power at 25 kV a.c. to the KCR electrified train.

Figure 24.31 The rectifier used at the telephone exchange.

The electrified KCR trains use the same traction motors as those on the MTR trains. However, power is transmitted to the train by overhead cables at 25 kV a.c. (Figure 24.30). Transformers and rectifiers are installed on the train to convert the a.c. to 1 500 V d.c. KCR transmits power by a.c. rather than by d.c. to minimize power loss in the overhead cables which extend from Hunghom to Lo Wu.

The Hong Kong Telephone Company also uses d.c. supply extensively. It takes power from the power companies at 346 V a.c. (Figure 24.31) and converts it to -50 V d.c. for the underground telephone cables.

Light emitting diode (LED)

The light emitting diode (Figure 24.32), or LED for short, is a diode which emits light when current flows through it in

Figure 24.32a A light emitting diode (LED).

Figure 24.32b The circuit symbol of an LED.

light emitting diode (LED) 發光二極管

the forward direction. <u>The intensity of light depends on the magnitude of the current</u>. An LED may be damaged if too large a current flows through it. The LED module shown in Figure 24.33 has a resistor in series with it to limit the current.

Figure 24.33a   An LED module.

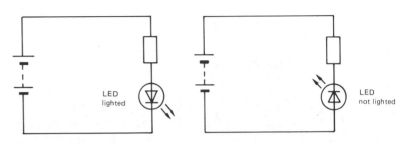

Figure 24.33b   An LED conducts only when it is connected in the forward direction.

LEDs are used in electronic circuits as indicators to show that a current is flowing. Two LED modules may be connected up as shown in Figure 24.34 as a polarity indicator for batteries. Seven-segment LEDs are widely used as numerical displays in calculators, clocks, cash registers, measuring instruments, etc. Each segment is an LED and depending on which segment has a current through it, the display lights up the numbers 0 to 9 (Figure 24.35).

Figure 24.35   A seven-segment LED display.

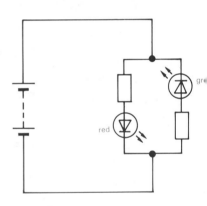

Figure 24.34   A polarity indicator for batteries.

<u>Light dependent resistor</u> (LDR)

A light dependent resistor (Figure 24.36), or LDR for short, is made of cadmium sulphide and its resistance varies with the intensity of light falling on it. <u>In the dark, an LDR has a high resistance</u>; <u>in bright light, its resistance falls to a low value</u>. LDRs are sometimes called **photocells** since it is sensitive to light.

Figure 24.36a   The circuit symbol of an LDR.

Figure 24.36b   A light dependent resistor (LDR).

light dependent resistor (LDR) 光敏電阻   photocells 光電管

When the LDR in the circuit in Figure 24.37 is covered, its resistance is so large that the LED is not lighted. When the LDR is uncovered, its resistance falls and the current through the circuit is large enough to make the LED emit light. LDRs are used in various types of light-operated circuits and in photographic exposure and light meters.

Phototransistor as a photo cell

A phototransistor (Figure 24.38) is a semiconductor device which is sensitive to light. It may be used as a photocell if only the two of its terminals, the *emitter* and the *collector*, are used while the third terminal, the *base*, is left unconnected (Figure 24.39). Used in this way, the phototransistor, like the LDR, has a high resistance in the dark and a low resistance in bright light. Phototransistors are widely used in light-operated circuits.

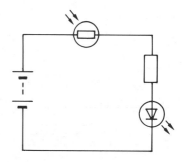

Figure 24.37   An LED is only lit when the LDR is illuminated by light.

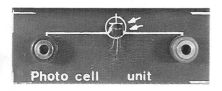

Figure 24.38a   A phototransistor used as a photo cell.

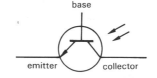

Figure 24.38b   The circuit symbol of a phototransistor.

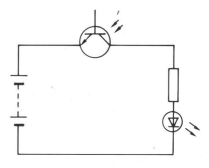

Figure 24.39   An LED is lighted only when the phototransistor is illuminated by light.

Thermistor → opposite to resistor

A thermistor (Figure 24.40) is made of a semiconducting metallic oxide and has a resistance which decreases as its temperature rises. In the circuit shown in Figure 24.41, the LED is not lighted when the thermistor is cold. Warming the thermistor reduces its resistance and allows a large enough current to flow to make the LED emit light. Thermistors are used in heat-operated circuits and in electronic thermometers.

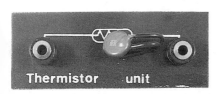

Figure 24.40a   A thermistor.

Figure 24.40b   The circuit symbol of a thermistor.

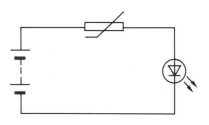

Figure 24.41   An LED is lighted only when the thermistor is warmed.

phototransistor 光電晶體管   thermistor 熱敏電阻

Reed switch

The reed switch (Figure 24.42) consists of two metal contacts, called the reeds, inside a glass envelope. The contacts are normally open and are made of materials which can easily be magnetised and demagnetised. To prevent corrosion of the contacts, the glass envelope is filled with an inert gas.

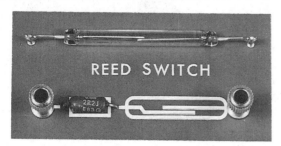

Figure 24.42   A reed switch.

When a magnet is brought close to a reed switch in a circuit as shown in Figure 24.43, the contacts are magnetised and attract each other. As a result, the reed switch closes and the buzzer sounds. On removing the magnet, the reed switch opens and the buzzer stops.

A reed switch can be used as a burglar alarm in the circuit as shown in Figure 24.44. When the door is closed, the magnet in the door cancels the effect of the fixed magnet in the door frame and the reed switch opens. When the door is opened, the fixed magnet closes the reed switch so that the alarm will sound if the set-alarm switch is closed.

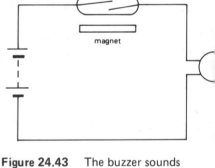

Figure 24.43   The buzzer sounds when a magnet is brought close to the reed switch.

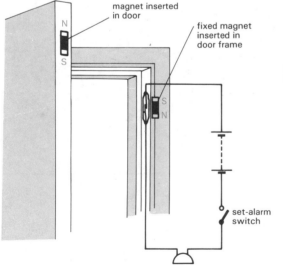

Figure 24.44   A reed switch burglar alarm.

reed switch 簧片開關

Reed relay

A reed relay (Figure 24.45) consists of a reed switch operated by a coil wound around it. When a current passes, the coil magnetises the contacts and the reed switch closes. In the circuit shown in Figure 24.46, the coil of the reed relay is connected to a push switch and a battery and the reed switch is connected to another battery and a motor in a *separate* circuit. When the push switch is pressed, a current flows in the coil and this closes the reed switch. As a result, the motor is operated. If an ammeter is used, it will be found that the current in the motor circuit is much greater than that in the coil circuit. Hence, a small current in one circuit can control another circuit of a much larger current.

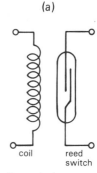

(a)

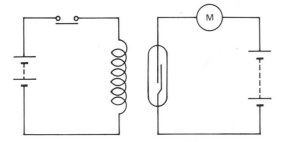

Figure 24.46 A reed relay: a small current in the coil circuit can control a large current in the reed switch circuit.

The circuit has many practical applications, for example, in the starter motor of a car. When the ignition switch of a car is closed, a small current flows in a relay coil and this switches on a much larger current for the starter motor. Serious overheating problems would result if the ignition switch were to operate the starter motor directly.

coil   reed switch

(b) circuit symbol

Figure 24.45 A reed relay module.

Electromagnetic relay

An electromagnetic relay (Figure 24.47) is similar in working principle to the reed relay but it has an L-shaped iron armature instead of a reed switch. When a current flows in the relay coil,

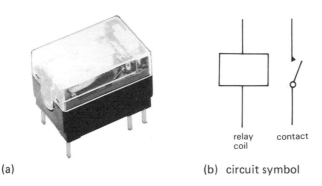

(a)   relay coil   contact   (b) circuit symbol

Figure 24.47 An electromagnetic relay unit.

reed relay 簧片繼電器   electromagnetic relay 繼電器

the armature is magnetised and is attracted to the coil (Figure 24.48). The armature turns about a pivot and closes the metal contacts. If the current stops flowing or falls below a certain value, the armature springs back and opens the contacts.

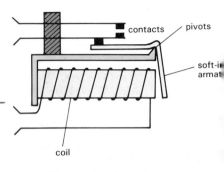

Potential divider

A variable resistor can be used as a potential divider for varying the p.d. applied across a device. In the circuit shown in Figure 24.49, the p.d. applied can vary from zero to the total p.d. of the battery by moving the sliding contact.

A potential divider can also be set up using a fixed resistor and an LDR or a thermistor. The p.d. across the LDR in the circuit shown in Figure 24.50 varies as LDR is covered, uncovered and illuminated by a torch light.

Figure 24.48 A relay: the contacts are closed when a current flows in the coil.

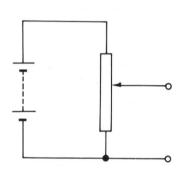

Figure 24.49 A potential divider built from a variable resistor.

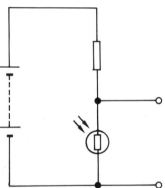

Figure 24.50 A potential divider built from a fixed resistor and an LDR.

Transistors and integrated circuits

A transistor is a semiconductor device with three terminals called the *emitter*, the *collector* and the *base*. Figure 24.51 shows several types of transistors and the circuit symbol. Since its invention in 1947, the transistor had been a major electronic device for building amplifiers, oscillators, switching circuits, etc.

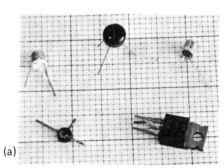

(a)

Figure 24.51 Some transistors.

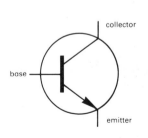

(b) circuit symbol

potential divider 分壓器　　transistor 晶體管　　base 基極　　collector 集電極　　emitter 發射極

In recent years, advances in semiconductor technology have made it possible to fabricate many transistors, diodes, resistors and other circuit components all on a small, thin layer of silicon. This silicon chip is called an **integrated circuit** (Figure 24.52), or IC for short, since it is a self-contained complete circuit. ICs are now widely used in place of transistors.

Figure 24.52a The production of integrated circuits in an electronics factory at the Tai Po Industrial Estate, N.T.

Figure 24.52b Some locally produced ICs.

LOGIC GATES

Modern electronics is about computers and computer controls. The basic building bricks of the computer are the logic gates. A logic gate is a switching circuit which can have a high or a low voltage at its output depending on the combination of voltages at its inputs. It is said to have two states, the *high* and *low* states (or *on* and *off* states). Some electronic devices also have two states, for example, a switch may be closed or open; an LED may be lighted or unlighted; a relay may be on or off; a buzzer may sound or not sound, and so on. These devices, called **digital devices**, can be easily controlled (i.e. switched on or off) by a logic gate or a combination of the gates.

Logic circuits from switches

Logic gates are now mostly made of ICs, but it is useful first to find out how some simple logic gates can be built from switches.

(a) **NOT circuit.** In the circuit shown in Figure 24.53, when the switch is closed the LED is off, and when it is open, the LED is on. A closed switch is considered to be at a high state and an open switch is at a low state. The behaviour of the NOT circuit can be summarized by the **truth table** below. The symbol for the NOT circuit is also given.

Switch A	LED
closed	off
open	on

Symbol

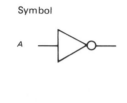

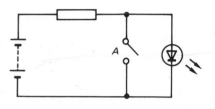

Figure 24.53   A NOT circuit switch.

The state of the LED is an *inversion* of the state of the switch.

(b) **AND circuit.** Two switches connected up as shown in Figure 24.54 form an AND circuit. The following is the truth table for the circuit and the symbol for the AND circuit.

Switch A	Switch B	LED
open	open	off
open	closed	off
closed	open	off
closed	closed	on

Symbol

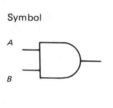

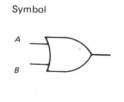

Figure 24.54   AND circuit switches.

The LED is on when both switch A *AND* switch B are closed.

(c) **OR circuit.** Two switches connected up as shown in Figure 24.55 form an OR circuit. The following is the truth table for the circuit and the symbol for the OR circuit.

Switch A	Switch B	LED
open	open	off
open	closed	on
closed	open	on
closed	closed	on

Symbol

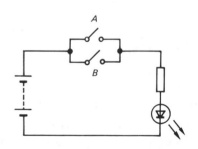

The LED is on when either switch A *OR* switch B is closed (or when both are closed).

Figure 24.55   OR circuit switches.

truth table 真值表

(d) **NAND circuit.** Two switches connected up as shown in Figure 24.56 form a NAND circuit. The following is the truth table for the circuit and the symbol for the NAND circuit.

Switch A	Switch B	LED
open	open	on
open	closed	on
closed	open	on
closed	closed	off

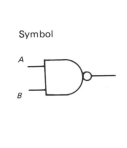

Symbol

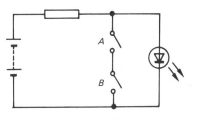

Figure 24.56 NAND circuit switches.

The LED is *NOT* on when both switch A *AND* switch B are closed. Comparing this truth table with that of the AND circuit, it can be seen that the NAND circuit is an inverted AND circuit.

(e) **NOR circuit.** Two switches connected up as shown in Figure 24.57 form a NOR circuit. The following is the truth table for the circuit and the symbol for the NOR circuit.

Switch A	Switch B	LED
open	open	on
open	closed	off
closed	open	off
closed	closed	off

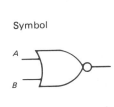

Symbol

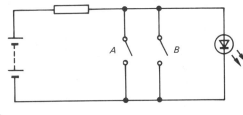

Figure 24.57 NOR circuit switches.

The LED is *NOT* on when either switch A *OR* switch B is closed (or when both are closed). The NOR circuit is an inverted OR circuit.

As an illustration, six switches can be connected up in a circuit as shown in Figure 24.58 to control a motor. The motor will operate when switches U, W and Y are closed, but if any one of the other switches is closed the buzzer will sound.

Figure 24.58 A motor control using switches.

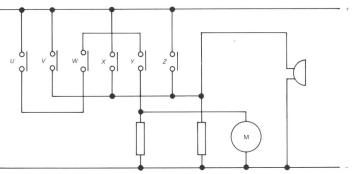

INTEGRATED CIRCUIT LOGIC GATES

ICs specifically designed as logic gates have been produced. These are used for making the logic gate modules for experiments.

NOT gate

Figure 24.59 shows a NOT gate module and its circuit diagram. The two horizontal lines are the positive and negative supply rails across which a power supply has to be connected. A flying

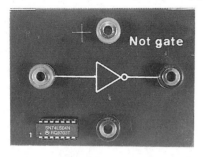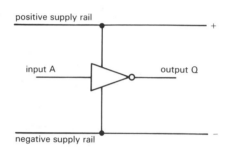

Figure 24.59 A NOT gate module.

lead is plugged into the input of the gate. The other end of the lead can be connected to the positive supply rail to make the input *high* or to the negative supply rail to make it *low* (Figure 24.60). An LED is connected between the output of the gate and the negative supply rail. The LED is lighted if the output is *high* and not lighted if the output is *low*. Note that, to keep the circuit diagram simple, the power supply and the connections of the gate to the supply rails are not shown.

By connecting the input high and low, the truth table for the NOT gate can be worked out. Here 1 stands for 'high' and 0 for 'low'.

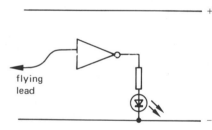

Figure 24.60 A NOT gate: the input can be made high or low by connecting to the positive or negative supply rail.

Truth table for NOT gate:

Input	Output
0	1
1	0

The output is high when the input is *NOT* high. The NOT gate is therefore an *inverter*. If the input is not connected it behaves as if it is high.

Figure 24.61 shows a NOT gate connected up as a fire alarm in a circuit. When the thermistor is cold, its resistance is high and

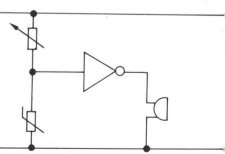

Figure 24.61 A NOT gate application: a fire alarm.

NOT gate 「非」門   integrated circuit 集成電路   inverter 反相器

so the p.d. across it is large. The input to the NOT gate is high and the output is low and so the buzzer does not sound. However, when the thermistor is heated, its resistance decreases and so does the p.d. across it. The input becomes low and the output high and so the buzzer sounds. The variable resistor can be adjusted to change the sensitivity of the circuit.

AND gate

Figure 24.62 shows an AND gate module and its circuit diagram. As before, the two inputs of the AND gate can be made high or low by connecting each to the positive or negative supply rails.

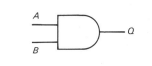
(a)

Truth table for AND gate:

Input A	Input B	Output Q
0	0	0
0	1	0
1	0	0
1	1	1

The output is high when both input A *AND* input B are high.

(b) circuit symbol

Figure 24.62 An AND gate module.

An AND gate can be connected up as a safety thermostat for a water heating system in the circuit shown in Figure 24.63. The thermistor and the contacts are placed near the top of the vessel which holds the water. When the water is cold (input A is high) and the contacts are covered with water (input B is also high), the relay is on and this switches on the heater. The variable resistor can be adjusted to set the temperature at which the heater switches off.

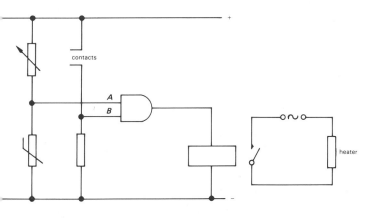

Figure 24.63 An AND gate application: a safety thermostat for water heating system.

AND gate 「與」門

OR gate

Figure 24.64 shows an OR gate module and the circuit diagram. By connecting the inputs high and low, the truth table can be worked out.

Truth table for OR gate:

Input A	Input B	Output Q
0	0	0
0	1	1
1	0	1
1	1	1

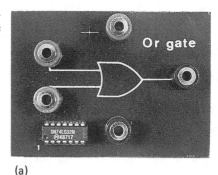

(a)

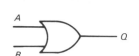

(b) circuit symbol

Figure 24.64 An OR gate module.

The output is high when either input A *OR* input B is high (or when both are high).

Figure 24.65 shows an OR gate connected up in a car door warning signal circuit. The two push switches are each installed on a car door and when either one is open, the input is unconnected and so behaves as if it is high. The output is high and the LED warning light is lighted.

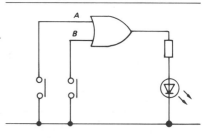

Figure 24.65 An OR gate application: a car door warning signal.

NAND gate

Figure 24.66 shows a quad NAND gate module consisting of four NAND gates on one board, and the circuit diagram for one NAND gate. By connecting the inputs high and low, the truth table can be worked out.

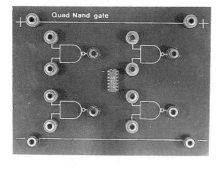

(a)

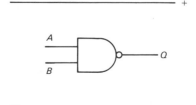

(b) circuit symbol

Figure 24.66 A Quad NAND gate module.

OR gate 「或」門   NAND gate 「與非」門

Truth table for NAND gate:

Input A	Input B	Output Q
0	0	1
0	1	1
1	0	1
1	1	0

The output is *NOT* high when both input A *AND* input B are high. Comparing this truth table with that of the AND gate, it can easily be seen that the NAND gate is an *inverted* AND gate.

Figure 24.67 shows a NAND gate connected up in a circuit for a simple burglar alarm. The buzzer will sound when either the LDR is illuminated (by the burglar's torch) or the switch is closed (by the burglar's foot).

Figure 24.67 A NAND gate application: a simple burglar alarm.

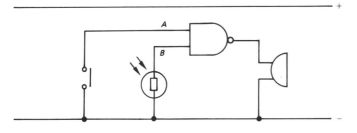

NOR gate

Figure 24.68 shows a NOR gate module and its circuit diagram. By connecting the inputs high and low the truth table can be worked out.

Truth table for NOR gate:

Input A	Input B	Output Q
0	0	1
0	1	0
1	0	0
1	1	0

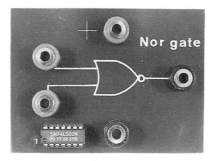

(a)

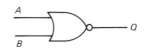

(b) circuit symbol

Figure 24.68 A NOR gate module.

NOR gate 「或非」門

The output in *NOT* high when either input A *OR* input B is high (or when both inputs are high). The NOR gate is an *inverted* OR gate.

Figure 24.69 shows a NOR gate connected up in a circuit for a night-time anti-theft device for cars. This circuit makes it impossible to operate the starter motor of the car at night. The motor would be on only when the ignition switch is pressed (input A is low) and it is day-time (LDR is illuminated, i.e. input B is also low).

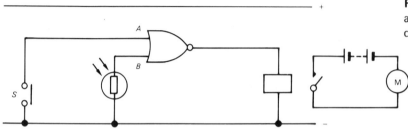

Figure 24.69   A NOR gate application: a night-time anti-theft device for cars.

Combination of gates

It is easy to see that a NAND gate can be built by joining an AND gate to a NOT gate (Figure 24.70) and that similarly a NOR gate can be built by joining an OR gate to a NOT gate (Figure 24.71). In fact, gates are often combined together in various ways for specific purposes.

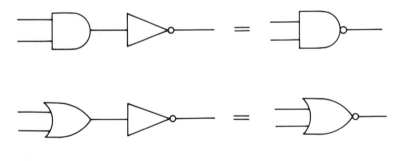

Figure 24.70   AND gate + NOT gate = NAND gate.

Figure 24.71   OR gate + NOT gate = NOR gate.

Example 4

Figure 24.72 shows two NOT gates joined to an AND gate. Find out how the combined circuit behaves by working out its truth table.

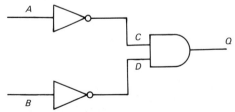

Figure 24.72   The combination of gates: two NOT gates joined to an AND gate is a NOR gate.

228

The truth table can be worked out step by step. In the table below, column C is column A inverted and column D is column B inverted. Columns C and D are the inputs of an AND gate and the output Q can be worked out accordingly.

A	B	C	D	Q
0	0	1	1	1
0	1	1	0	0
1	0	0	1	0
1	1	0	0	0

It can be seen that the combined circuit is in fact a NOR gate.

Some applications also require more than one gate. Figure 24.73 shows a circuit for a street light which turns on automatically when it is dark. The circuit uses a NOT gate joined to one of the inputs of an OR gate. When it is dark, the resistance of the LDR is high, and so is the the p.d. across it. Input A of the OR gate is high and so is the output and the light turns on. The switch connected to input B via a NOT gate is used to turn on the light at any time when so required.

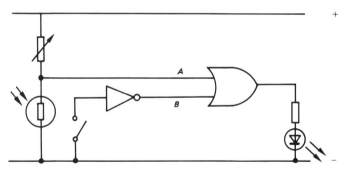

Figure 24.73   An application: an automatic street light.

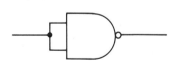

Figure 24.74   A NOT gate from a NAND gate.

NAND gate — a fundamental building brick

Of all the gates, the NAND gate is regarded as a fundamental building brick since all other gates can be built from it. If a NAND gate has its two inputs joined together as one input, it becomes a NOT gate (Figure 24.74). This NOT gate can be joined to a NAND gate to turn it into an AND gate (Figure 24.75). The OR gate and the NOR gate can also be built from NAND gates although the combined circuit is slightly more complex.

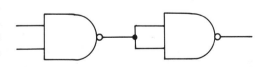

Figure 24.75   An AND gate from two NAND gates.

THE BISTABLE CIRCUIT

Figure 24.76 shows a bistable unit built from two NAND gates. The connections are such that output Q of gate 1 is joined to an input of gate 2 and the output $\overline{Q}$ of gate 2 is joined to an input of gate 1.

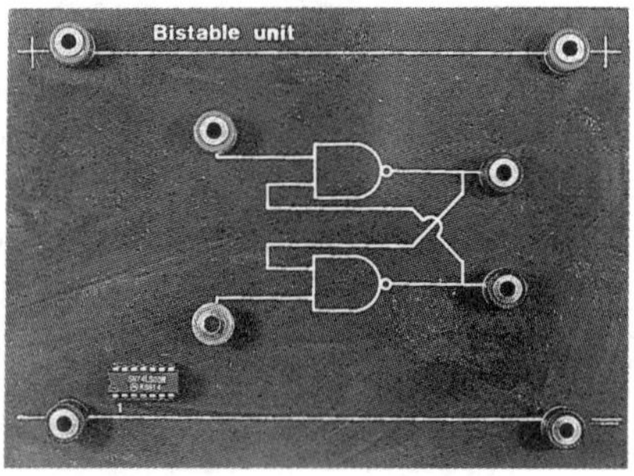

Switching the bistable

To study its behaviour, the bistable unit is connected up as shown in Figure 24.77. The following results are obtained when the RESET and SET switches are pressed in turn.

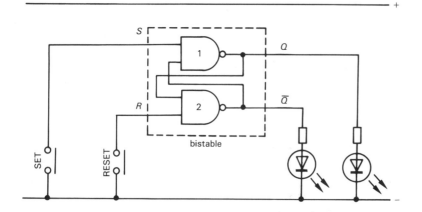

Figure 24.76   A bistable unit.

Figure 24.77   Switching the bistable circuit.

(a)   On pressing and releasing the RESET switch, the output $\overline{Q}$ goes high (LED lighted) and the output Q goes low (LED unlighted). Further depressions of the RESET switch produce no change to the outputs.

(b)   On pressing and releasing the SET switch, the output Q goes high and the output $\overline{Q}$ goes low. This is opposite to that obtained by pressing and releasing the RESET switch. Again, further depressions of the SET switch produce no change to the outputs.

Explaining the two stable states

To explain why the bistable behaves the way it does, consider the circuit initially in a state as shown in Figure 24.78a. When

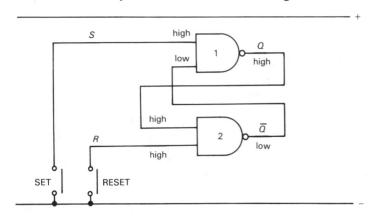

Figure 24.78   Explaining the two stable states.

(a)   Initial state of a bistable,

bistable circuit 雙穩電路

the RESET switch is pressed, the R input of gate 2 is taken low and so the output $\overline{Q}$ goes high. This high output of gate 2 is fed back to an input of gate 1. Both inputs of gate 1 are now high and so the output Q goes low. This low output of gate 1 goes to an input of gate 2. With both inputs of gate 2 low, the output $\overline{Q}$ remains high. This new state is shown in Figure 24.78b. Releasing the RESET switch makes the R input of gate 2 high (an unconnected input behaves as high), but since the other input is low, the output does not change from high. Pressing and releasing the RESET switch further again produces no change.

(b) RESET switch is pressed,

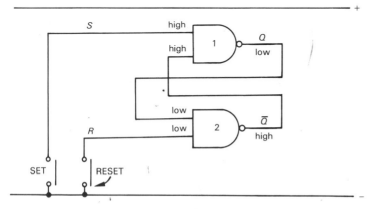

The bistable can be switched to the other state by pressing the SET switch. This takes the S input of gate 1 low and so output Q goes high (Figure 24.78c). Both inputs of gate 2 are high so that output $\overline{Q}$ is low. This low output of gate 2 is fed back to an input of gate 1 and this keeps the output Q high even if the SET switch is released. For the same reason, further depressions of the SET switch produce no change.

(c) SET switch is pressed.

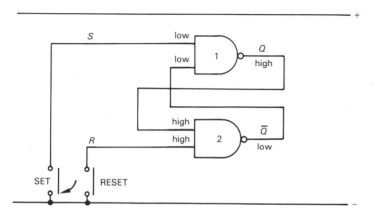

Properties of the bistable circuit

In summary, the bistable has the following properties:

(a) The bistable has two stable states:

the SET state when Q is high and $\overline{Q}$ is low
the RESET state when Q is low and $\overline{Q}$ is high.

(b) On switching on, the bistable will be randomly set to one of its stable states.

(c) To change from the SET state to the RESET state, the R input must be taken momentarily low. If R is taken low again, no change occurs.

(d) To change from the RESET state to the SET state, the S input must be taken momentarily low. If S is taken low again, no change occurs.

(e) When S and R are both high, the state remains unchanged.

(f) When S and R are both low, the circuit has no stable state and this should be avoided.

Truth table of the bistable circuit:

S	R	Q	$\overline{Q}$
1	1	as before	
0	1	1	0
1	0	0	1
0	0	disallowed	

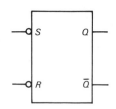

Figure 24.79 The circuit symbol for a bistable.

The bistable is another very useful building brick used in electronic circuits. Its symbol is given in Figure 24.79.

Applications

A burglar alarm can be set up as shown in Figure 24.80 using a bistable, two push switches and a buzzer. In this circuit, when the TRIP switch is pressed (by the burglar's foot), the alarm sounds and cannot be turned off by releasing the switch or by depressing it again. The output is said to be 'latched'. To turn off the alarm, the RESET switch must be pressed. This latched burglar alarm is better than the one built from a NAND gate which is considered earlier. In a practical system, the TRIP switch is contained in a pressure pad and put under a mat or carpet somewhere in the house.

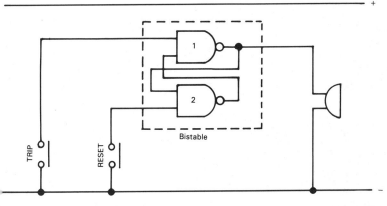

Figure 24.80 A bistable application: a latched burglar alarm.

Figure 24.81 shows the circuit of a 'latched' fire alarm built from a bistable. Once triggered, the alarm will continue to sound until it is reset.

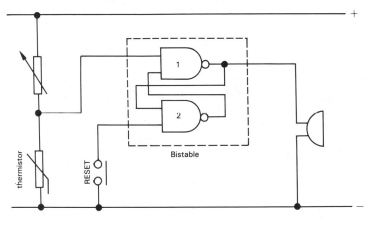

Figure 24.81 A bistable application: a latched fire alarm.

THE IMPACT OF MICROELECTRONICS

Technology in the manufacture of integrated circuits has greatly improved in recent years. The first IC, made in 1958, contained only a handful of components, but now more than one million components can be put on a silicon chip of 5 square millimetres! Not only are ICs incredibly small in size and have a large number of components, they are cheap, very reliable and can be made very complex. Electronics which deals with such small-sized devices is called microelectronics.

The latest development in ICs is the microprocessor (Figure 24.82). This combines the functions of a whole range of ICs and can be programmed to do a wide variety of jobs. The microprocessor forms the heart of the micro-computers (Figure 24.83) which have recently been put to an increasing number of applications: computer games in the home; educational programs in schools; word processing, accounting and database system in the office; operation of robots in factories (Figure 24.84), etc. Microelectronics will very soon drastically change the way we live, work and spend our leisure time.

Figure 24.82 This coin-sized microprocessor contains almost 150 000 transistors.

Figure 24.84 An industrial robot writing Chinese character.

Figure 24.83 A microcomputer.

SUMMARY

Electrons

Electrons are emitted when a tungsten filament is heated to white hot by passing a current through it in a vacuum (thermionic emission). An electron beam can readily be deflected by a magnetic and an electric field.

Cathode ray oscilloscope (CRO)

The CRO consists of 3 main parts:

(a) Electron gun — for producing a fine electron beam sharply focused on the screen.

(b) Deflection plates — time base applied across the X-plates sweeps the electron beam across the screen; voltages applied across the Y-plates are amplified and displayed on the screen.

(c) Fluorescent screen.

Uses: display waveforms, measure voltages (a.c. and d.c.), measure frequency.

Electronic devices

A semiconductor diode is a two-terminal device which conducts when it is connected in the forward direction but not the reverse direction. It is used as a rectifier for changing an *a.c.* to a *d.c.*

A light emitting diode (LED) is a diode which emits light when current passes in the forward direction.

A light dependent resistor (LDR) is a resistor made of cadmium sulphide which decreases its resistance when illuminated by light.

A phototransistor can be converted into a photocell if only two of its terminals, the emitter and the collector, are connected. The photocell decreases its resistance when illuminated by light.

A thermistor is a resistor made of a semiconducting metallic oxide which decreases its resistance when the temperature rises.

A reed switch is a special switch consisting of two metal contacts inside a glass envelope which is closed when magnetised and opened when demagnetised.

A reed relay consists of a reed switch operated by a coil wound around it. A small current in the coil circuit can control a large current in the reed switch circuit.

An electromagnetic relay consists of a coil which attracts an armature and closes two metal contacts when a current passes.

A potential divider provides a variable p.d. from a power supply. It can be set up using a variable resistor or a fixed resistor in series with an LDR or thermistor.

Logic gates

Logic gates are the building bricks of the computer and computer controlled circuits. The output of a gate can be at a high or a low voltage level, depending on the voltage level at the input(s).

NOT gate: its output is high when the input is NOT high.

AND gate: its output is high when both input A AND input B are high.

OR gate: its output is high when either input A OR input B is high (or when both are high).

NAND gate: its output is NOT high when both input A AND input B are high.

NOR gate: its output is NOT high when either input A OR input B is high (or both inputs are high).

The NAND gate is a fundamental gate from which all other gates can be built.

Logic gates and devices can be connected in circuits to do a variety of useful jobs.

Bistable circuit

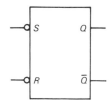

The bistable circuit has two stable states: the SET state (Q high and $\overline{Q}$ low) and the RESET state (Q low and $\overline{Q}$ high). To change from the SET state to the RESET state, the R input must be taken low momentarily; to change from the RESET state to the SET state, the S input must be taken momentarily. The bistable can be used to build 'latched' burglar alarm and 'latched' fire alarm circuits.

PROBLEMS

1. A diode tube is connected in a circuit as in Figure 24.85.
   (a) Name the parts of the diode tube labelled *A*, *K* and *F*.
   (b) What are the functions of the parts *A*, *K* and *F*?
   (c) What are the conditions under which a current will flow through the circuit?

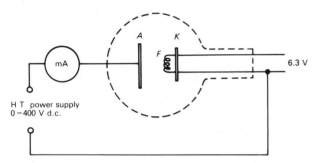

Figure 24.85

2. Figure 24.86 represents the screen and the deflecting plates of a CRO. The time base is switched off and a spot appears at the centre of the screen. By applying different voltages across the X-plates and Y-plates and/or adjusting the controls of the CRO, state how the trace in Figure 24.87a—g can be obtained.

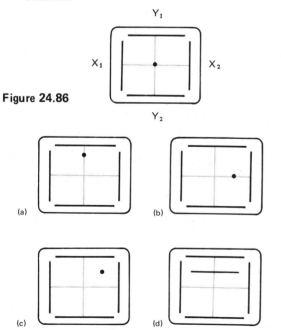

Figure 24.86

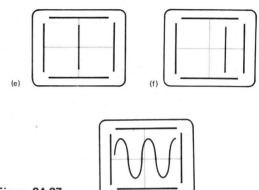

Figure 24.87 (g)

3. Figure 24.88 shows how the time base voltage applied across the X-plates of a CRO varies with time.
   (a) Explain what happens to the spot (i) between points *A* and *B*, and (ii) between points *B* and *C* on the graph.
   (b) Ideally, what should the part *BC* of the graph be like?

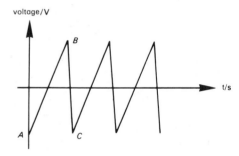

Figure 24.88

4. The time base of a CRO is switched off and a spot appears at the centre of the screen. When a certain voltage is input to the CRO, the spot is deflected up by 3 cm (Figure 24.89).
   (a) What type of voltage is input to the CRO? a.c. or d.c.?
   (b) If the gain control is set at 50 mV/cm, what is the size of the input signal?
   (c) What happens to the spot if the time base is now switched on and set at a certain high sweep time?

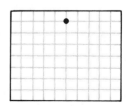

time base switched off
gain at 50 mV/cm

Figure 24.89

5. Figure 24.90 shows the waveform produced on the screen when a certain signal is input to a CRO. If the controls of the CRO are set at 1 ms/cm and 0.2 V/cm, find (i) the frequency and (ii) the peak voltage of the signal.

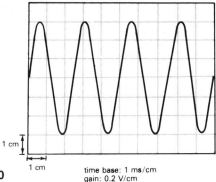

1 cm

1 cm   time base: 1 ms/cm
             gain: 0.2 V/cm

Figure 24.90

6. Figure 24.91 shows the waveform of a certain signal input to a CRO.
   (a) If the controls on the CRO are set at 0.5 V/cm and 2 ms/cm, find (i) the peak voltage and (ii) the frequency of the signal.
   (b) If the gain control is changed to 1 V/cm, how would this affect the trace on the screen? Sketch the trace.
   (c) If the time base control is changed to 5 ms/cm, how would this affect the waveform on the screen? Sketch the trace on the screen.

time base: 2 ms/cm
gain: 0.5 V/cm

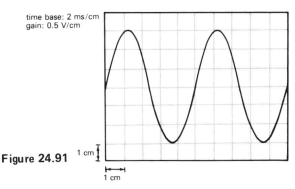

Figure 24.91 1 cm

1 cm

7. (a) Figure 24.92 shows the essential features of a CRO.
   (i) What is the function of the filament F?
   (ii) How is the deflection of the electron beam controlled?
   (iii) A variable voltage is applied to the X-plates to provide a time base for the CRO. Sketch a graph showing how this voltage varies with time.

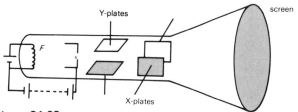

Y-plates   screen

F

X-plates

Figure 24.92

(b) Figure 24.93 shows a square wave displayed on the screen of a CRO with time base set at 1 ms cm^{-1}. What is the frequency of the wave?

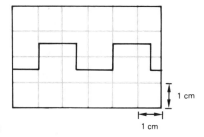

Figure 24.93   1 cm

1 cm

(c) The points P and Q across a 10 Ω resistor in a given circuit are connected to the Y-input of a CRO as shown in Figure 24.94. The CRO is at a sensitivity of 0.5 V cm^{-1}. The line AB on the screen of the CRO is shifted to CD as shown in Figure 24.95 when the connection is made.
   (i) What is the potential difference across PQ?
   (ii) Calculate the resistance of R.

(HKCEE 1978)

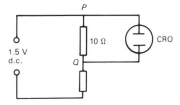

P

1.5 V d.c.   10 Ω   CRO

Q

Figure 24.94

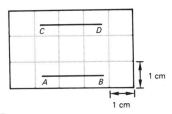

C D

A B 1 cm

1 cm

Figure 24.95

8. (a) The following pieces of apparatus (as shown in Figure 24.96) are provided: an a.c. power supply, a CRO and a transformer.
By means of a diagram, show how you would connect the pieces of apparatus below to display a 10 V a.c. on the CRO.

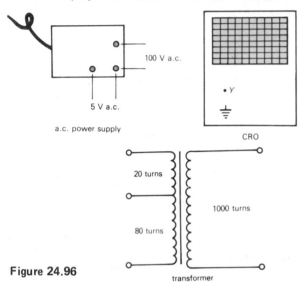

Figure 24.96

(b) If an a.c. signal is input to the CRO with a time base set at 1 ms cm^{-1} and a vertical voltage sensitivity set at 2.5 V cm^{-1}, the wave pattern displayed is shown in Figure 24.97.
   (1) From the wave pattern obtained, estimate the peak voltage of the input signal.
   (2) Estimate the time taken for the spot on the screen to produce one complete cycle.
   (3) What is the frequency of the input signal?
   (4) If the diode is used to rectify the above a.c. signal, sketch the wave pattern that would be displayed on the CRO.
                                        (HKCEE 1982)

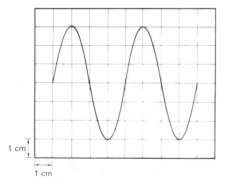

Figure 24.97

9. A semiconductor diode is connected in series with a variable resistance to an a.c. supply as in Figure 24.98. Terminals Y and Z of the variable resistance are connected to the CRO as shown.
   (a) Sketch the trace on the screen when the CRO is set at a suitable time base.
   (b) What happens to the trace if the sliding contact Y of the variable resistance is moved towards X?
   (c) Which terminal of the variable resistor is positive? X or Y?

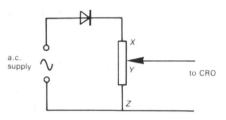

Figure 24.98

10. (a) Figure 24.99 shows some of the important features of a cathode ray tube. State *two* other important features, not indicated, which are necessary if a cathode ray beam is to be produced and observed.
Which part of the tube is known as the *electron gun*? Suggest a reason why it is so called. Explain
   (i) the purpose of S, and how this purpose is achieved,
   (ii) why T is maintained at a high positive potential relative to R,
   (iii) what you would do and expect to observe when using the plates U to determine the sign of the charge on the particles emitted by R.

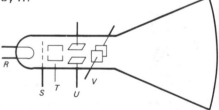

Figure 24.99

(b) A student centralizes the beam of a cathode ray oscilloscope and, with the time base switched *off*, then applies certain potential differences to the instrument. The traces obtained are shown in Figure 24.100a and b. With the time base switched *on*, the student applies potential differences to the instrument. The traces obtained are shown in Figure 24.100c and d.

238

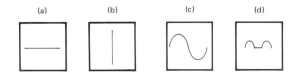

(a)   (b)   (c)   (d)

Figure 24.100

In each case, describe the nature of the potential difference applied and state whether it was applied to the U or the V plates of the tube shown in Figure 24.99.

(London Jan 1983)

11. (a) Using all of the components shown in Figure 24.101, draw a circuit diagram to show an experimental set-up which is used to provide a low d.c. voltage across the load resistor and to display its waveform.
    (b) Sketch the waveform of the output voltage as displayed on the CRO in (i).   (HKCEE 1987)

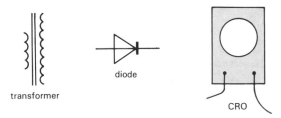

diode

transformer

CRO

high voltage
a.c. source

load
resistor

Figure 24.101

12. Figure 24.102 shows a circuit and a CRO. X_1 and X_2 are cells of the same emf. C is connected periodically to A and B at a steady frequency f. Figure 24.103 shows the trace on the CRO when the time-base is switched on.

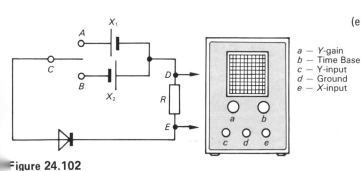

a — Y-gain
b — Time Base
c — Y-input
d — Ground
e — X-input

Figure 24.102

(a) Draw lines on Figure 24.102 to show how D and E should be connected the terminals of the CRO in order to produce a trace on the CRO as shown in Figure 24.104.

(b) Which cell produces the potential difference across R shown in Figure 24.104?

(c) If the Y-gain and the time-base of the CRO are set to be 0.5 V div^{-1} and 2.5 ms div^{-1} respectively, find
    (i) the maximum potential difference across R, and
    (ii) the frequency f
    when the CRO produces a trace as shown in Figure 24.104.

(d) If the diode shown in Figure 24.102 is reversed, sketch in Figure 24.105 the trace on the CRO that would be produced.

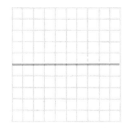

Figure 24.103

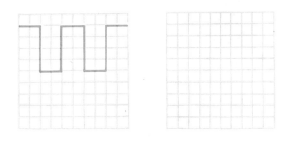

Figure 24.104   **Figure 24.105**

(e) If you are given an electromagnet, a low voltage a.c. supply, an iron strip and the necessary connecting wires, draw a diagram to show how to construct a simple device that would allow C to be connected periodically to A and B at a steady frequency.

(HKCEE 1986)

13. Diodes and lamps are connected up in several different ways in the circuits in Figure 24.106. State which lamp lights and which do not. Explain briefly.

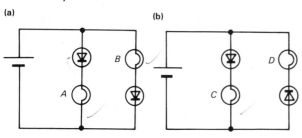

(a) (b)

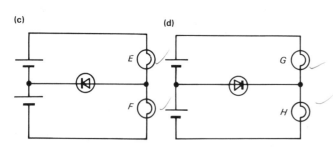

(c) (d)

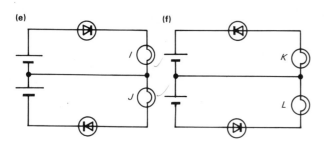

(e) (f)

Figure 24.106

14. In the circuit in Figure 24.107, when the thermistor is cold the ammeter reading is 60 mA. When the thermistor is warmed with an hair dryer, the ammeter reading rises to 600 mA.
    (a) Does the resistance of the thermistor becomes greater or smaller when it is warmed?
    (b) Calculate the resistance of the thermistor when it is cold and when it is warmed.

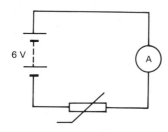

Figure 24.107

15. In the circuit in Figure 24.108 state which switch(es) should be closed and which should be open so that the LED emits light.

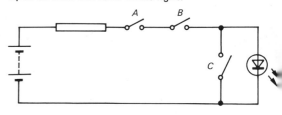

Figure 24.108

16. Complete the truth table for the combination of two NOT gates and a NAND gate connected up as shown in Figure 24.109.

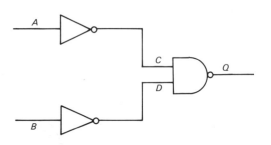

Figure 24.109

Input A	Input B	C	D	Output Q
0	0			
0	1			
1	0			
1	1			

What sort of circuit is this combination?

17. Figure 24.72 shows how a NOR gate can be built by joining two NOT gates to an AND gate. Build the same NOR gate using a combination of NAND gates only. How many NAND gates are need? (Hint: A NOT gate can be built by joining the two inputs of a NAND together as one input.)

240

18. Work out the truth table for the combination of gates in Figure 24.110.

Input A	Input B	C	D	Output Q
0	0	1	1	1
0	1	1	0	1
1	0	0	1	1
1	1	0	0	0

What sort of circuit is this combination?

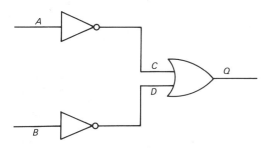

Figure 24.110

19. You do not want to be awakened at night. Design a circuit which will sound a doorbell (buzzer) when a push switch is pressed and it is day-time. (Hint: use a NOR gate.)

20. You work night shifts and do not want to be awakened while you are asleep during the day. Design a circuit which will sound a doorbell when a push switch is pressed and it is dark.

21. Design a circuit which will switch on the cooling fan of a car engine when the engine gets too hot. The fan should only operate when the ignition switch of the car is on. The motor for the fan is connected to a relay.

22. An entry to a car park is a single-lane road which is controlled by a set of stop-go traffic lights. A car entering the car park activates a switch in the road so that the lights go red. Once inside the car park, the car activites another switch so that the lights go green. Design a circuit for this purpose. (Hint: use a bistable, two push switches and a red and a green LED.)

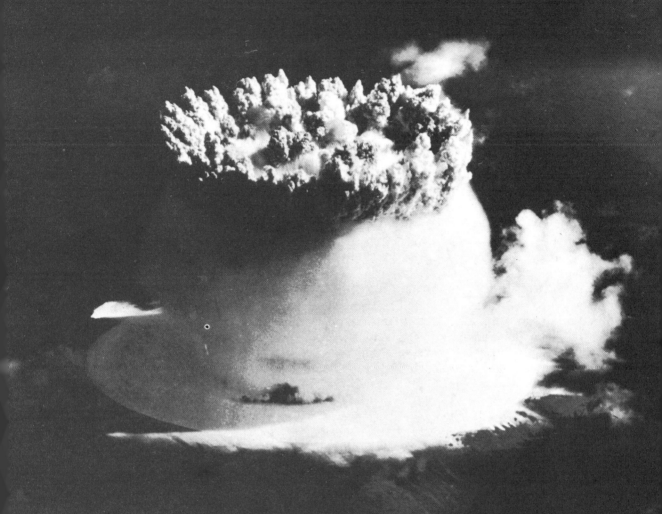

section F
NUCLEAR PHYSICS

Radioactivity I

Materials which spontaneously emit penetrating and highly dangerous radiations are said to be radioactive. The phenomenon is called radioactivity.

DISCOVERY OF RADIOACTIVITY

Radioactivity was discovered accidentally by the French scientist, Henri Becquerel (Figure 25.1) in 1896. He found that uranium salt fluoresced (glowed) when exposed to sunlight and suspected that it might be emitting X-rays. To test this, he wrapped a photographic plate in black paper, put some uranium salt on top, and took the plate out under strong sunlight. When the plate was developed, it was found to have turned black. It therefore appeared that, when exposed to sunlight, the uranium salt emitted X-rays which penetrated the black paper.

To confirm his result, Becquerel decided to repeat the experiment but the weather was cloudy, and so he put the apparatus away in a drawer. Several days later, he found, much to his surprise, that the plate had turned black even though the uranium salt had not been exposed to sunlight. After further experiments, Becquerel concluded that the radiation from the uranium salt occurred naturally, and was not due to sunlight or any other outside influence.

Becquerel's experiment can be repeated in the school laboratory (Figure 25.2a) by holding a *sealed* radioactive

Figure 25.1 Henri Becquerel (1852–1908) accidentally discovered radioactivity.

Figure 25.2 Becquerel's experiment.

radioactivity 放射現象   fluoresce 發螢光

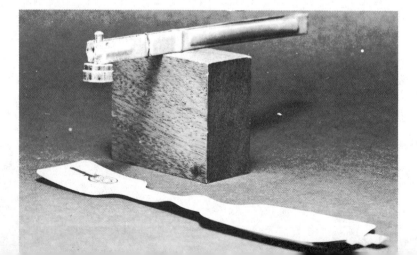

source above a dental X-ray film (or a polaroid film) with a key on it. The apparatus is left for about one hour. The developed film is shown in Figure 25.2b. The radiation has penetrated the wrapping of the film but not the metal key (exposed part black).

In 1898 Marie Curie and her husband (Figure 25.3) succeeded in extracting a strongly radioactive element, radium, from uranium ore. Since then, many other radioactive materials have been discovered.

The radiation emitted by a radioactive material is often referred to as *nuclear* radiation because it comes from the nuclei of the atoms in the material.

Figure 25.3   The Curie family: Marie, Pierre and daughter Irene.

IONIZING EFFECT OF NUCLEAR RADIATION

When molecules in a gas lose or gain electrons, ions are produced and the gas is said to be ionized. Molecules which have lost electrons become *positive* ions; those which have gained electrons become *negative* ions. Positive and negative ions always occur in pairs because the electron lost by one molecule becomes the electron gained by another molecule (Figure 25.4). One method of ionizing a gas is by the action of a point — electric charge concentrated at pointed conductor (see p.103).

When a lighted match is brought near the cap of a charged electroscope, the leaf falls and the electroscope is discharged. The match can discharge an electroscope charged either positively or negatively. The small flame ionizes the air around it, producing ion pairs. Ions with a charge different from that on the electroscope are attracted to the cap where they neutralize the charges on it; thus the leaf falls (Figure 25.5).

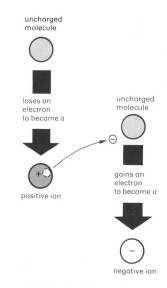

Figure 25.4   Positive and negative ion are formed when electron is transferred from one molecule to another.

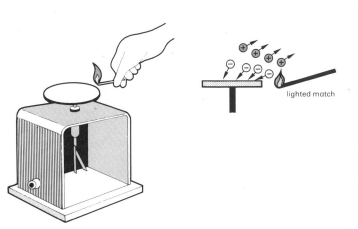

Figure 25.5   Discharging electroscope by ions in a flame.

radioactive source 放射源   radium 鐳   uranium 鈾   nuclear radiation 核輻射   ion 電離子   **245**

The same result is obtained when a radioactive radium source is brought near the cap of a charged electroscope (Figure 25.6). The radiation from the source also ionizes the air. The more intense the radiation the more ions are produced and the faster the electroscope is discharged.

RADIATION DETECTORS

There are many methods for detecting nuclear radiation. Detectors used in the school laboratory are described below.

Figure 25.6 Discharging electroscope by radioactive source.

Photographic method

Becquerel's experiment provides a means of detecting nuclear radiation. This is used today by radiation workers to measure their level of exposure to radiation in the course of their work. They are required to wear a sealed badge (Figure 25.7) containing a photographic film. The film is replaced and developed at regular intervals of time and the amount of blackening of the film indicates the level of exposure. If the level is too high the working area must be checked for leakage of radiation and the worker must go for a medical check-up.

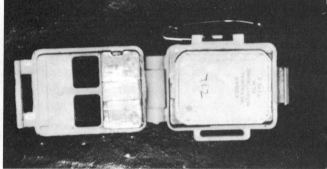

Figure 25.7 Radiation badge.

Spark counter

A spark counter consists of a wire gauze with a fine wire mounted 1 to 2 mm below it. On applying a voltage of about 4.5 kV between the gauze and the wire, sparking occurs. The voltage is then reduced until sparking *just* stops (usually at about 4 kV). When a radium source is held about 1 to 2 cm above the gauze, sparking occurs at random (Figure 25.8). This is due to radiation from the source ionizing the air between the gauze and the wire. The **range** of the radiation can be found by slowly raising the source until sparking just

range 射程

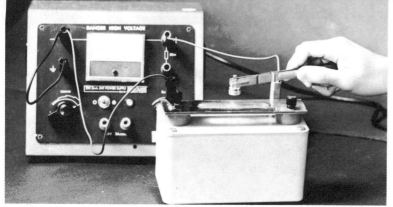

Figure 25.8 Radioactive source held above spark counter.

stops. If a sheet of paper is inserted between the source and the gauze, sparking stops. This means that the radiation that the spark counter detects cannot penetrate the paper.

Geiger-Muller (GM) tube

The **Geiger-Muller tube** (Figure 25.9) has two electrodes across which a voltage of about 400 V is applied. A central wire acts as the anode and the cylindrical metal wall of the tube forms the cathode. The tube is filled with argon gas at a low pressure. It has a thin mica window at one end through which radiation can enter.

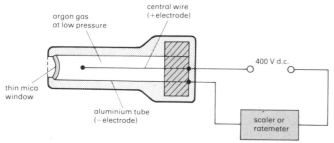

Figure 25.9 Geiger-Muller tube.

When radiation enters the tube it produces argon ions and electrons. These are accelerated towards the respective electrodes, causing more ionization by colliding with other argon atoms. This movement of ions and electrons causes a momentary electrical pulse in the circuit.

The GM tube is connected either to a **scaler** or a **ratemeter**. A scaler records the total number of counts whereas a ratemeter gives the count rate in number of pulses or counts per second. Figure 25.10 shows an instrument which functions both as a scaler and a ratemeter. The GM tube and a scaler or ratemeter are usually referred to as a **Geiger counter**.

mica 雲母   scaler 脈衝計數器   ratemeter 定率計   counter 計數器

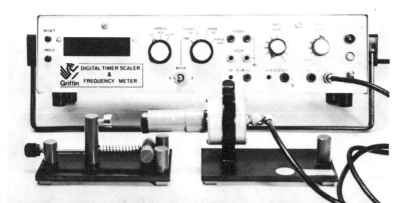

Figure 25.10 Geiger counter detecting radiation from sealed source.

ABSORPTION OF RADIATION

Around 1900 many experiments were carried out to study the ionizing power and penetrating ability of the newly-discovered nuclear radiation. The results suggested that the radiation was of three types which were called alpha (α), beta (β) and gamma (γ). (α, β, and γ are the first three letters in the Greek alphabet.)

Using a Geiger counter the penetrating ability of the radiation from a radium source can be studied and the different types of radiation emitted identified (Figure 25.11). When the source is placed very close to the GM tube and a sheet of paper is inserted between them, the count rate on the scaler is unaffected. As a sheet of paper stops the sparking produced by a radium source in a spark counter, the count recorded on the scaler must be due to another type or types of radiation. The type of radiation from the radium source which is stopped by a sheet of paper (and so cannot penetrate the thin mica end-window of the GM tube) is called **alpha** radiation.

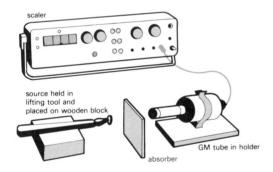

Figure 25.11 Investigating absorption of radiation.

When an aluminium sheet about 5 mm thick is inserted between the source and the GM tube, the count rate drops. This is due to absorption of a second type of radiation, **beta** radiation. When a thick sheet of lead is next inserted, the count rate drops further. This is due to a third type of radiation, **gamma** radiation, being absorbed. When more lead sheets are inserted, the count rate drops even further but does not fall to zero. Gamma radiation is highly penetrating and cannot be completely absorbed.

A radium source emits alpha, beta and gamma radiations, but there are also pure sources which emit only one type of radiation. Those commonly used in the school laboratory are:

1. *americium* source for alpha radiation,

2. *strontium* source for beta radiation,

3. *cobalt* source for gamma radiation.

americium 鎇   strontium 鍶   cobalt 鈷

The absorption experiment can be repeated using these pure sources. The results (Figure 25.12) again show that:

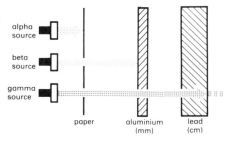

alpha radiation is stopped by a sheet of paper,

beta radiation is absorbed by an aluminium sheet 5 mm thick,

gamma radiation is reduced to about half by a lead sheet 25 mm thick.

Figure 25.12   Absorption of α, β and γ radiations.

DEFLECTION OF RADIATION

During the early study of radioactivity, experiments were also carried out to find out if the radiation could be deflected by a magnetic field. Figure 25.13 shows the effect of magnetic field on the three types of radiation. The fact that alpha and and beta radiations are deflected shows that they consist of charged particles. Using Fleming's left-hand rule the direction of deflection of the radiation suggests that alpha particles carry positive charge and beta particles carry negative charge. Alpha particles are deflected only by a small amount whereas beta particles are strongly deflected. Alpha particles are therefore more massive than beta particles. Gamma radiation is not deflected and so is neutral.

The magnetic deflection of beta particles can be demonstrated by arranging a strontium source and a Geiger counter as in Figure 25.14. With the GM tube facing the source and without the magnet, the count rate is noted. When the magnet is inserted the count rate drops but it rises again when the GM tube is moved to a new position as shown.

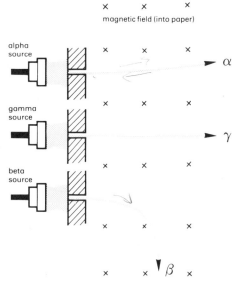

DEFLECTION NOT TO SCALE

Figure 25.13   Action of magnetic field on α, β and γ radiations.

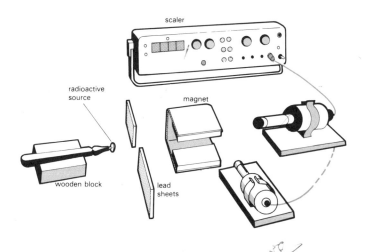

Figure 25.14   Magnetic deflection of β particles.

Magnetic deflection of alpha particles cannot be shown easily because it requires an extremely strong magnetic field.

ALPHA, BETA AND GAMMA RADIATION

The three types of radiation were identified by their different penetrating ability and behaviour in magnetic fields. More is now known about their nature and properties.

Alpha particles

These are deflected by electric and magnetic fields, in directions which suggest they are positively charged particles. Measurement of their charge-to-mass ratio by J.J. Thomson at the beginning of this century indicated that they were helium nuclei. This was confirmed in 1909 by Rutherford and Royds when they detected helium gas in a specially sealed apparatus containing an alpha source.

Alpha particles emitted from any one source all travel at nearly the same speed — up to about one-tenth of the speed of light. They tend to attract electrons away from nearby atoms and so cause intense ionization in a gas. They are, however, the least penetrating; they have a range of a few cm in air and can be stopped by a sheet of paper.

Beta particles

These can easily be deflected by electric and magnetic fields. Measurement of their charge-to-mass ratio shows that they are fast moving electrons. Beta particles emitted from any one source travel with various speeds which can be as high as nine-tenths the speed of light. They are much lighter than alpha particles (about $\frac{1}{7200}$ of their mass). They are much less ionizing but are more penetrating. The fastest beta particles have a range in air of several metres and are stopped by about 5 mm of aluminium.

Gamma rays

These are electromagnetic waves of very short wavelengths (very high frequencies). Their nature was not established until 1914 when they were shown to have interference and diffraction effects. Their wavelengths are those of very short X-rays.

Like X-rays, gamma rays are extremely penetrating, but their ionizing power is very low. They are never completely absorbed but their intensity can be reduced to about half by 25 mm of lead.

The nature and properties of the three types of radiation are summarized in Table 25.1.

Table 25.1

Radiation	Nature	Charge	Ionizing effect	Range in air	Absorbed by	Deflection in E & B fields
Alpha (α) particles	helium nuclei	+2	strong	5 cm	a sheet of paper	very small
Beta (β) particles	fast moving electrons	−1	weak	5 m	5 mm aluminium	large
Gamma (γ) rays	EM waves of short wavelengths	neutral	very weak	100 m	25 mm lead reduces intensity to half	zero

DETECTION OF ALPHA, BETA AND GAMMA RADIATION

Ionization power depends on (i) Charge (ii) Mass

Not all the radiation detectors described previously can detect all three types of radiations.

A photographic plate detects alpha, beta and gamma radiations.

A spark counter detects alpha particles only.

A GM counter detects beta and gamma radiations and only energetic alpha particles.

The ionizing effects of beta and gamma radiations are not strong enough to produce sparks in a spark counter. The school type GM tube does not have a thin enough mica end-window to admit the low energy alpha particles from a radium or americium source. Also, where there is more than one type of radiation, these detectors cannot distinguish one type from the other.

There are other types of very advanced detectors, e.g. solid-state detector and scintillation counter.

solid-state detector 固態探測器   scintillation counter 烔爍計數器

CLOUD CHAMBER

A **cloud chamber** enables the tracks of nuclear radiation to be seen, especially alpha particle tracks. It was invented in 1911 by the Scottish scientist, C.T.R. Wilson, who was inspired by watching the formation of clouds when he was on holiday in the Scottish mountains. Figure 25.15 shows the cloud chamber used by Wilson. A modified version, the **diffusion cloud chamber**, was invented by Langsdorf in 1936.

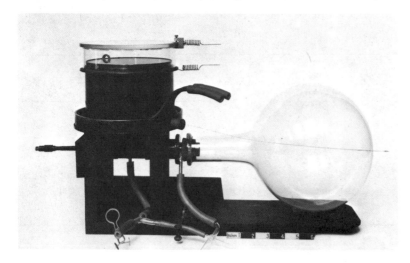

Figure 25.15   Wilson's cloud chamber.

Figure 25.16 shows a simple diffusion cloud chamber. The bottom of the chamber is cooled, using dry ice, to approximately −80°C. A felt ring inside the top of the chamber is soaked in alcohol. As the alcohol vapour diffuses downwards, it is cooled and is ready to condense. Each time a particle is emitted from the source it produces ions along its path and the alcohol vapour then condenses around these ions. The condensed alcohol droplets reflect light and so can be seen as a narrow white line.

Figure 25.16   Diffusion cloud chamber.

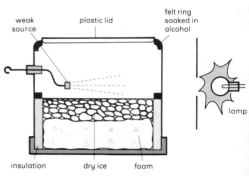

cloud chamber 雲室

Cloud chamber photographs

Figure 25.17 shows photographs of cloud chamber tracks of alpha, beta and gamma radiations.

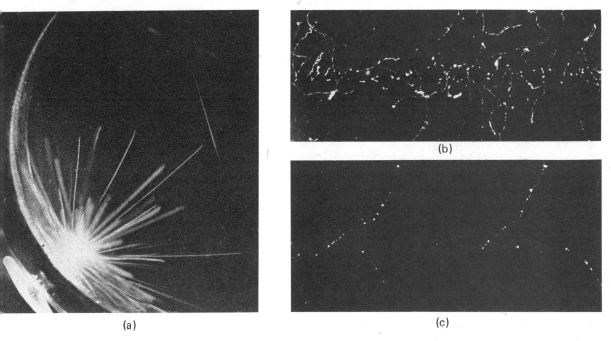

(a)

(b)

(c)

Figure 25.17   Cloud chamber photographs of (a) α, (b) β and (c) γ tracks.

Alpha particles give straight, thick tracks which are of about the same length. Note that the tracks are seen one after another along random directions; the photograph shows a number of tracks emitted over a period of time.

Beta particles give thin and twisted tracks. They cause much less ionization and, being small in mass, they are pushed off course each time they collide with an air molecule.

Gamma rays eject electrons from air molecules. These electrons behave rather like beta particles and produce tracks spreading out from the gamma rays.

The cloud chamber tracks provide evidence that 'something' is being shot out from the radioactive materials. Note however that we are not observing the actual radiation, but only the alcohol droplets which form on the ions produced by such radiation. Of all the radiations, only the alpha particle tracks can readily be seen when the cloud chamber is observed directly.

Alpha particles are massive and cannot easily be deflected by a magnetic field. Figure 25.18 shows alpha particle tracks in a *very strong* magnetic field.

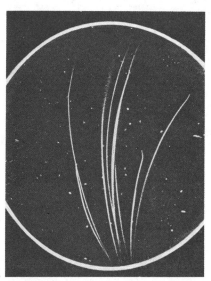

Figure 25.18   α tracks in very strong magnetic field – about 1000 times that of a magnadur magnet.

253

Nowadays, high speed nuclear particles are studied using a **bubble chamber** (Figure 25.19). In this, tracks of the particles are seen as a trail of bubbles in a liquid.

Right-angled fork tracks

Figure 25.20 shows a special alpha track in a cloud chamber filled with helium gas. The right-angled fork track indicates some sort of collision between an alpha particle and a helium molecule. Such a collision occurs *very rarely*; only a few fork tracks can be found from several tens of thousands of cloud chamber photographs.

The right-angled fork track can be explained by an analogue experiment. A small magnetic puck is placed in the middle of a glass picture frame covered with a thin layer of polystyrene beads. An identical puck is pushed so that it collides with the stationary puck (Figure 25.21). After collision, the two pucks always move off at right angles to each other. However, if the pucks are of different masses, they would move off at a different angle to each other. The alpha particle and the helium molecules in the cloud chamber are therefore of the same mass. This confirms that alpha particles are, in fact, helium nuclei.

Figure 25.19   Bubble Chamber at European Council for Nuclear Research (CERN).

Figure 25.20   Right-angled fork α tracks in cloud chamber filld with helium gas.

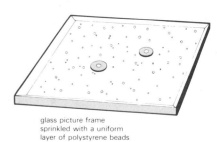

glass picture frame
sprinkled with a uniform
layer of polystyrene beads

Figure 25.21   Magnetic analogue for right-angled fork α tracks.

RADIATION HAZARDS

Nuclear radiations are potentially very dangerous. They may damage or even destroy living cells and lead to cancer and eye cataracts later in life. They may also cause genetic damage which affects future generations. Furthermore the effects are cumulative so that a small daily exposure may add up over a long period of time to a dangerously high total dose of radiation. Marie Curie is believed to have died of cancer as a result of over exposure to radiation through working with radioactive materials for many years.

Alpha particles have so short a range that they cannot penetrate even the surface of the skin. They are the least hazardous type of radiation, provided that alpha-emitting materials are not taken into the body through the lungs or stomach. Beta particles are more penetrating but they can be stopped by a sheet of aluminium or perspex. Gamma rays are the most dangerous because they can penetrate to tissues deep within the body.

Hazardous as nuclear radiations are, we are all exposed to a small amount of **background radiation**. If a Geiger counter is set up, the counter records a low count rate even with no source near it. This is due to background radiation produced by **cosmic radiation** from space and by small amounts of radioactive substances present in the rocks.

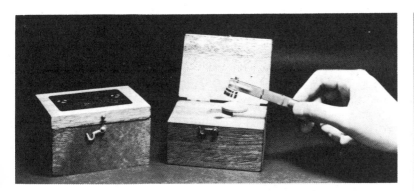

Figure 25.22   Lead 'castle' to store radioactive source.

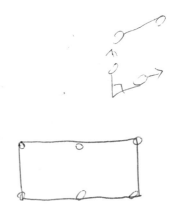

(a)

The sealed sources permitted for use in schools for teaching purposes, are all *weak* sources. Nevertheless, they should be treated with great care. They should always be handled with forceps or a special lifting tool and should be pointed away from the human body, especially the eyes. When not in use the source should be kept in a special lead 'castle' cased in a wooden box (Figure 25.22). Strong sources are stored in thick-walled lead castles surrounded by concrete blocks (Figure 25.23). All storage places for radioactive materials are marked with a sign as shown in Figure 25.24.

(b)

Figure 25.23   Storage of radioactive source at Queen Mary Hospital. (a) Thick-walled room. (b) Lead bricks surrounding radioactive material.

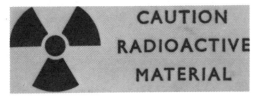

Figure 25.24   Danger! Radioactive material!

background radiation 本底輻射   cosmic radiation 宇宙輻射

SUMMARY

Properties of radiation

Radiation	Nature	Charge	Ionizing effect	Range in air	Absorbed by	Deflection in E & B fields
Alpha (α) particles	helium nuclei	+2	strong	5 cm	a sheet of paper	very small
Beta (β) particles	fast moving electrons	−1	weak	5 m	5 mm aluminium	large
Gamma (γ) rays	EM waves of short wave wavelengths	neutral	very weak	100 m	25 mm lead reduces intensity to half	zero

Natural radioactivity was accidentally discovered in 1896 by Becquerel.

Types of radiation

Alpha (α) radiation/particle
Beta (β)   radiation/particle
Gamma (γ) rays

Detection of radiation

A photographic plate detects alpha, beta and gamma radiation.

A spark counter detects alpha particles only.
A GM counter detects beta and gamma radiation and high energy alpha particles.
A cloud chamber detects mainly alpha particles.

Radiation hazards

Nuclear radiation is potentially very dangerous; it causes damage to and destruction of living cells, and even genetic changes in the cells, as well as the delayed effects of cancers and eye cataracts.

PROBLEMS

1. Becquerel's experiment is repeated using a photographic film and a radioactive source. Of the four sealed sources used in the school laboratory (radium, americium, strontium and cobalt), which can be used? Explain your answer.

2. State which type of nuclear radiation
   (a) carries a positive charge,
   (b) is an electromagnetic wave,
   (c) is the most penetrating,
   (d) has the strongest ionization effect,
   (e) can be stopped by a sheet of paper,
   (f) is not deflected by an electric field,
   (g) is made up of helium nuclei,
   (h) is made up fast-moving electrons,
   (i) has the same characteristics as X-rays,
   (j) discharges a charged gold-leaf electroscope.

3. Of the four sealed sources used in the school laboratory (radium, americium, strontium and cobalt), which can produce sparks in a spark counter? Explain your answer.

4. Why is nuclear radiation dangerous? What damages would nuclear radiation cause to the living cells? Which type of radiation is potentially the most dangerous?

5. State the safety precautions which must be observed when using radioactive sources.

6. How would you show that a radium source emits all three kinds of nuclear radiations, alpha, beta and gamma?

7. A cobalt source emits only gamma radiations. How would you check if it emits neither alpha nor beta radiations?

8. A radioactive source is placed in front of a Geiger-Muller tube which can detect alpha, beta and gamma radiations. A sheet of paper, 5 mm thick aluminium, and 25 mm thick lead are placed in turn in front of the Geiger-Muller tube and the following results are obtained:

Absorber	Counts min^{-1}
—	800
paper	720
aluminium	720
lead	320

Deduce the type(s) of radiation emitted by the source.

9. How do tracks made by alpha particles in a cloud chamber differ from those made by beta particles?

10. What happens to the tracks of alpha particles in a cloud chamber if the air pressure in the chamber is reduced? Explain your answer.

11. A radium source which emits alpha, beta and gamma radiations is placed in a lead block (Figure 25.25). The beam of radiation emitted is split into three parts by a strong magnetic field acting in the direction shown, each part being indicated by the mark it makes on a photographic film. Which type of radiation is responsible for the marks X, Y and Z?

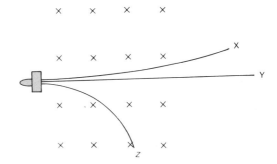

Figure 25.25

12. (a) How would you show by experiment that a given radioactive source is an emitter of *both* beta and gamma radiation?
    (b) A method of detecting alpha-particles is to use a spark counter which consists of a knife edge situated close to a metal mesh with a high voltage maintained between the knife edge and the mesh.
       (i) Explain why sparks are obtained when a source of alpha-particles is placed close to the counter.
       (ii) If a radium source, which emits alpha, beta and gamma radiations, is slowly moved away from the counter, what would you expect to happen to the sparking? Explain your answer.
       (iii) Sparking can also take place if the flame from a match is gently blown near to the mesh. Explain this.
       (iv) Sparking occasionally takes place when the spark counter is left on its own with a high voltage across the terminals. Explain this.

(c) In a cloud chamber experiment to view alpha-particles, very occasionally forked tracks are seen, as in Figure 25.26.
   (i) Why are there two tracks X and Y?
   (ii) If the angle between the tracks is $90°$, what can you deduce from this?

(O&C Nov 1977)

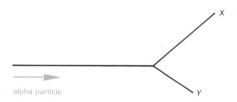

Figure 25.26

13. A Geiger-Muller tube attached to a scaler is placed on a bench in the laboratory. Over three consecutive minutes the scaler reads 11, 9 and 16 counts per minute.
   When a radioactive source is placed near to the Geiger-Muller tube the counts over three consecutive minutes are 1310, 1270, and 1296 per minute.
   When a piece of thick paper is placed between the source and the tube the counts are 1250, 1242, and 1236 per minute.
   When the paper is replaced by a sheet of aluminium 2 mm thick the counts are 13, 12 and 11 per minute.
   (a) Why is there a reading when no source is present?
   (b) Why do the three readings in any one group differ?
   (c) What can be deduced about the nature of the emission? Give reasons for your answer.

(London June 1979)

14. A Geiger counter G_1, placed as shown (Figure 25.27) at a distance of 25 cm from a radioactive source, S, records an average count of 250 per minute. A similar counter G_2 placed above G_1, but also at 25 cm from S, records three successive minute-interval counts of 21, 18 and 23. When a horseshoe magnet is suitably positioned the count rate of G_1 decreases to approximately half its former value and the count rate of G_2 shows an appreciable increase.
   (a) Account for the three successive minute-interval counts recorded by G_2 and explain why these figures are not constant.
   (b) Why, in experiments with radioactive sources, is a knowledge of these figures important? Indicate how they are used.

(c) What is the nature of the radiation emitted by S? Give reasons for your answer.
(d) Describe, as exactly as you can, the position of the horse-shoe magnet. (A diagram may help.)
(e) State clearly the direction of the magnetic field.
(f) What is the purpose of the metal tube?

(London Jan 1980)

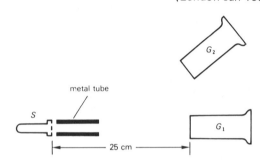

Figure 25.27

15. A weak radioactive source was thought to emit β-radiation. In an attempt to confirm this a student arranged a Geiger-Muller tube, connected to a ratemeter, close to the source and then placed sheets of different materials as absorbers between the source and tube. Three readings of the ratemeter were taken at 10-second intervals for each sheet and the results were tabulated as follows:

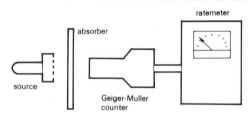

Figure 25.28

Absorber material	Ratemeter reading /counts per minute		
	1	2	3
Air	120	110	130
Paper	100	120	110
Cardboard	130	130	100
Aluminium (0.5 mm thick)	110	120	110
Aluminium (5 mm thick)	50	60	40
Lead (5 mm thick)	40	50	50
Lead (50 mm thick)	50	40	50

(a) Give reasons for confirming that the source does not emit α-rays or γ-rays but must emit β-radiation.

(b) Suggest another test, not involving absorption, you could perform to further confirm that the source emitted β-radiation.

(c) As only β-radiation was emitted, account for the ratemeter readings for the 50-mm thick lead absorber.

(d) Why were identical readings not obtained each time for the same absorber?

(e) If the source had been emitting either α-radiation or γ-radiation a different set of readings would have been obtained. Copy the table below for an α-source and a γ-source and complete the table by inserting suitable estimated values you would expect to obtain for each absorber.

(London June 1981)

Absorber material	Ratemeter reading /counts per minute	
	α-source	γ-source
Air Paper Cardboard Aluminium (0.5 mm thick) Aluminium (5 mm thick) Lead (5 mm thick) Lead (50 mm thick)	120	120

Radioactivity II 26

By the beginning of this century the old belief that atoms were the smallest and indivisible particles was no longer accepted. The discovery that charged particles were emitted by radioactive materials suggested that atoms could be made up of yet smaller particles carrying positive and negative charges.

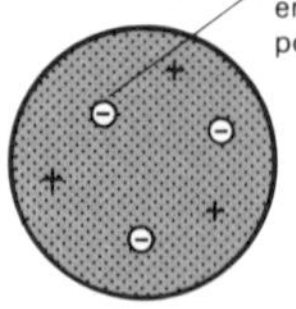

Figure 26.1 Thomson's plum pudding model.

RUTHERFORD'S SCATTERING EXPERIMENT

Following the discovery of the electron, J.J. Thomson proposed the so-called **'plum-pudding' model** of the atom. In this model (Figure 26.1), the atom was assumed to be a positively charged sphere in which negative electrons were embedded, rather like plums in a pudding. Many scientists, including Ernest Rutherford (Figure 26.2), were doubtful about this model. In 1911 Geiger and Marsden, under the direction of Rutherford, carried out a series of experiments using alpha particles to bombard a thin gold foil. This experiment led to the overthrow of Thomson's model.

Figure 26.3 shows a simplified form of the apparatus used by Geiger and Marsden. A radium source in a lead container emitted a narrow beam of alpha particles through a slit. When the alpha particle struck a zinc sulphide screen they produced tiny flashes of light (scintillations), which were observed through a microscope. The experiment was conducted in vacuum so that the collisions of the alpha particles with air molecules were avoided.

Figure 26.2 Ernest Rutherford 1871–1937.

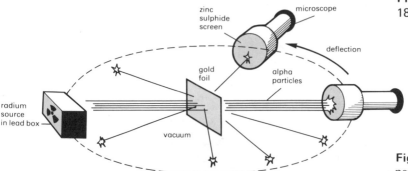

Figure 26.3 Scattering experiment performed by Geiger and Marsden.

With the gold foil in position, Geiger and Marsden counted the number of scintillations produced on the screen over a certain period of time and found that it was nearly the same as that produced without the gold foil.

Geiger and Marsden then rotated the detector to look for alpha particles which might have been deflected from their course. Much to their surprise they found that a small number of alpha particles were deflected through various angles and a few even bounced back! Some of the results are shown in Table 26.1.

When Rutherford learnt of the results, he was so astonished that he said at the time, 'It was almost as incredible as if you had fired a 15-inch shell at a piece of tissue paper and it came back and hit you!'

RUTHERFORD'S NUCLEAR ATOM

Thomson's 'plum-pudding' model could not explain the rare, large deflection of the alpha particles. Being a positively charged sphere the pudding would allow all the alpha particles to pass through without deflection. Rutherford proposed a new model of the atom where most of it was empty space and all the positive charge and most of the mass were concentrated in a tiny core or **nucleus**. The negative electrons orbited the nucleus at a distance.

When positively charged alpha particles were fired at the gold foil, most of them passed straight through the empty space of the gold atoms. The few which happened to come close to the positively charged nucleus were acted on by a strong electrostatic force of repulsion and as a result, were deflected or even bounced back (Figure 26.4).

Rutherford's model provided more than a qualitative explanation of the scattering of the alpha particles. By considering the electrostatic repulsion between an alpha particle and a gold nucleus, Rutherford derived a mathematical formula to predict the number of alpha particles that would be deflected through different angles. Rutherford's prediction was confirmed by Geiger and Marsden's results given in in Table 26.1.

From the scattering experiment, Rutherford also estimated the diameter of the nucleus to be around 10^{-14} metre or a millionth of a millionth of a centimetre! The diameter of an atom, from an earlier estimate, was around 10^{-10} m. Hence the diameter of the nucleus was at least 10 000 times smaller than that of an atom. If an atom were the size of a concert

Table 26.1

Angle of deflection	Number of scintillations observed in a time interval
5°	8 289 000
10°	502 700
15°	120 570
30°	7 800
45°	1 435
60°	477
75°	211
105°	69
120°	52
135°	43
150°	33

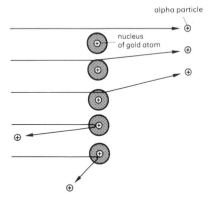

Figure 26.4   Rutherford explained why some α particles bounced back.

hall, its nucleus would be no bigger than a peanut. You can well imagine the amount of empty space there is in an atom.

SCATTERING ANALOGUES

Figure 26.5 shows a **gravitational analogue** of the Rutherford scattering experiment. A ball-bearing is rolled down a ramp onto a curved 'hill'. As the ball approaches the 'hill' it has to climb uphill against gravitational force. The ball is deflected and the angle of deflection depends on its direction of approach. In particular, when the ball is aimed at the centre of the 'hill', it is deflected through a large angle or may even return along its original path.

Figure 26.5 Gravitational α scattering analogue.

A **magnetic analogue** can also be set up as in Figure 26.6. The magnet attached to the end of the string represents the alpha particle and the magnet positioned in the middle of the paper represents the gold nucleus. The 'alpha particle' is made to approach the 'nucleus' along different paths as shown.

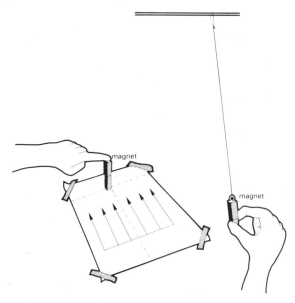

Figure 26.6 Magnetic α scattering analogue.

PROTONS AND NEUTRONS

In 1919, Rutherford bombarded nitrogen gas with fast moving alpha particles and found that positively charged particles were emitted from the nitrogen nuclei. These particles carried a charge of the same size but different in sign to that of an electron, and they had a mass 1840 times greater. Rutherford called these particles **protons**.

In 1932, James Chadwick found that uncharged particles of the same mass as a proton were ejected as a result of bombarding beryllium with alpha particles. Chadwick named these particles **neutrons**.

As a result of these and other experiments, Rutherford's model of the atom was modified. It is now believed that the nucleus is made up of protons and neutrons which are bound together by a **strong nuclear force** and that fast-moving electrons orbit the nucleus. Different types of atoms have different numbers of protons and neutrons in their nuclei. In a neutral atom, the number of protons is the same as the number of electrons (Figure 26.7).

Atomic number and mass number

All naturally-occurring materials are made up from about 90 basic substances called **elements**. Some of these are listed in Table 26.2 together with their chemical symbols. Atoms of different elements have different numbers of protons and neutrons in their nuclei and therefore different numbers of electrons in orbit.

> The atomic number or proton number of an atom is the number of protons in its nucleus.

In a neutral atom the atomic number is also the number of electrons in orbit. The electrons in an atom, and hence the atomic number, determine the chemical properties. When elements are arranged in increasing order of atomic number in the periodic table, they fall into groups of similar chemical properties.

The protons and neutrons in the nucleus are called **nucleons**.

> The mass number or nucleon number of an atom is the total number of protons and neutrons in the atom.

If an atom of chemical symbol X has a mass number A and an atomic number Z, its nucleus is represented by the symbol $_Z^A X$. For example, helium nucleus is represented as $_2^4 He$.

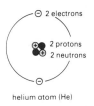

Figure 26.7 Model of helium atom.

Table 26.2

Element	Symbol	Atomic number Z
Hydrogen	H	1
Helium	He	2
Lithium	Li	3
Beryllium	Be	4
Carbon	C	6
Nitrogen	N	7
Oxygen	O	8
Sodium	Na	11
Potassium	K	19
Cobalt	Co	27
Krypton	Kr	36
Strontium	Sr	38
Iodine	I	53
Barium	Ba	56
Lead	Pb	82
Radium	Ra	88
Actinium	Ac	89
Thorium	Th	90
Protactinium	Pa	91
Uranium	U	92

atomic number 原子序   proton number 質子數   nucleon 核子   mass number 質量數

The difference between the mass number and the atomic number gives the number of neutrons in the nucleus. For example, the neutron number of helium is (4 − 2) or 2.

Nuclides and isotopes

All atoms of a particular element have the same number of protons in their nuclei, but they may differ in the number of neutrons. For example, lithium exists naturally in two forms — one form has 3 neutrons and the other has 4, but both forms have 3 protons each. Since both have the same atomic number they have identical chemical properties. The nuclei of the two forms are represented by the symbols $^6_3$Li and $^7_3$Li.

An element with a particular mass number and atomic number is called a **nuclide** and is referred to by its mass number, for example, lithium-6 and lithium-7. A nuclide which is radioactive is called a **radionuclide**.

Nuclides with the same atomic number but different mass number are called **isotopes**. Most elements occur naturally as a mixture of isotopes.

To illustrate the different terms used:

> **Lithium is an element.**
>
> **Lithium-6 is a nuclide; lithium-7 is also a nuclide.**
>
> **Lithium-6 and lithium-7 are isotopes.**

RADIOACTIVE DECAY

Radioactivity is due to unstable nuclei which break up, emitting alpha, beta particles or gamma rays as they do so. The process is called **radioactive decay** or **disintegration**. The emission of particles results in changes in the numbers of protons and neutrons in the nucleus. Hence when a nucleus decays it becomes a nucleus of another element. The nucleus which decays is called the **parent** nucleus and that which results is called the **daughter** nucleus. The daughter nucleus together with the emitted particles are called decay products.

Alpha emission

An alpha particle is a helium nucleus. It consists of 2 protons and 2 neutrons and is represented by $^4_2$He or $^4_2\alpha$. When a nucleus emits an alpha particle, it is left with 2 protons and 2 neutrons less than before. Its atomic number therefore decreases by 2 and its mass number by 4.

nuclide 核素   radionuclide 放射性核素   isotope 同位素   radioactive decay 放射衰變
disintegration 蛻變   parent nucleus 母核   daughter nucleus 子核   decay products 衰變產物

Figure 26.8 shows a typical alpha decay process in which an uranium-238 nucleus (atomic number 92) emits an alpha particle. The daughter nucleus that results has an atomic number 90 and a mass number 234. According to Table 26.2, thorium has an atomic number 90 and so it is a nucleus of thorium-234 which is formed.

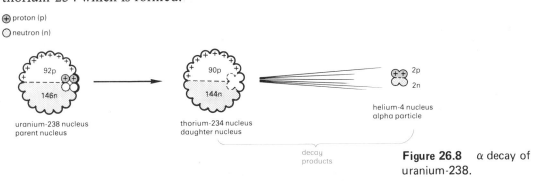

⊕ proton (p)

○ neutron (n)

uranium-238 nucleus
parent nucleus

thorium-234 nucleus
daughter nucleus

helium-4 nucleus
alpha particle

decay products

Figure 26.8 α decay of uranium-238.

The decay process can be written in the form of an equation:

$$^{238}_{92}\text{U} \longrightarrow {}^{234}_{90}\text{Th} + {}^{4}_{2}\text{He}$$

Note that the top and bottom numbers balance on both sides of the equation: $238 = 234 + 4$; $92 = 90 + 2$. This means that during the decay process the total number of nucleons and the total charge remain the same.

> When a nuclide decays by alpha emission, it becomes a nuclide with an atomic number 2 and a mass number 4 less than before.

Beta emission

A beta particle is an electron. It has negligible mass compared with a proton or a neutron and carries a charge of −1 unit. It can be represented by $^{0}_{-1}\text{e}$ or $^{0}_{-1}\beta$. When a nucleus decays by beta emission, one of its neutrons changes into a proton and an electron. The proton remains in the nucleus and the electron is emitted as a beta particle. As a proton has now replaced a neutron in the nucleus, the mass number of the nucleus remains unchanged, but the atomic number increases by 1. It is important to note that the beta particle comes from the nucleus and is *not* one of the electrons orbiting the nucleus.

Figure 26.9 shows a typical beta decay process in which a nucleus of thorium-234 (atomic number 90) emits a beta particle. The daughter nucleus has the same mass number as the parent nucleus (234) but its atomic number increases to 91. According to Table 26.2 this is a nucleus of protactinium-234.

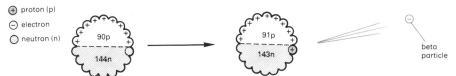

proton (p)
electron
neutron (n)

90p
144n

thorium-234 nucleus

91p
143n

protactinium-234 nucleus

beta
particle

Figure 26.9 β decay of thorium-234.

The decay process can be written as:

$$^{234}_{90}\text{Th} \longrightarrow ^{234}_{91}\text{Pa} + ^{0}_{-1}\text{e}$$

Again the top and bottom numbers balance on both sides of the equation: $234 = 234 + 0$, $90 = 91 - 1$. This means that during the decay process, there is no change in the number of nucleons or in the total charge.

> **When a nuclide decays by beta emission, it becomes a nuclide with an atomic number 1 greater than before, but with the same mass number.**

Example 1

The nuclide radium-226 (atomic number 88) decays by alpha emission. Name the daughter nuclide formed and write down the equation for the decay process.

Let the unknown nuclide be represented by $^{A}_{Z}\text{X}$. The alpha emission can be written as:

$$^{226}_{88}\text{Ra} \longrightarrow ^{A}_{Z}\text{X} + ^{4}_{2}\text{He}$$

Since the top and bottom numbers balance on both sides of the equation,

$$226 = A + 4 \quad \text{and} \quad 88 = Z + 2$$

$$\Rightarrow \qquad A = 222 \quad \text{and} \quad Z = 86$$

According to Table 26.2 X is radon-222. The equation can be rewritten as:

$$^{226}_{88}\text{Ra} \longrightarrow ^{222}_{86}\text{Rn} + ^{4}_{2}\text{He}$$

Gamma radiation

After emitting an alpha or beta particle some nuclei are left in an excited state with more energy than normal. As the protons and neutrons in the nucleus rearrange to become more stable, the extra energy is emitted as short-wavelength electromagnetic waves.

> **Gamma emission does not change either the atomic number or the mass number.**

excited state 受激態

RADIOACTIVE SERIES

When a nucleus of uranium-238 decays by alpha emission it changes to a nucleus of thorium-234 which is itself unstable. The daughter nucleus emits a beta particle and changes to a nucleus of protactinium-234. The decay process carries on for many more stages until a final *stable* nucleus of lead-206 is formed. This is a radioactive series which can be written, *in part*, as:

$$\ce{^{238}_{92}U} \xrightarrow{\alpha} \ce{^{234}_{90}Th} \xrightarrow{\beta} \ce{^{234}_{91}Pa} \xrightarrow{\beta} \ce{^{234}_{92}U}$$

$$\longrightarrow \cdots \ce{^{210}_{84}Po} \xrightarrow{\alpha} \ce{^{206}_{82}Pb}$$

The complete series can be represented by the chart in Figure 26.10 in which the mass number of the atoms in the series is plotted against the atomic number.

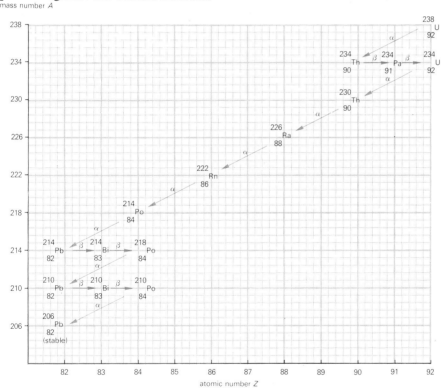

Figure 26.10 Radioactive series of uranium-238 to stable lead-206.

Example 2
Part of a radioactive series is shown below:

$$\ce{^{232}_{90}Th} \longrightarrow \ce{^{228}_{88}Ra} \longrightarrow \ce{^{228}_{89}Ac} \longrightarrow \ce{^{228}_{90}Th}$$

(a)   What kind of particle is emitted at each decay?

radioactive series 放射系

(b) If the stable end-product of the complete series is lead-208, how many alpha particles are emitted from thorium-232 to the end of the series?

(a) An alpha particle is emitted in a decay when the mass number of the daughter nucleus is 4 less than the parent nucleus, and the atomic number 2 less; a beta particle is emitted when the mass number remains the same but the atomic number is 1 greater.

Hence

$$\ce{^{232}_{90}Th} \xrightarrow{\alpha} \ce{^{228}_{88}Ra} \xrightarrow{\beta} \ce{^{228}_{89}Ac} \xrightarrow{\beta} \ce{^{228}_{90}Th}$$

(b) Since beta emission does not affect the mass number of a nucleus, there are altogether $\dfrac{(232-208)}{4}$ or 6 alpha particles emitted in the complete series.

RANDOM DECAY

Experiments with radioactive sources have shown that the emission of nuclear radiation occurs *at random*. In a cloud chamber the alpha particle tracks appear at irregular time intervals. When a GM tube points, for example, at a strontium source, the count rate reading on the scaler fluctuates.

Radioactive decay is a random process. Of all the undecayed nuclei in the source it is not possible to know when one particular nucleus will disintegrate. Nevertheless, when all the nuclei are considered, the average number of disintegrations per second can be predicted reasonably accurately. The number of disintegrations per second is called the **activity** of the source.

Dice decay analogue

Radioactive decay can be simulated by throwing a large number of dice (Figure 26.11). The dice represent nuclei and after throwing, those with for example side 'one' facing uppermost represent nuclei which have decayed. The 'decayed' dice are removed and the remaining 'undecayed' dice are thrown again. This procedure is repeated many times until there are only a few dice left.

Dice throwing is a random process. It is not possible to know when a particular die will turn its side 'one' uppermost, yet if the number of dice is large, on average about one-sixth of dice 'decays' at each throw.

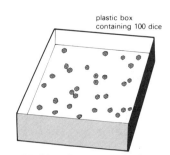
plastic box containing 100 dice

Figure 26.11 Dice analogue to illustrate random nature of decay process.

random 無規   activity 放射性

Table 26.3 is a typical set of results obtained by throwing
100 dice.

Table 26.3

Number of throws	0	1	2	3	4	5	6	7	8	9	10
Number of dice removed	0	11	18	17	8	9	9	4	4	2	2
Number of dice remaining	100	89	71	54	46	37	28	24	20	18	16

When number of dice remaining is plotted against the number
of throws, a curve is obtained as in Figure 26.12. The following
points can be noted from the curve:

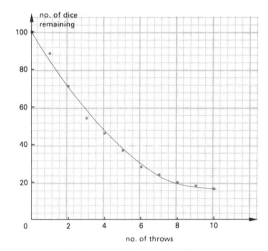

Figure 26.12 'Decay' curve of throwing dice.

1. The points plotted do not fall exactly on the curve; the
   fluctuations are due to the random nature of dice throwing.

2. The number of dice 'decayed' depends on the number
   of dice thrown; it decreases as the number of remaining
   dice decreases.

3. After about 3.5 throws the number of dice is reduced
   from 100 to 50; after another 3.5 throws it is reduced
   from 50 to 25. Hence a 'time' of 3.5 throws is needed for
   half of the remaining dice to 'decay'. All random decay
   processes follow such a characteristic pattern of having a
   fixed time interval for half of the undecayed material to
   decay.

Half-life

The decay of a sample of radium-226 to radon-222 is illustrated
in Figure 26.13. Suppose there are 40 million undecayed

nuclei at the start. 1620 years later, 20 million of these have disintegrated. Since the number of undecayed nuclei is now halved, only 10 million nuclei will decay over the next 1620 years. The decay process continues in this manner with the number of undecayed nuclei halving every 1620 years.

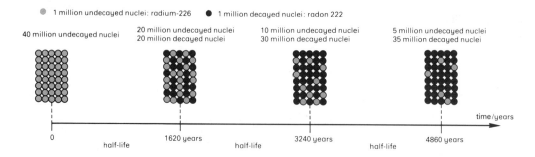

Figure 26.13   Decay of radium-226.

> **The half-life of a radionuclide is the time taken for half of the nuclei present in any given sample to decay.**

When the number of undecayed nuclei is plotted against time, a **decay curve** is obtained as in Figure 26.14. It is important to note that the total number of nuclei, parent and daughter, in the sample always stays the same (40 million).

Example 3
The half-life of iodine-131 is 8 days. Starting with 16 g of iodine how much iodine will have decayed in 24 days?

> The half-life of iodine is 8 days and so the amount of iodine is halved every 8 days. The decay process is illustrated in Figure 26.15. 14 g of iodine will have decayed in 24 days and 2 g will remain undecayed.

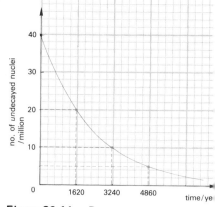

Figure 26.14   Decay curve.

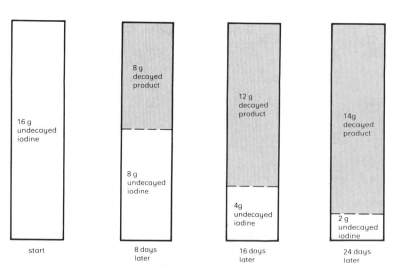

Figure 26.15   Decay of iodine-131.

half-life 半衰期   decay curve 衰變曲綫

In the dice decay analogue the number of dice that 'decay' depends on the number of dice thrown. The activity of a radioactive source (number of disintegrations per second) is proportional to the number of undecayed nuclei present. It follows that the activity also falls to half its original value after a half-life. Here then we have another definition of half-life.

The half-life of a radionuclide is the time taken for the activity of any given sample to fall to half its original value.

Example 4

Sodium-24 has a half-life of 15 hours. A sample of sodium-24 is found to have an activity of 800 disintegrations per second. What will be its activity 2.5 days later?

The activity of sodium is halved every 15 hours.

Hence   800 disint./s $\xrightarrow[\text{later}]{15\text{ h}}$ 400 disint./s

$\xrightarrow[\text{later}]{15\text{ h}}$ 200 disint./s $\xrightarrow[\text{later}]{15\text{ h}}$ 100 disint./s

$\xrightarrow[\text{later}]{15\text{ h}}$ 50 disint./s

The activity of the sample falls to 50 disintegrations per second after 60 hours or 2.5 days.

Half-lives of radionuclides vary greatly. Table 26.4 shows the half-lives of some radionuclides.

It is useful to know the half-life of a radionuclide to find out how long it will remain radioactive. A measurement of the half-life is also useful for identifying unknown radionuclides since each radionuclide has a characteristic half-life.

The half-life of a radionuclide can be found from its decay curve. The activity of the radionuclide is recorded at regular time intervals using a Geiger counter. Each count-rate reading recorded has to be corrected by subtracting from it the background count-rate. The *corrected* count-rate is then plotted against time and a smooth curve is then drawn through (or between) the points. From this decay curve the half-life of the radionuclide can be determined. In the school laboratory it is only possible to measure short half-lives, for example those of protactinium-234 and radon-220, but not those as short as a fraction of a second.

Nuclide	Half-life
Uranium-235	7×10^8 years
Carbon-14	5600 years
Radium-226	1620 years
Iodine-131	8 days
Sodium-24	15 hours
Protactinium-234	72 s
Radon-220	52 s

Table 26.4

Example 5

A Geiger counter is used to measure the activity of a sample of radioactive substance. The total number of counts in successive 20 s intervals is recorded in the table below:

Time/s	0-20	20-40	40-60	60-80	80-100	100-120	120-140	140-160
Total number of counts in each 20 s interval	248	208	174	148	126	108	92	80

The background radiation is measured to be 84 counts per minute. Use the results to plot a decay curve and deduce from it the half life of the radioactive substance.

The background radiation is 84 counts per minute or 28 counts in each 20 s interval.

The recorded number of counts is corrected for background radiation by subtracting from it the background count.

Time/s	0-20	20-40	40-60	60-80	80-100	100-120	120-140	140-160
Corrected total number of counts in each 20 s interval	220	180	146	120	98	80	64	52

The results are plotted as in Figure 26.16. The corrected total number of counts in each 20 s interval is taken to be the count in the middle of the time interval, that is, at 10, 30, 50 s, ... From the decay curve, the radioactive substance takes 70 s to halve its activity from 220 to 110 counts. Hence its half life is 70 s.

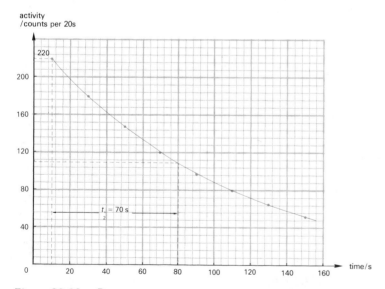

Figure 26.16 Decay curve.

ARTIFICIAL RADIOACTIVITY

In 1934 Irene Joliot-Curie (Marie Curie's daughter) and her husband bombarded aluminium with alpha particles and obtained an unstable nuclide of phosphorus. This was the first artificially produced radionuclide. Since then, radionuclides of practically every element have been produced using similar methods.

Artificial radionuclides are being used in an increasing number of ways in medicine, industry and agriculture.

Radiotherapy

Nuclear radiation is dangerous and can destroy living cells, but this very property is valuable for treating cancers. Strong

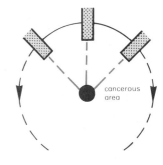

Figure 26.17 Gamma rays from radioactive cobalt-60 kill malignant cancer cells.

gamma rays from cobalt-60 are used to kill malignant cancer cells in the human body (Figure 26.17). To avoid destroying other healthy cells, the source is made to rotate in a circle. The cancerous areas of the patient is positioned exactly at the centre of the circle and so it receives the highest dose of radiation. The surrounding healthy cells receive a much smaller doses of radiation, not sufficient to cause much damage.

Tracers

A small amount of weak radionuclide injected into a system can be detected by a GM tube or other detectors. The progress of the radionuclide through the system can then be traced. Radionuclides used in this way are called **tracers**.

Tracers have many uses in medicine. Blood clots can be located by injecting radioactive sodium-25 into the bloodstream and using a detector to find where the flow stops. Iodine-131 is added to the human body to study its uptake by the thyroid gland. A photograph of a brain scan, shown in Figure 26.18,

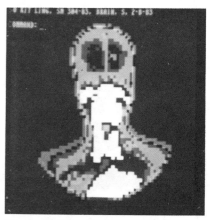

Figure 26.18 Brain scan: trace of radioactive technetium is used.

artificial radioactivity 人為放射性　　radiotherapy 放射治療　　malignant cancer cells 惡性癌細胞　　**273**

tracer 示踪物　　bloot clot 血塊　　thyroid gland 甲狀腺

provides useful information about the functioning of the organ.

In agriculture, tracers are used to determine the amount of fertilizer required for a crop. Radioactive phosphorus-30 is added to the fertilizer and its rate of uptake by the plant can be determined using a GM counter.

All tracers have short half-lives so that there are no after-effects on the system to which the tracers are added.

Thickness gauge

Radionuclides are used in industry to control the thickness of materials while they are being manufactured. In Figure 26.19, a strontium-90 source is placed on one side of the tyre cord. The beta radiation which penetrates the tyre cord is measured by a Geiger counter. If the level of radiation is high, the cord is too thin; if the level is low the cord is too thick. The machine making the cord will then adjust the thickness automatically.

Figure 26.19 Radioactive strontium-90 is used to control thickness of tyre.

'Radioactive' lightning conductor

Conventional lightning conductors use a pointed earthed metal rod to draw lightning discharge to it. The charge is conducted to the ground via an insulated cable, thus causing no damage to the building. An advanced type of lightning conductor (Figure 26.20a) uses alpha-emitting sources (e.g. an americium source) to produce an intense ionization of air around the pointed earthed rod. The sealed sources are held in radial arms (Figure 26.20b) and direct a large number of positive ions and electrons at the earthed tip. This facilitates the discharge action and so provides better protection to the building. Such lightning conductors have now been installed in many tall buildings, telecommunication stations and power transmission pylons in Hong Kong.

Figure 26.20a The 'radioactive' lightning conductor (circled in the figure).

Figure 26.20b Sealed americium sources held in radial arms produce an intense ionization of air around the earthed tip.

CARBON DATING

Carbon dioxide in the atmosphere contains two isotopes: the common, stable carbon-12 and the rare radioactive carbon-14. Living plants both absorb and give out carbon dioxide and so the percentage of carbon-14 present in the tissues remains constant. However, when a plant dies, the carbon-14 trapped in it decays by beta emission with a half-life of 5600 years. Hence by measuring the activity of the carbon-14 present in dead plants' tissue it is possible to estimate their age. This method is called **carbon dating** and is used by archaeologists to determine the age of ancient remains (Figure 26.21) and palaeontologists to date fossils.

NUCLEAR FISSION

In 1938 Hahn and Strassman, continuing the work by Enrico Fermi, carried out a series of experiments using neutrons to bombard uranium and found that the uranium nucleus was split into two fragments. Being uncharged, a neutron is not repelled on approaching the uranium nucleus and so can easily cause disruption of the uranium nucleus. This process is called **nuclear fission**.

Naturally occurring uranium consists of two radioactive isotopes, 99.3% is uranium-238 and 0.7% is uranium-235. It is the nucleus of the rare isotope, uranium-235, which undergoes fission when it is struck by a *slow* neutron (Figure 26.22a). The nucleus can split in several ways, but fission fragments of barium and krypton nuclei are commonly produced. The fission can be written as.

$$^{235}_{92}\text{U} + {}^{1}_{0}\text{n} \longrightarrow {}^{144}_{56}\text{Ba} + {}^{90}_{36}\text{Kr} + {}^{1}_{0}\text{n} + {}^{1}_{0}\text{n} \text{ (+ energy)}$$

The energy released per fissioned atom of uranium is enormous. It is about 500 million times greater than that obtained from the burning of carbon.

Neutrons emitted during fission can carry on splitting other nuclei and a **chain reaction** may result (Figure 26.22b) releasing an enormous amount of energy in a short time. In practice, many fission neutrons escape without causing further fission. The percentage of neutrons escaping decreases as the mass of uranium increases. For a chain reaction to occur the mass of the uranium-235 has to exceed a certain value, called the **critical mass**.

The atomic bomb

Work on nuclear fission led to the development of the atomic

Figure 26.21 The King Arthur's round table was carbon-dated.

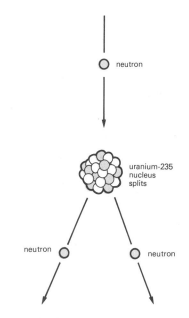

Figure 26.22a The nuclear fission.

bomb. Natural uranium contains too low a proportion of uranium-235 for use in a bomb and it has to be *enriched* by a very elaborate process. In principle, the first atomic bomb contained two lumps of enriched uranium and when they were brought together the critical mass was exceeded and an *uncontrolled* chain reaction resulted. The bomb exploded not only with the most devastating blast, but it also produced radiations and radioactive fall-out which were harmful to living things even for long time after the explosion.

The first atomic bomb (Figure 26.23) was exploded in 1945 at a test site in New Mexico, U.S.A. Shortly afterwards atomic bombs were dropped on Hiroshima and Nagasaki in Japan causing complete destruction of the two cities (Figure 26.24). 115 000 died in the explosions and many others suffered radiation after-effects of the radiation. The dropping of the these atomic bombs ended the Second World War.

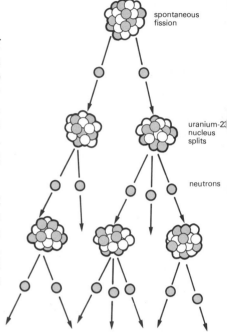

Figure 26.22b   The chain reaction.

Figure 26.23   The first atomic bomb test on 16 July, 1945. The photograph shows the huge pile and crew.

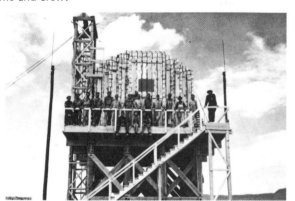

Figure 26.24   Nagasaki, September 1945.

Nuclear reactor

Nuclear fission can be used to generate electricity for peaceful use. The world's first commercial nuclear power station was opened in 1956 at Calder Hall, England.

In a nuclear power station (Figure 26.25), fission in a **nuclear reactor** provides energy to make steam to drive a turbine, which in turn drives a generator to produce electricity. A controlled chain reaction takes place in the nuclear reactor releasing energy at a steady rate.

Figure 26.26 shows a simplified diagram of a **pressurized water reactor (PWR)**, a common type of thermal reactor used in nuclear power stations. The fuel element contained in a steel

Figure 26.25   A nuclear power station.

nuclear reactor 核反應堆   pressurized water reactor (PWR) 壓水式反應堆

pressure vessel is uranium oxide enriched with a little extra uranium-235. 1 kg of the enriched uranium fuel can produce as much energy as 55 tonnes of coal.

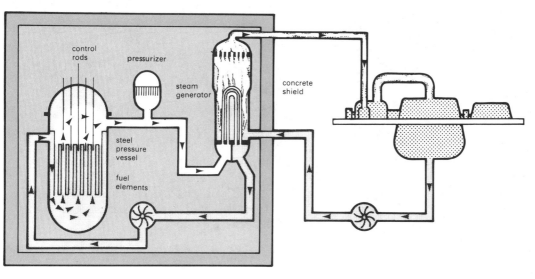

Figure 26.26   A simplified pressurized water reactor.

Energy released in fission is carried by water at high pressure to the steam generator. The pressurized water also acts as a **moderator** to slow down the fission neutrons so that a chain reaction is maintained.

Boron-steel **control rods** inserted in the fuel elements are used to control the chain reaction. The boron absorbs neutrons and so controls the number of neutrons which can cause fission. The chain reaction, and hence the temperature of the reactor, can be changed by raising or lowering the rods. In an emergency, all the rods are lowered to shut down the reactor.

The steel pressure vessel containing the fuel elements and control rods, the pressurizer and the steam generator are all enclosed in a concrete shield to contain any nuclear radiation which may leaked out in case of an accident.

Used fuel elements (Figure 26.27) are removed from the reactor and sent to a reprocessing plant. There, unused uranium is separated from the nuclear waste, together with small quantities of plutonium-239. The nuclear waste presents serious handling and storage problems as some of it remains active for thousands of years.

Plutonium-239 is currently mainly used in the production of nuclear weapons, but it can be used as a fuel in a new type

control rods 控制桿   moderator 減速劑   **277**

Figure 26.27   A remote-controlled mechanical arm handling radioactive fuel rods.

of reactor, the **fast breeder reactor**. In this reactor, the chain reaction is maintained by *fast* neutrons and so no moderator is necessary. Uranium-238 nuclei absorb excess neutrons in the reactor, producing plutonium-239 to replace the plutonium-239 that has been used up, hence the name **breeder**.

Uranium-235 only makes up 0.7% of natural uranium and so it is wasteful to use only uranium-235 as a fuel. If only uranium-235 were used, it is estimated that the world's reserves of uranium would run out by early next century. The fast-breeder reactor will solve this problem of shortage because it makes use of the plentiful uranium-238 and 'breeds' more plutonium than it consumes.

NUCLEAR FUSION

The union of two light nuclei into a heavier nucleus can also lead to the release of an enormous amount of energy. This process is called **nuclear fusion**.

Figure 26.28 shows the fusion of nuclei of hydrogen-2 (deuterium) and hydrogen-3 (tritium) to form a nucleus of helium-4 and a neutron. The reaction can be written as:

$$_{1}^{2}\text{H} + _{1}^{3}\text{H} \longrightarrow _{2}^{4}\text{He} + _{0}^{1}\text{n} \text{ (+ energy)}$$

For fusion to occur, the two hydrogen nuclei have to approach each other at very high speed in order to overcome the electrical

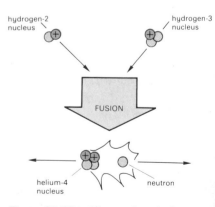

Figure 26.28   The nuclear fusion.

fast breeder 快速增值反應堆   nuclear fusion 核聚變

repulsion between them. On a large scale, this can be achieved by raising the temperature of the hydrogen gas, but a staggering 100 million K is needed to start the fusion!

Nuclear fusion is believed to occur on the Sun and is responsible for the Sun's energy output. Man-made *uncontrolled* fusion has resulted in the **hydrogen bomb**. The initial high temperature required is obtained by using uncontrolled fission (atomic bomb) to trigger off the fusion.

Research is going on to find a method of producing controlled fusion (Figure 26.29), but there is still a long way to go. If controlled fusion ever became a practical reality, it would be a very cheap, abundant and safe source of energy. The hydrogen nuclides used as fuel are plentiful in sea-water, and the waste product, helium, is inert and non-radioactive.

Figure 26.29   ORMAK – fusion research device.

THE NUCLEAR DEBATE

Modern industrial societies depend heavily on oil, natural gas and coal. However, known reserves of these fossil fuels are likely to be run out early in the next century. It is not likely that alternative sources of energy, such as solar energy, hydroelectric power, wind and tidal power, will be sufficiently developed to be of widespread use, at least not in the near future. It appears that the solution to the world's future energy shortage lies with the nuclear power. Used in fast-breeder reactors, reserves of uranium will last for hundreds of years.

hydrogen bomb 氫彈

Therefore, there appears to be a strong case for the development of the nuclear power. However, there are serious social and environmental problems which must be considered.

Nuclear power is potentially hazardous. Should an accident happen, nuclear radiation which leaked out from the reactor will contaminate the environment, destroy or damage all forms of life and may even cause genetic disorders. Hazards could arise from the transportation of radioactive fuel, the operation of the reactor, the reprocessing of spent fuel and the disposal of nuclear waste.

A serious accident happened on March 28, 1979 at the Three Mile Island nuclear power plant in Pennsylvania, U.S.A. (Figure 26.30). This resulted in the melt-down of the core of the reactor. Fortunately, the nuclear radiation leaked out from the core of the reactor was contained inside the concrete shield and there was no harmful release to the surrounding. It was found out later that the accident was caused by a series of human errors rather than by the malfunctioning of the nuclear plant.

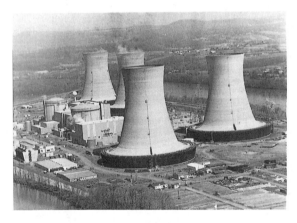

Figure 26.30 The Three Mile Island nuclear power plant accident occurred on 28 March 1979.

Figure 26.31 The Chernobyl nuclear power plant disaster occurred on 26 April, 1986. The arrow shows the part destroyed by the explosion of the reactor core.

The worst nuclear accident in history happened on April 26, 1986 at the nuclear power plant in Chernobyl, U.S.S. R. (Figure 26.31). An explosion occurred in the reactor, resulting in the melt-down of the core and the release of a large amount of radiation to the surrounding. The disaster claimed 31 lives, injured 500 people and contaminated soil, water and crops all across Europe. Tens of thousands of people had to be evacuated from the surrounding areas which have become inhabitable for several years.

The second consideration is the use of nuclear fuels, particularly plutonium, for the production of nuclear weapons. Any country which operates a reactor has the potential capability to produce nuclear weapons. The widespread use of nuclear power will lead to the growth of nuclear weapons and threaten the world peace (Figure 26.32).

Figure 26.32 Down with nuclear weapons!

For or against?

In deciding whether or not to go into nuclear power, the advantages must be weighed against the disadvantages. Supporters of nuclear power put forward the following arguments:

(a) Oil and coal will run out in the not-too-distant future and nuclear power is the *only* solution to the world's energy shortage crisis.

(b) Compared with oil and coal, nuclear power is clean and cheap.

(c) There are adequate safety features built into all nuclear reactors to contain any accident which may occur.

Opponents to nuclear power, on the other hand, have the following counter-arguments:

(a) Nuclear power constitutes an unacceptable hazard to the public. The chance of an accident happening is very small, but the consequence is far too serious to be taken lightly.

(b) Nuclear power will not be cheap if large sums of money have to be spent on maintaining and upgrading the safety standards of the reactor.

(c) Nuclear power is not necessary. All future energy needs can be met by an increasing use of alternative energy sources and by conservation.

The Daya Bay nuclear power plant

A nuclear power plant is now being constructed at Daya Bay, Shenzhen, across the border from Hong Kong (Figure 26.33). The plant is powered by a pressurised water reactor (PWR) which drives two generators each of 900 MW. The project is jointly financed and owned by the power companies of Guangdong Province and Hong Kong. This plant will supply electricity to both territories in the future and is scheduled to be completed by 1992.

Figure 26.33 A model of the nuclear power plant to be built at Daya Bay.

The construction of this nuclear power plant has been a hotly debated social and political issue in Hong Kong, especially after the Chernobyl disaster in 1986. There were mass movements in Hong Kong, requesting that the nuclear power plant be abandoned (Figure 26.34), delayed or relocated, but to no avail. Do Guangdong and Hong Kong really need nuclear power? Will the nuclear power plant, which is situated at 50 km from the city centre (Figure 26.35), pose a threat to the safety and environment of our densely populated city?

Figure 26.34 A public rally in Hong Kong, opposing the construction of the Daya Bay nuclear power plant.

Figure 26.35 The Daya Bay nuclear power plant is situated at 50 km from the city centre of Hong Kong.

Physics and the nuclear weapon

The atomic bomb came into being as a result of research in physics. Its demonstrated destructive power burdens the conscience of many scientists. No longer is scientific research 'pure' and 'for-the-sake-of-knowledge'. Scientists must therefore examine their work in the light of the sort of use it might be put to. Advances in science could lead to the destruction of mankind if they were put to military uses.

A CHRONOLOGY

The following is a chronology of some of the developments in radioactivity.

1895   Rontgen discovered X-rays.

1896   Becquerel discovered natural radioactivity in uranium salt.

1897   Thomson measured the charge-to-mass ratio of an electron.

1898   Marie Curie and her husband extracted radium from uranium ore.

1900   Three types of nuclear radiation were identified; they were named alpha, beta and gamma radiation.

1909　Rutherford and Royds showed that alpha particles were helium nuclei.

1911　Geiger and Marsden, under the direction of Rutherford, detected the scattering of alpha particles by gold foil. Rutherford subsequently proposed a new 'nuclear' model of the atom.
In the same year Wilson invented the cloud chamber.

1919　Rutherford discovered the proton by bombarding nitrogen with alpha particles; as a result nitrogen was transformed into oxygen.

1932　Chadwick discovered the neutron by bombarding beryllium with alpha particles, transforming beryllium into carbon.

1934　Irene Joliot-Curie and her husband produced the first artificial radionuclide by bombarding stable nuclei with alpha particles.

1936　Langsdorf invented the diffusion cloud chamber.

1938　Hahn and Strassman produced nuclear fission by bombarding uranium with neutrons.

1942　Fermi achieved controlled nuclear fission.

1945　The first atomic bomb was exploded at a test-site in New Mexico, U.S.A. Shortly afterwards, bombs were dropped on Hiroshima and Nagasaki.

1952　The first hydrogen bomb was exploded in the Pacific ocean.

1956　The world's first nuclear power station was opened in Calder Hall, England.

SUMMARY

The atom

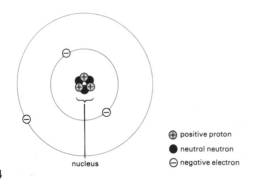

⊕ positive proton
● neutral neutron
⊖ negative electron

Rutherford's scattering experiment showed that most of an atom is empty space and that all the positive charge and most of the mass of an atom are concentrated in a tiny nucleus.

Approximate atomic diameter $= 10^{-10}$ m

Approximate nuclear diameter $= 10^{-14}$ m

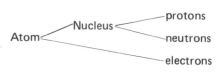

$$\frac{\text{mass of proton}}{\text{mass of electron}} \approx 1840$$

$$\frac{\text{mass of proton}}{\text{mass of neutron}} \approx 1$$

Charge on proton $= +1$
Charge on electron $= -1$
Charge on neutron $= 0$

Atomic number Z = no. of protons in atom

Mass number A = no. of protons + no. of neutrons

For an atom of chemical symbol X, its nucleus is:
$^A_Z X$

Nuclide and isotope

An element with a particular mass number and atomic number is called a nuclide. Nuclides with the same atomic number but different mass number are called isotopes. Nuclides which are radioactive are called radionuclides.

Radioactive decay

Radioactive decay is due to unstable nuclei which break up, emitting alpha or beta particles or gamma rays in the process.

Alpha emission

Alpha emission can be represented by:

$$^A_Z X \longrightarrow {}^{A-4}_{Z-2} Y + {}^4_2 He$$

where X is the parent nucleus and Y the daughter nucleus. The mass number decreases by 4 and the atomic number decreases by 2.

Beta emission

Beta emission can be represented by:

$$^A_Z X \longrightarrow {}^A_{Z+1} Y + {}^0_{-1} e$$

The mass number remains unchanged and the atomic number increases by 1.

Gamma emission

Gamma emission does not change either the atomic number or the mass number.

Nature of radioactivity

Radioactive decay is a random process.

The activity of a source is the number of disintegrations per second.

The half-life of a radionuclide is the time taken for half of the nuclei present in any sample to decay. It is also the time for the activity of any given sample to fall to half its original value.

Artificial radioactivity

Artificial radionuclides can be produced by bombarding stable nuclides with atomic particles in a nuclear reactor. Artificial radionuclides are used in medicine, industry and agriculture.

Nuclear fission

When a nucleus of uranium-235 is bombarded by neutrons, it splits into two smaller nuclei, releasing enormous amounts of energy in the process.

Such nuclear fission, if occurring in a controlled way in a nuclear reactor, can be used to generate electricity.

Uncontrolled nuclear fission produces an atomic bomb.

Nuclear fusion

Nuclear fusion is the union of two light nuclei into a heavier nucleus, during which enormous quantities of energy are released. For example:

$$^2_1 H + {}^3_1 H \longrightarrow {}^4_2 He + {}^1_0 n \quad (\text{+ energy})$$

Uncontrolled nuclear fusion results in the hydrogen bomb.

Nuclear energy and man

Methods have yet to be found to harness the fusion energy in a controlled way to generate electricity.

Nuclear power will help to solve the world's future energy shortage crisis, but there are serious social and environmental problems involved.

PROBLEMS

If necessary, refer to Table 26.2 for the names of radionuclides, their symbols and atomic numbers.

1. The nucleus of a radium nuclide is represented by $^{226}_{88}$Ra.
   How many (i) protons, (ii) neutrons and (iii) electrons does the radium atom contain?
   What is the symbol of the nucleus of another radium nuclide containing two more neutrons?

2. Thorium-228 decays by alpha emission. What nuclide is formed as a result? Write down an equation for the decay process.

3. Iodine-131 decays by beta emission. What nuclide is formed as a result? Write down an equation for the decay process.

4. A radioactive decay series starts with uranium-238 and ends with stable lead-206 after many stages of decay. How many alpha particles are emitted in the complete series?

5. The following represents part of a radioactive series:

   $$^{216}_{84}\text{Po} \longrightarrow {}^{212}_{82}\text{Pb} \longrightarrow {}^{212}_{83}\text{Bi} \longrightarrow$$

   $$^{212}_{84}\text{Po} \longrightarrow {}^{208}_{82}\text{Pb}$$

   State what particle is emitted at each decay.

6. A GM tube detects the radiation from a certain source. If the corrected count rate drops from 192 to 12 counts per second in 208 s, what is the half-life of the source?

7. Sodium-24 has a half-life of 15 hours. How long will it take for 100 g of sodium-24 to reduce to 6.25 g?

8. The proposed nuclear power station in Daya Bay, Shenzhen will generate electric power at 380 MW.
   (a) Calculate the energy the power station will supply in 1 hour.
   (b) The energy extracted from 1 kg of uranium fuel in the reactor is 5.4×10^{12} J. If the power station is 33.3% efficient, calculate the mass of uranium fuel consumed in 1 hour.

9. An experiment was carried out to measure the activity of a certain radionuclide over a period of time. The number of counts per minute recorded was plotted against time in a graph (Figure 26.36).
   (a) Estimate the average background radiation in counts per minute.
   (b) Find the half-life of the radionuclide from the graph.

10. An artificial radiouclide is found to have an activity of 1600 counts per minute, after allowing for background radiation, immediately after its manufacture. The graph in Figure 26.37 shows how its activity varies with time thereafter.
    (a) What is the half-life of this radionuclide?
    (b) When its activity falls below the average background count rate of 50 counts per minute, the radionuclide can be considered suitable for disposal. After how many days after its manufacture can the radionuclide be considered suitable for disposal? .

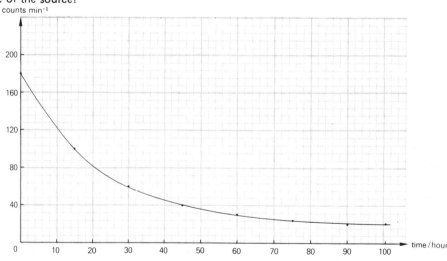

Figure 26.36

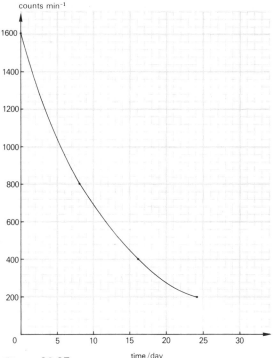

counts min⁻¹ values: 1600, 1400, 1200, 1000, 800, 600, 400, 200

time/day axis: 0, 5, 10, 15, 20, 25, 30

Figure 26.37

11. (a) A manufacturer wishes to check that the thickness of the steel sheets he produces is uniform. Describe how this could be done, using a radioactive source and a counter.
What radiation would you expect the source to emit?

(b) You are told that a radioactive source has a half-life of twenty-four hours. State what you understand by *half-life*.
Assuming that you had a counter and could use it over a period of three days, describe how you would check that the half-life was twenty-four hours.

(c) The following symbols represent five nuclides (nuclei):

$$^{58}_{29}A; \quad ^{54}_{27}B; \quad ^{59}_{29}C; \quad ^{58}_{30}D; \quad ^{59}_{30}E.$$

(i) Which nuclides are isotopes of each other?

(ii) Which nuclide could be produced from which other by the emission of an α particle?

(iii) Which nuclide could be produced from which other by the emission of a β particle?

(iv) One nuclide emits γ rays. Is it possible to determine which one from the above information? If so state which one; if not give a reason for your answer.

(v) Which nuclide possesses the most neutrons?

(London Jan 1979)

12. What do you understand by the *half-life* of a radioactive element?
Figure 36.38 is plotted from readings taken with a radioactive source at daily intervals.
Use the graph to deduce the half-life of the source. Hence give the count rate after five days, and the time when the count is 160 per minute.
Would you expect the mass of the source to have changed significantly after 4 days? (Give a reason for your answer.)

(London June 1978)

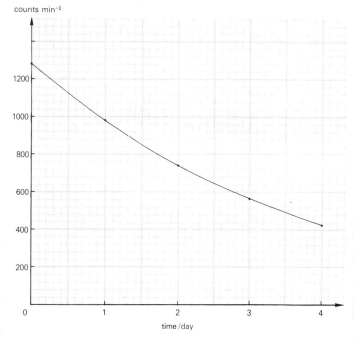

counts min⁻¹ values: 1200, 1000, 800, 600, 400, 200

time/day axis: 0, 1, 2, 3, 4

Figure 26.38

13. (a) What is meant by the half-life of a radioactive substance?

(b) Carbon 14 (atomic number 6) disintegrates by the emission of β particles. What will be the atomic number and mass number of the resulting nucleus?

(c) It is known that 1 gram of carbon from a living plant which contains a definite proportion of carbon 14 decays at a rate of 15 disintegrations per minute. In 1978, a specimen which was formed from a living

287

plant a long time ago shows 15 disintegrations every 4 minutes from 1 gram of carbon present in it. Given that the half-life of carbon 14 is 5600 years, estimate the age of the specimen.

(d) The half-lives of three radioactive isotopes *X*, *Y* and *Z* are respectively 1 second, 15 hours and 1620 years. By considering their half-lives, which should be used for injection into a patient's vein to investigate his blood circulation? Explain briefly.

(HKCEE 1978)

14. A radioactive source *R* is contained at the bottom of a narrow lead cylinder. The source emits radiation which passes between two poles of a strong magnet. Two similar Geiger-Muller tubes, connected to separate counters, are placed at *P* and *Q* as shown in Figure 36.39. The two tubes point towards the gap between the poles of the magnet.

The number of counts per minute, indicated by each counter, is recorded at 10-minute intervals. The results are tabulated below.

Time/minutes	Counts per minute at:	
	Counter P	Counter Q
0	585	42
10	405	39
20	290	40
30	205	38
40	155	43
50	120	37
60	95	41

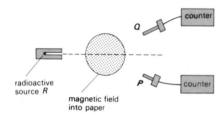

Figure 26.39

(a) Explain why the count rate is so much higher at *P* than it is at *Q*.

(b) Plot two graphs on the same axes to show how the count rates (*y*-axis) change with time (*x*-axis).

(c) Suggest a reason for the shape of each graph. What radiation is being detected in each case?

(d) Estimate the count rate at counter *P* after one hour more.

(e) Estimate the count rate at counter *Q* after one hour more.

(f) What experimental results would you expect to get if the magnetic field were
(i) reversed,
(ii) removed altogether?

(g) Estimate the half-life of the radioactive source.

(O&C June 1979)

15. (a) Figure 26.40 shows the first 4 nuclear disintegrations of a natural radioactive series (a series of nuclear changes originating from the radioactive nucleus *A* of atomic number 90 and mass number 232). *B, C, D* and *E* are the successive decay products.

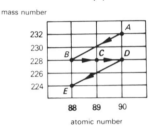

Figure 26.40

What particles will be emitted from the nuclei in the following nuclear disintegrations?
(i) *A → B*
(ii) *B → C*
(iii) *C → D*
(iv) *D → E*

(b) A neutral particle decays in a very short time into a proton and a negative particle. Figure 36.41 shows the initial and the subsequent paths of the particles in a magnetic field.

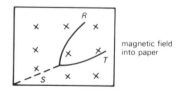

Figure 26.41

(i) Identify the paths *R, S* and *T* for the three particles.
(ii) Explain briefly why the paths *R* and *T* are curved.

(c) In a certain β decay:

$$X \xrightarrow{\beta} Y$$

X is the radioactive substance, and Y is the stable decay product. If the initial mass of X is 8 g, what are the respective masses of X and Y after a time of 2 half-lives of this decay has elapsed?

(HKCEE 1979)

16. (a) $^{238}_{92}U$ is a radioactive source giving α, β and γ radiations.
    (i) If $^{238}_{92}U$ decays by emitting four α particles and two β particles, what will be the atomic number and mass number of the resulting nucleus?
    (ii) A Geiger counter is placed at A as shown in Figure 26.42 about 20 cm from the source. What type(s) of radiation can be received by the counter at A?
    (iii) An electric field is applied across the metal plates M and N as shown in Figure 26.43 so that M is at a higher potential and N at a lower potential. The Geiger counter is now moved to B about 20 cm from the source. Describe and explain what happens to the count rate.

Figure 26.42

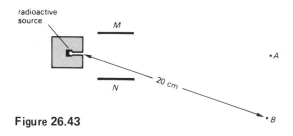

Figure 26.43

(b) A small volume of solution containing a radioactive isotope with an activity of 4400 disintegrations per minute is injected into the blood stream of a patient. After 20 hours the activity of 10 cm^3 of blood is 2 disintegrations per minute. If the half-life of the isotope is 10 hours, estimate the volume of blood inside the person.

(HKCEE 1981)

17. (a) What are the mass numbers of
    (i) α particles,
    (ii) β particles,
    (iii) neutrons?

(b) Figure 26.44 shows a radioactive decay series:
$$A \longrightarrow B \longrightarrow C \longrightarrow D \longrightarrow E$$
    (i) State what particles are emitted at each stage.
    (ii) What is the mass number of C?

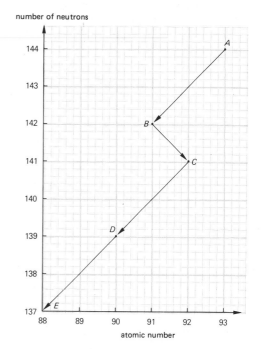

Figure 26.44

(c) Figure 26.45 shows the decay curves of two radioactive elements X and Y both emitting β particles. N_0 is the number of radioactive atoms present at time $t = 0$ and N is the number at the end of t minutes.

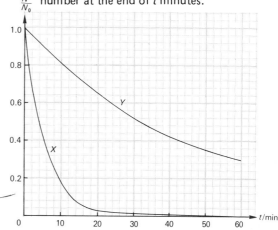

Figure 26.45

(i) What are the half-lives of X and Y?

(ii) A mixture of X and Y is placed in front of a Geiger counter. Initially, they have the same number of radioactive atoms. Which of the two, X or Y, will be mainly responsible for the reading shown on the Geiger counter during the first four minutes? Estimate the fraction of the total number of counts due to that element.

(HKCEE 1982)

18. (a) A Geiger counter is placed on a bench.

(i) Explain why the counter registers a reading even when no radioactive source is placed nearby.

(ii) When a radioactive source is placed near the counter, the counter registers 520, 510 and 514 counts per minute in the first three consecutive minutes. Explain why the three readings differ from each other?

(iii) When a piece of paper is placed between the source in (ii) and the counter, the counter registers 504, 510 and 512 counts per minute in the first three consecutive minutes. However, when the paper is replaced by an aluminium sheet, the counts are reduced to 7, 9 and 8 respectively. What type(s) of radiation (α, β or γ) is/are being emitted by the source? Give a reason for your answer.

(b) The radioactivity from a sample of $^{224}_{88}$Ra is measured at two-day intervals. The readings are tabulated below:

Time/days	0	2	4	6	8	10
Activity	100	68	47	32	22	15

(i) Plot the decay graph to show the activity against time and from the graph, find
(1) the activity of the sample after 5 days, and
(2) the half-life of the sample.

(ii) If an α particle is emitted from an atom of $^{224}_{88}$Ra during the decay process, what will be the mass number and the atomic number of the daughter atom?

(HKCEE 1983)

19. In an experiment to determine the half-life of radon-220 ($^{220}_{86}$Rn) the following results were obtained, after allowing for the background count:

Time/s	0 10 20 30 40 50 60 70
Count rate/s^{-1}	30 26 23 21 18 16 14 12

(a) By plotting the count rate (vertically) against the time (horizontally), determine the half-life of $^{220}_{86}$Rn. Show clearly on your graph how you obtain your answer.

(b) (i) What is the origin of the background count?

(ii) How is the background count determined?

(c) $^{220}_{86}$Rn emits α-particle.

(i) What is an α-particle?

(ii) When $^{220}_{86}$Rn emits an α-particle it becomes an isotope of the element polonium (Po). Write an equation to represent this change.

(d) When carrying out experiments with radioactive sources, students are instructed that

(i) the source should never be held close to the human body,

(ii) no eating or drinking is allowed in the laboratory. Why is it important to follow these instructions?

(London Jan 1982)

20. (a) The radioactivity in a room containing a radioactive source is measured by a GM counter. Figure 26.46 shows the variation of count rate with time. Find from the figure,

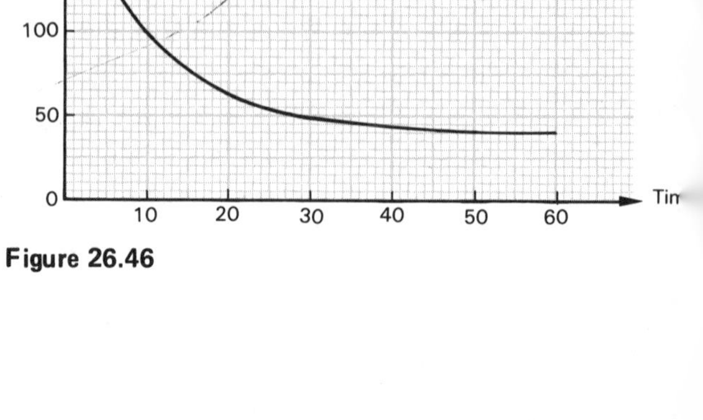

Figure 26.46

(i) the background count rate of the room,
(ii) the count rate due only to the radioactive source at time 0, and
(iii) the half-life of the radioactive source.
(b) A factory aims at producing aluminium sheets of 1 mm thickness. A radioactive source and a detector is used to monitor the thickness of the aluminium sheet manufactured as shown in Figure 26.47.
 (i) State what type of source (α, β or γ) should be used.
 (ii) Explain briefly why the other two types of source are not used.
(c) Some people propose that nuclear energy should eventually replace oil and coal as sources of energy supply. Do you agree with this? List 3 reasons to support your argument.

(HKCEE 1986)

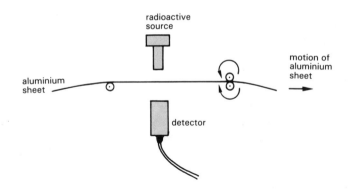

Figure 26.47

291

SI Units

The International System of Units (or SI for short) is used throughout the course. This is a comprehensive system of units of measurement of all physical quantities for scientific as well as general use. It is based on seven **base units** from which **derived units** are obtained by combining two or more base units together in some way. There is only one unit, base or derived, for each physical quantity.

BASE UNITS

The following are the five base units used in this course.

Physical quantitiy	Symbol	Unit	Symbol
length	l	metre	m
mass	m	kilogram	kg
time	t	second	s
electric current	I	ampere	A
thermodynamic (absolute) temperature	T	kelvin	K

They are defined, as follows, in a very precise way in terms of reproducible measurements of physical phenomena. *The definitions are quoted here for reference only and need not be remembered by heart. Indeed, some definitions are not easy to understand and should be referred to after the relevant topics have been covered in the text.*

The **metre** is the length equal to 1 650 763.73 wavelengths in vacuum corresponding to the transition between the levels $2p_{10}$ and $5d_5$ of the krypton-86 atom.

The **kilogram** is the unit of mass; it is equal to the mass of the international prototype of the kilogram.

The **second** is the duration of 9 192 631 770 periods of the radiation corresponding to the transition between the two hyperfine levels of the ground state of the caesium-133 atom.

The **ampere** is that constant current which, if maintained in two straight parallel conductors of infinite length, of negligible circular cross-section, and placed 1 metre apart in vacuum, would produce between these conductors a force equal to 2×10^{-7} newton per metre of length.

The **kelvin**, unit of thermodynamic temperature, is the fraction $\frac{1}{273.16}$ of the thermodynamic temperature of the triple point of water.

DERIVED UNITS

Derived units are obtained from base units by multiplying or dividing one unit by another. For example, the unit for area is square metre and that for speed is metre per second. For symbols of derived units the negative index notation is preferred to the notation using the solidus (stroke). Hence m s^{-1} is used, rather than $\frac{m}{s}$, as the symbol for the unit of speed. Some derived units are given special names and symbols.

The following are some of the derived units used in this course.

Physical quantity	Symbol	Unit	Symbol
area	A	square metre	m^2
volume	V	cubic metre	m^3
density	ρ	kilogram per cubic metre	$kg\ m^{-3}$
frequency	f	hertz	$Hz\ (1\ Hz = 1\ s^{-1})$
wavelength	λ	metre	m
distance, displacement	s or d	metre	m
speed, velocity	v	metre per second	$m\ s^{-1}$
acceleration	a	metre per second squared	$m\ s^{-2}$
force	F	newton	$N\ (1\ N = 1\ kg\ m\ s^{-2})$
pressure	p	pascal	$Pa\ (1\ Pa = 1\ N\ m^{-2})$
work, energy	W, E	joule	$J\ (1\ J = 1\ N\ m)$
power	P	watt	$W\ (1\ W = 1\ J\ s^{-1})$
common temperature	t	degree Celsius	$°C$

Physical quantity	Symbol	Unit	Symbol
specific heat capacity	c	joule per kilogram degree Celsius or joule per kilogram kelvin	$\text{J kg}^{-1}\,{}^{\circ}\text{C}^{-1}$ or $\text{J kg}^{-1}\,\text{K}^{-1}$
specific latent heat	l	joule per kilogram	J kg^{-1}
electric charge	Q	coulomb	C (1 C = 1 A s)
potential difference, e.m.f.	V, E	volt	V $(1\text{V} = 1\text{ J C}^{-1}\text{ or W A}^{-1})$
electric resistance	R	ohm	$\Omega\ (1\,\Omega = 1\text{ V A}^{-1})$
nucleon number (mass number)	A	–	–
proton number (atomic number)	Z	–	–
neutron number	N	–	–

PREFIXES

Larger or smaller multiples of the units are obtained by combining the unit with an appropriate prefix which is expressed as a power of ten. The following are some of the commonly used prefixes.

Prefix	Multiple	Symbol
nano	10^{-9}	n
micro	10^{-6}	μ
milli	10^{-3}	m
centi	10^{-2}	c
kilo	10^{3}	k
mega	10^{6}	M
giga	10^{9}	G

Examples:
1 microsecond (μs) $= 10^{-6}$ s
1 millimetre (mm) $= 10^{-3}$ m
1 kilometre (km) $= 10^{3}$ m
1 megawatt (MW) $= 10^{6}$ W
1 gigahertz (GHz) $= 10^{9}$ Hz

Answers to Problems

Chapter 14

2. (a) 2.8 m s^{-1}
   (b) 0.7 m
3. 0.1 m s^{-1}
4. (a) 0.25 Hz
   (b)

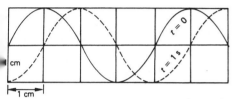

5. (a) (i) 0.015 m
       (ii) 2.0 m
       (iii) 20 m s^{-1}
       (iv) 10 Hz
   (b) (i) X and Z
       (ii) W and Y
       (iii) W
       (iv) Y
6. (a) 4.0 m
   (b) 1.5 Hz
7. (a) 4 cm
   (b) 10 Hz
   (c) 40 cm s^{-1}
   (d) A moving downwards,
       B moving upwards
   (e) 2 cm, 10 Hz
8. (a) (i) 2 cm
       (ii) 8 cm
       (iii) 4 s
       (iv) 0.25 Hz
   (b) (i) R, S
       (ii) P, T
       (iii) Q
   (c) 2 cm below its present
       position.

Chapter 15

1. Frequency, wavelength and wave
   speed all remain unaltered on
   reflection.
2.

3.

4. (a)

   (b)

   (c)

   (d)

5. 5 Hz, 2.5 Hz
6. (a) 40 Hz
   (b) 0.025 s
   (c) Cover up 5 slits so that the
       strobe has 5 evenly spaced
       slits.
7. (a) 24 rev s^{-1}
   (b) (i) Stopped in 1 position

   (ii) Stopped in 2 positions

8. (a) 40 sightings per second
   (b) 0.025 s
   (c) 40 rev s^{-1}
   (d) 5 rev s^{-1}
   (e) 10, 15, 20, 25, 30, 45, 50,
       . . . rev s^{-1}
9. 12 Hz
10. (a) 20 cm s^{-1}
    (b) 20 cm s^{-1}, 1 cm
11. (a) 12.5 cm s^{-1}
    (b) 2.5 cm
12. (b)

    (c)

13.

14.

15. (a)

    (b)

(c) With longer wavelength, there is more diffraction.
16. (c) (i) 2.5 cm behind
17. (a) (i) 9 Hz
    (ii) 18 cm s^{-1}
18. (a) (i) 20 cm s^{-1}
19. (c) (i) 0.3 m s^{-1}
    (ii) 0.2 m s^{-1}
    (e) 19.5°

Chapter 16

1. 3.33 × 10^{-6} s
2. (a)

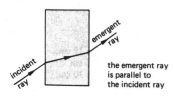

the emergent ray is parallel to the incident ray

   (b) When light passes from air to glass
       wave speed decreases,
       wavelength decreases,
       frequency unchanged.
3. Red light most widely spaced; blue light most closely spaced.
4. (b) Fringe separation increases.
5. (a) $S_1O = S_2O$
   (b) $S_2P - S_1P = \frac{1}{2}$ wavelength of light
   (c) $S_2Q - S_1Q = 1$ wavelength of light

Chapter 17

1. (a)

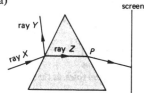

   (b) (i) No change in wavelength
       (ii) No change in wave speed
   (c) (i) Wavelength decreases.
       (ii) Wave speed decreases.
   (d) The white light is dispersed into its constituent colours and a spectrum is seen on the screen. Each coloured light has a slightly different wave speed in the prism and so is refracted and deviated to different extent.
2. The Earth also radiates energy away.
3. (a) Ultraviolet
   (b) Gamma rays
   (c) Short radio waves
   (d) X-rays
4. 2.5 × 10^9 Hz
5. 287 m
6. (a) (i) 10^{10} Hz
       (ii) 0

Chapter 18

1. 1.7 km
2. 320 m s^{-1}
3. The wave trace on the oscilloscope is transverse, whereas the sound wave controlling it is longitudinal.
4. (a) C
   (b) C
5. (a) Half the length.
   (b) Increase the tension to four times.
6. (a) 0.8 m
   (b) 1.33 m
7. 332 m s^{-1}
8. (a) 1.34 m
   (b) 343 m s^{-1}
9. (a) $S_1Q = \sqrt{8^2 + (1.5)^2} = 8.14$ m
       $S_2Q = \sqrt{8^2 + (2.5)^2} = 8.38$ m
   (b) 0.24 m
   (c) 0.24 m
   (d) 336 m s^{-1}
10. (a) (ii) 680 Hz
11. (b) 25 Hz
    (d) 4 m s^{-1}

Chapter 19

1. (a) Positive charge: acetate, perspex
   (b) Negative charge: polythene, PVC
2. So that charge produced is not conducted away. Charge will be conducted to earth via human body as quickly as it is produced.
3. (a) (i) The 2 strips attract each other.
       (ii) The 2 strips become uncharged on touching each other and lie vertically; + and − charges neutralize each other (charge sharing).
    (b) (i) The 2 strips repel each other.
        (ii) The 2 strips remain repelling each other and lie inclined to the vertical; no charge sharing takes place as both strips have charge of the same quantity and same sign.
4. Polystyrene ball attracted towards charged metal sphere; repelled on touching the sphere.
5. The positively charged acetate strip attracts the negative induced charge on the near side of the water stream and repels the positive induced charge on the far side, the latter force being the smaller of the two forces.
6. (a) See Figure.

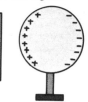

   (b) Sphere is touched momentarily with finger while negatively charged rod is held in position. When the charged rod is next removed, sphere is left with positive charge.
7. (a) See Figure.

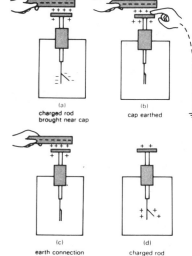

(a) charged rod brought near cap
(b) cap earthed
(c) earth connection removed
(d) charged rod removed

       (iii) Electrons would have flown back.
       (iv) No
    (b) (i) Leaf rises further.
        (ii) Leaf falls slightly.
        (iii) Leaf falls slightly.
8. —
9. (a) See Figure.

(b) Non-conducting semolina particles become charged in the electric field and settle into positions showing the field pattern.

(c) Water, or any other liquid which is conducting, short-circuits the E.H.T. supply and this could be dangerous. Castor oil is non-conducting.

(d) Pattern remains unchanged except that there are now more lines of particles between the parallel electrodes. Decreasing the gap between the electrodes increases the strength of the electric field.

10. 0.2 J
11. 12 V
12. (c) 10^{-8} C
13. –
14. (a) Negative
    (b) –

    (c) Ions in the surrounding air have been drawn towards the pin because of point action.
    (d) No

Chapter 20

1. 300 C
2. (a) 2 C
   (b) 12 J
   (c) 24 J
   (d) 15 s
3. (a) 3 A
   (b) 6 V
4. (a) See Figure 20.78.
   (b) (i) 16.7 Ω
       (ii) 34.5 Ω
   (c) Resistance of lamp filament increases with temperature.
5. –
6. (a) 12 Ω
   (b) 0.75 A
7. (a) 16 Ω
   (b) 3 Ω
   (c) 8 Ω
   (d) 6 Ω
8. (a) 6 Ω
   (b) 1 A, 0.75 A, 0.25 A
   (c) 3 V, 3 V, 3 V
9. 8 Ω, 8 Ω
10. (a) 0.75 A, 0.75 A
    (b) 3 A, 1 A
11. 20 Ω, 10 A
12. (a) 5 A
    (b) 6 Ω, 4 Ω
    (c) 1.2 A
        Lamps dimly lighted
13. 3 Ω
14. (a) 2 A
    (b) 4 A
    (c) 6 A

(d) 6 V
(e) 1 Ω
15. (a) (i) 0.2 A
        (ii) 1000 Ω
    (b) Whole set of lamps goes out.
    (c) 12.5 V
    (d) 0.25 A (larger current)
        Resistance of lamp filament increases as it is heated up more by larger current.
16. (a) (i) 110 Ω
        (ii) 2 A
    (b) (i) 1.82 A
        (ii) 364
    (c) 17.4%
17. (a) 8 W
    (b) 16 W
    (c) 24 W
18. (a) 500 Ω, 1 000 Ω
        1 000 Ω is the true value of R.
    (b) The circuit in Figure 20.45.
19. (b) (i) 3 : 8
        (ii) 8 : 3
20. –
21. –
22. –
23. –
24. (c) (i) 440 mA
        (ii) 2.5 V
        56.8 Ω

Chapter 21

1. 1.08×10^7 J
2. 3×10^5 J
3. 168 s
4. (a) $0.35
   (b) $14
   (c) $1.05
5. See p. 50.
6. 3 A fuse
7. (a) (i) 667
        (ii) 0.3 A
   (b) 16
8. (b) $90
9. (b) (ii) 2
   (c) (i) 4 min 40 s
       (ii) 4.67 cents
10. (b) 5 kWh; $3.0; 40 A
11. (a) 6 A
    (c) $108
12. –
13. (b) (i) 222 Ω
        (ii) 0.9 A

Chapter 22

1. (a)   (b)

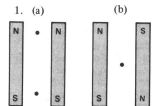

2 neutral points   1 neutral point

2. (a)

(b) Y is a neutral point.

3. (a)

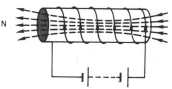

(b) Field strength increases in all 3 cases, (i), (ii) and (iii).

4. (a)

(b) Needle points in direction of the resultant field of the Earth and the solenoid.
(c) Increase current; incease number of turns; place a soft-iron core in the solenoid.
5. (a) Force upwards
   (b) (i) Force downwards
       (ii) Force downwards
       (iii) Force upwards
6. (a), (b) and (c) See Figure.

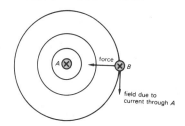

(d) Two parallel wires carrying current in the same direction attract one another.
7. (a)

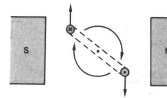

(b) (i) Maximum turning effect when coil is horizontal (parallel to the magnetic field direction).
(ii) Zero turning effect when coil is vertical (at right angles to the magnetic field direction).
(c) Increase current; increase number of turns of coil; use stronger magnet; increase area of coil.

8. –
9. –
10. (a) 1.001 Ω
(b) 1 Ω
(c) 9 kΩ
(d) 10 kΩ
11. (a) 90 Ω, 900 Ω
12. (a) (i) 25 mA
(b) (i) 12 mA
(ii) 11.7 mA
13. –
14. –
15. (ii) 1.001 Ω

Chapter 23

1. (a) See Figure.

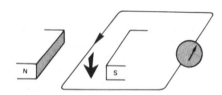

(b) (i) Direction of induced current reversed.
(ii) No induced current flows.
(iii) Induced current increases.
(iv) No induced current flows.
(v) Induced current increases.
2. (a) See Figure.

(b) Any three of the following:
(i) moving magnet at a higher speed,
(ii) using a stronger magnet,
(iii) increasing the number of turns in the coil,
(iv) inserting a soft-iron core in the coil.
3. –

4. (a) See Figure.

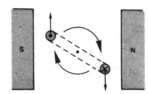

(b) (i) When the coil is horizontal.
(ii) When the coil is vertical.
(c) (i) Using a stronger magnet.
(ii) Increasing the number of turns in the coil.
(iii) Winding the coil on a soft-iron armature.
(iv) Rotating the coil at a higher speed.
5. (a) The galvanometer pointer oscillates about the zero mark.
(b) The damping effect of eddy currents flowing in the coil brings the oscillating magnet rapidly to a standstill.
6. –
7. –
8. See Figure.

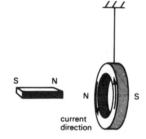

current direction

9. –
10. (c) 83.3%
11. (a) 120
(b) 4 A
(c) 0.12 A
12. (a) (i) 4 A
(ii) 40 : 1
(iii) 0.1 A
(b) (i) 1.5 Ω
(ii) 234 V
(iii) 58.5 Ω
(iv) 936 J
13. (a) 200 J
(b) 1 A, 2 J
14. –
15. –
16. (a) (i) 100 A
(ii) 10 kW
(iii) 100 W
17. (a) 4 A
(b) 0.2 A
(c) 0.4 W
(d) 24.4 W
(e) 120 V, 1 V, 1 V, 122 V
(f) 6.1 V

18. –
19. (a) (i) $1\frac{1}{4}$
(ii) 10 Hz
(b) 30%
20. –
21. (a) 6 Ω
(c) (i) 1.67 A
(ii) 16.7 W
22. (a) (i) 30 W
(ii) 3.6 W
(iii) 12%

Chapter 24

1. (a) A: anode; K: cathode; F: filament
(b) A: connected to the + terminal of supply; attracts electrons emitted by filament.
K: connected to the − terminal of supply; repels electrons emitted by filament.
F: emits electrons when heated.
(c) Current flows when filament is heated; A connected to + terminal and K to the − terminal of supply.
2. (a) d.c. voltage across Y-plates with Y_1 positive.
(b) d.c. voltage across X-plates with X_2 positive.
(c) Conditions (a) and (b).
(d) d.c. voltage across Y-plates with Y_1 positive and time base switched on.
(e) a.c. voltage across Y-plates.
(f) a.c. voltage across Y-plates and d.c. voltage across X-plates with X_1 positive.
(g) Time base switched on and a.c. voltage across Y-plates.
3. (a) (i) Spot sweeps across screen at constant speed.
(ii) Spot flies back to the start of the sweep.
(b) BC vertical
4. (a) d.c.
(b) 150 mV
(c) The spot becomes a horizontal line 3 cm above zero line.
5. (a) 400 Hz
(b) 0.6 V
6. (a) (i) 1.5 V
(ii) 100 Hz
(b) Amplitude of waveform reduced to 1.5 cm.
(c) Number of complete waves increases to 5.
7. (a) 333.3 Hz
(c) (i) 1 V
(ii) 5 ohms
8. (c) (i) (1) 7.5 V
(2) 4 ms
(3) 250 Hz

9. (a)

   (b) Amplitude of waveform increases.
   (c) *X*

10. –
11. –
12. (c) (i) 2 V
     (ii) 100 Hz
13. Lamps *A*, *B*, *C*, *E*, *F*, *G*, *H*, *I* and *J* are lighted.
14. (a) Resistance becomes smaller when warmed.
   (b) 100 Ω when cold, 10 Ω when warmed.
15. Switches *A* and *B* closed and *C* open.

16.

Input	Input			Output
A	*B*	*C*	*D*	*Q*
0	0	1	1	0
0	1	1	0	1
1	0	0	1	1
1	1	0	0	1

OR gate

17. 4 NAND gates

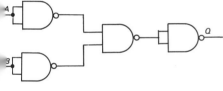

18.

Input	Input			Output
A	*B*	*C*	*D*	*Q*
0	0	1	1	1
0	1	1	0	1
1	0	0	1	1
1	1	0	0	0

NAND gate

19.

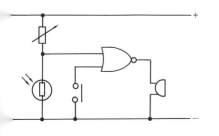

20.

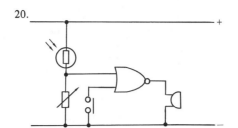

21.

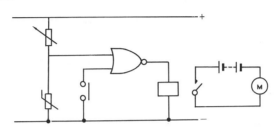

22.

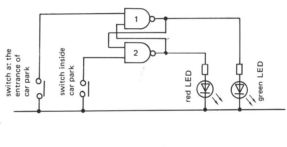

Chapter 25

1. Radium, strontium and cobalt source. Alpha particles emitted by americium source cannot penetrate wrapping of photographic film.
2. (a) α
   (b) γ
   (c) γ
   (d) α
   (e) α
   (f) γ
   (g) α
   (h) β
   (i) γ
   (j) α
3. Radium and americium source. These sources emit alpha radiation which has high enough ionizing power to produce sparks in spark counter.
4. –
5. –

6. Place a sheet of paper, a 5 mm thick aluminium sheet and a 25 mm thick lead sheet in turn between radium source and detector and note that the count rate decreases but never to zero.
7. A sheet of paper and a 5 mm thick aluminium sheet placed between source and detector have no appreciable effect on the count rate.
8. Alpha and gamma radiations. Beta is not emitted as there is no change in count rate when aluminium sheet is placed between source and detector.
9. Tracks of alpha particles are thick and straight and of equal length (about 3 to 5 cm long); tracks of beta particles are thin and twisted.

10. Tracks will be thinner and longer as there are now fewer air molecules per cm track length for alpha particles to ionize. An alpha particle stops when all its energy is lost in ionizing air molecules.
11. X: alpha, Y: gamma, Z: beta
12. –
13. –
14. –
15. –

Chapter 26

1. (a) 88 protons
   (b) 138 neutrons
   (c) 88 electrons
   $^{228}_{88}Ra$
2. Radium-224 $^{228}_{90}Th \rightarrow {}^{224}_{88}Ra + {}^{4}_{2}He$
3. Xenon-131 $^{131}_{53}I \rightarrow {}^{131}_{54}Xe + {}^{0}_{-1}e$
4. $\dfrac{238 - 206}{4} = 8$

5. $\alpha, \beta, \beta, \alpha$
6. $192 \rightarrow 96 \rightarrow 48 \rightarrow 24 \rightarrow 12$ counts s^{-1}
   The count rate drops from 192 to 12 counts s^{-1} in 4 half-lives.
   Half-life $= \dfrac{208}{4} = 52$ s
7. 100 g $\rightarrow 50$ g $\rightarrow 25$ g $\rightarrow$
   12.5 g $\rightarrow 6.25$ g
   Time: 4 half-lives or 60 hours
8. (a) 380 MW $\times$ 60 $\times$ 60 s
       $= 1.37 \times 10^{12}$ J
   (b) $\dfrac{1.37 \times 10^{12}}{5.4 \times 10^{12}} \times 3 = 0.76$ kg
9. (a) 20 counts min^{-1}
   (b) 15 hours
10. (a) 8 days
    (b) 5 half-lives or 40 days
11. –
12. 2.5 days, 320 counts min^{-1},
    7.5 days
13. (b) 7, 14
    (c) 112 000 years

14. –
15. (a) (i) α
        (ii) β
        (iii) β
        (iv) α
    (c) 2 g, 6 g
16. (a) (i) 86, 222
        (ii) β, γ
    (b) 5500 cm^3
17. (a) (i)   4
        (ii) 0
        (iii) 1
    (b) (i) $\alpha, \beta, \alpha, \alpha$
        (ii) 233
    (c) (i)   4 min, 32 min
        (ii) X, 0.86
18. (a) (iii) β (or β and γ)
    (b) (i) (1) 39.5 days
             (2) 3.7 days
        (ii) 220, 86
19. –
20. (a) (i)   40 counts min^{-1}
        (ii) 160 counts min^{-1}
        (iii) 7 s

Index